The
Collected
Poems of
William
Carlos
Williams

Volume I
1909-1939

BY WILLIAM CARLOS WILLIAMS

William Carlos Williams, 1926. Photograph by Charles Sheeler.
Reproduced by permission of William Eric Williams.

The Collected Poems of William Carlos Williams

Volume I
1909-1939

Edited by A. Walton Litz and Christopher MacGowan

First published in Great Britain by Carcanet Press Limited in 1987
208-212 Corn Exchange
Manchester M4 3BQ

ISBN 0-85635-717-0

The Publisher acknowledges financial assistance from the
Arts Council of Great Britain.

Contents

xi

Preface

This is the first volume of a two-volume edition of all of William Carlos Williams' published poetry excluding *Paterson*. We have followed Williams in recognizing 1939 as the turning point in his poetic life, and the volume ends in that year. Looking back from the perspective of the 1950s, Williams saw his *Complete Collected Poems* of late 1938 as the "whole picture" of his early career, "all I had gone through technically to learn about the making of a poem." After this volume appeared he shifted his attention to the experiments that would lead to *Paterson*. When *The Collected Later Poems* containing his work of the last dozen years was published in 1950 the dust jacket announced that the 1938 collection would "be re-issued in a revised and enlarged edition in 1951 as [a] companion volume," and this is roughly true. However, in preparing *The Collected Earlier Poems* (1951) Williams included a number of post-1938 poems that he had unintentionally omitted from *Collected Later Poems* and radically rearranged the sequence of the 1938 volume. In February 1938 he had told his publisher James Laughlin of New Directions that he wanted the poems "to come out in subdivisions of the original books as they appeared, chronologically," and *The Complete Collected Poems* (1938) follows this pattern for all but the longer poems, which are grouped together at the end. At first Williams intended to organize *Collected Earlier Poems* in the same way, but in February 1950 he reported "a hell of a good idea for the *Collected*," and by the end of November he could tell James Laughlin that the "revised and corrected and enlarged Earlier Collected Poems is ready for you for next year—you'll be surprised how much it is an improvement on the 1938 edition—in content, that is and arrangement." And in March 1951 he bragged to Laughlin that "you would hardly know the old gal in her new dress as of 1938. It'll be a different and a far better book than that one, good as that one was."

Williams' "good idea" for *Collected Earlier Poems* resembles some of his later schemes for organizing his complete works under thematic and stylistic headings, or "modes of attack," while preserving some sense of chronology. One of his chief aims was obviously to spread the longer poems throughout the volume. Unfortunately, in arranging *Collected Earlier Poems* Williams greatly obscured the order of publication and therefore the record of his poetic development. Many of the placements are extremely misleading. For example, "Portrait of a Lady"—like the other "Transitional" poems in *Complete Collected Poems*—is printed as if it were a part of Williams' 1913 volume *The Tempers*, although it was first published in August 1920. (Williams may have been trying to claim priority over T. S. Eliot's "Portrait of a Lady," which was first published in 1915.) In making this new edition we decided to reject Williams' 1951 arrangement and print the poems in chronological order, retaining (as Williams wished in 1938) the integrity of the individual volumes of poetry. This seemed to us the most satisfactory way to present his entire poetic achievement. Those wishing to know the order of *Collected Earlier Poems* will find the table of contents in Appendix C, along with those of the earlier 1938 and 1934 collections.

We begin this edition with the first volume of poems that Williams wished to preserve, *The Tempers* (1913), and print the successive volumes through *Adam & Eve & The City* (1936) with the original contents intact. Between each volume we print the uncollected poems of that period in order of first publication (exceptions to this practice are noted in Appendix A). Poems not found in the individual volumes that were included in *Collected Poems, 1921-1931* (1934), *Complete Collected Poems* (1938), *Collected Later Poems* (1950), and *Collected Earlier Poems* (1951) appear in order of first publication. The one exception to our policy of printing all the published poetry is Williams' first volume of apprentice verse, *Poems* (1909). He explicitly told his publisher James Laughlin that these poems were not to be reprinted and we have followed his wish, although we would have liked to include the volume both for the sake of completeness and as a demonstration of Williams' extraordinary advances in technique over the next few years. We have, however, been able to print three poems from the 1909 volume that were published elsewhere, and these along with other poems of the 1909-1913 period give a clear sense of where Williams began and how far he had to go.

A detailed description of the editorial procedures for this volume may be found in Appendix A, "A Note on the Text." The reader should keep these general principles in mind:

(1) Although the poems are printed in order of first publication, our corrected text of *Collected Earlier Poems* and *Collected Later Poems* is used for the poems that appeared in those volumes. The poems not in-

cluded in these two collections are printed in their original published forms, and are identified in the Annotations.

(2) In order to give a sense of the changes in style and visual arrangement that took place during Williams' early career, we have printed within the text several poems in both a first version and a later revised version. Other examples of significant revision are provided in the Annotations (Appendix B). In general, the changes in Williams' poetry that occur between periodical and book publication are marked by an increasing emphasis on consolidation and regularity.

(3) Poems in manuscript or typescript have not been included in this text (with the exception of those written after 1909 which have been published elsewhere since Williams' death).

(4) *Spring and All, The Descent of Winter*, and shorter prose/poetry compositions of the 1920s have been printed in full, since the relationship between prose and poetry is a central theme in Williams' art.

(5) This volume closes with the revised version of "The Last Words of My English Grandmother" (Summer 1939) which can be compared with the first version of March 1924. The last five poems in the volume are part of the partially-published sequence *Detail & Parody for the poem Paterson* (March 1939), and prepare the way for the opening poems of Volume II.

(6) The Annotations (Appendix B) include significant textual variants and background information on the individual poems drawn from both published and unpublished sources. Explanatory notes are not provided for items of general cultural knowledge that can be found in the standard dictionaries or encyclopedias. The page numbers in the running heads for Appendix B are keyed to the titles of the poems in the main text.

A.W.L. and C.M.

THE TEMPERS
1913

THE TEMPERS

BY

WILLIAM CARLOS WILLIAMS

LONDON
ELKIN MATHEWS, CORK STREET
M CM XIII

PEACE ON EARTH

The Archer is wake!
The Swan is flying!
Gold against blue
An Arrow is lying.
There is hunting in heaven—
Sleep safe till tomorrow.

The Bears are abroad!
The Eagle is screaming!
Gold against blue
Their eyes are gleaming!
Sleep!
Sleep safe till tomorrow.

The Sisters lie
With their arms intertwining;
Gold against blue
Their hair is shining!
The Serpent writhes!
Orion is listening!
Gold against blue
His sword is glistening!
Sleep!
There is hunting in heaven—
Sleep safe till tomorrow.

POSTLUDE

Now that I have cooled to you
Let there be gold of tarnished masonry,
Temples soothed by the sun to ruin
That sleep utterly.

3

Give me hand for the dances,
Ripples at Philae, in and out,
And lips, my Lesbian,
Wall flowers that once were flame.

Your hair is my Carthage
And my arms the bow,
And our words arrows
To shoot the stars
Who from that misty sea
Swarm to destroy us.

But you there beside me—
Oh how shall I defy you,
Who wound me in the night
With breasts shining
Like Venus and like Mars?
The night that is shouting Jason
When the loud eaves rattle
As with waves above me
Blue at the prow of my desire.

O, prayers in the dark!
O, incense to Poseidon!
Calm in Atlantis.

FIRST PRAISE

Lady of dusk-wood fastnesses,
    Thou art my Lady.
I have known the crisp, splintering leaf-tread with thee on before,
White, slender through green saplings;
I have lain by thee on the brown forest floor
    Beside thee, my Lady.

Lady of rivers strewn with stones,
    Only thou art my Lady.
Where thousand the freshets are crowded like peasants to a fair;

Clear-skinned, wild from seclusion
They jostle white-armed down the tent-bordered thoroughfare
   Praising my Lady.

HOMAGE

Elvira, by love's grace
There goeth before you
A clear radiance
Which maketh all vain souls
Candles when noon is.

The loud clangor of pretenders
Melteth before you
Like the roll of carts passing,
But you come silently
And homage is given.

Now the little by-path
Which leadeth to love
Is again joyful with its many;
And the great highway
From love
Is without passers.

THE FOOL'S SONG

I tried to put a bird in a cage.
   O fool that I am!
   For the bird was Truth.
Sing merrily, Truth: I tried to put
   Truth in a cage!

And when I had the bird in the cage,
   O fool that I am!
Why, it broke my pretty cage.

Sing merrily, Truth: I tried to put
Truth in a cage!

And when the bird was flown from the cage,
O fool that I am!
Why, I had nor bird nor cage.
Sing merrily, Truth: I tried to put
Truth in a cage!
Heigh-ho! Truth in a cage.

FROM "THE BIRTH OF VENUS," SONG

Come with us and play!
See, we have breasts as women!
From your tents by the sea
Come play with us: it is forbidden!

Come with us and play!
Lo, bare, straight legs in the water!
By our boats we stay,
Then swimming away
Come to us: it is forbidden!

Come with us and play!
See, we are tall as women!
Our eyes are keen:
Our hair is bright:
Our voices speak outright:
We revel in the sea's green!
Come play:
It is forbidden!

IMMORTAL

Yes, there is one thing braver than all flowers;
Richer than clear gems; wider than the sky;

Immortal and unchangeable; whose powers
Transcend reason, love and sanity!

And thou, beloved, art that godly thing!
Marvelous and terrible; in glance
An injured Juno roused against Heaven's King!
And thy name, lovely One, is Ignorance.

MEZZO FORTE

Take that, damn you; and that!
And here's a rose
To make it right again!
God knows
I'm sorry, Grace; but then,
It's not my fault if you will be a cat.

AN AFTER SONG

So art thou broken in upon me, Apollo,
Through a splendor of purple garments—
Held by the yellow-haired Clymene
To clothe the white of thy shoulders—
Bare from the day's leaping of horses.
This is strange to me, here in the modern twilight.

CRUDE LAMENT

Mother of flames,
The men that went ahunting
Are asleep in the snow drifts.
You have kept the fire burning!
Crooked fingers that pull
Fuel from among the wet leaves,
Mother of flames

You have kept the fire burning!
The young wives have fallen asleep
With wet hair, weeping,
    Mother of flames!
The young men raised the heavy spears
And are gone prowling in the darkness.
    O mother of flames,
    You who have kept the fire burning!
    Lo, I am helpless!
Would God they had taken me with them!

THE ORDEAL

O crimson salamander,
Because of love's whim
           sacred!
Swim
    the winding flame
    Predestined to disman him
And bring our fellow home to us again.
    Swim in with watery fang,
    Gnaw out and drown
The fire roots that circle him
Until the Hell-flower dies down
    And he comes home again.

Aye, bring him home,
O crimson salamander,
That I may see he is unchanged with burning—
Then have your will with him,
    O crimson salamander.

THE DEATH OF FRANCO OF COLOGNE:
HIS PROPHECY OF BEETHOVEN

It is useless, good woman, useless: the spark fails me.
God! yet when the might of it all assails me

It seems impossible that I cannot do it.
Yet I cannot. They were right, and they all knew it
Years ago, but I—never! I have persisted
Blindly (they say) and now I am old. I have resisted
Everything, but now, now the strife's ended.
The fire's out; the old cloak has been mended
For the last time, the soul peers through its tatters.
Put a light by and leave me; nothing more matters
Now; I am done; I am at last well broken!
Yet, by God, I'll still leave them a token
That they'll swear it was no dead man writ it;
A morsel that they'll mark well the day they bit it,
That there'll be sand between their gross teeth to crunch yet
When goodman Gabriel blows his concluding trumpet.
Leave me!
            And now, little black eyes, come you out here!
Ah, you've given me a lively, lasting bout, year
After year to win you round me darlings!
Precious children, little gambollers! "farlings"
They might have called you once, "nearlings"
I call you now, I first of all the yearlings,
Upon this plain, for I it was that tore you
Out of chaos! It was I bore you!
Ah, you little children that go playing
Over the five-barred gate, and will still be straying
Spite of all that I have ever told you
Of counterpoint and cadence which does not hold you—
No more than chains will for this or that strange reason,
But you're always at some new loving treason
To be away from me, laughing, mocking,
Witlessly, perhaps, but for all that forever knocking
At this stanchion door of your poor father's heart till—oh, well
At least you've shown that you can grow well
However much you evade me faster, faster.
But, black eyes, some day you'll get a master,
For he will come! He shall, he must come!
And when he finishes and the burning dust from
His wheels settles—what shall men see then?
You, you, you, my own lovely children!
Aye, all of you, thus with hands together

Playing on the hill or there in a tether,
Or running free, but all mine! Aye, my very namesakes
Shall be his proper fame's stakes.
And he shall lead you!
And he shall meed you!
And he shall build you gold palaces!
And he shall wine you from clear chalices!
For I have seen it! I have seen it
Written where the world-clouds screen it
From other eyes
Over the bronze gates of paradise!

PORTENT

Red cradle of the night,
   In you
   The dusky child
Sleeps fast till his might
   Shall be piled
Sinew on sinew.

Red cradle of the night,
   The dusky child
Sleeping sits upright.
   Lo! how
      The winds blow now!
   He pillows back;
The winds are again mild.

When he stretches his arms out,
Red cradle of the night,
   The alarms shout
From bare tree to tree,
   Wild
      In afright!
Mighty shall he be,
Red cradle of the night,
   The dusky child! !

CON BRIO

Miserly, is the best description of that poor fool
Who holds Lancelot to have been a morose fellow,
Dolefully brooding over the events which had naturally to follow
The high time of his deed with Guinevere.
He has a sick historical sight, if I judge rightly,
To believe any such thing as that ever occurred.
But, by the god of blood, what else is it that has deterred
Us all from an out and out defiance of fear
But this same perdamnable miserliness,
Which cries about our necks how we shall have less and less
Than we have now if we spend too wantonly?
Bah, this sort of slither is below contempt!
In the same vein we should have apple trees exempt
From bearing anything but pink blossoms all the year,
Fixed permanent lest their bellies wax unseemly, and the dear
Innocent days of them be wasted quite.
How can we have less? Have we not the deed?
Lancelot thought little, spent his gold and rode to fight
Mounted, if God was willing, on a good steed.

AD INFINITUM

Still I bring flowers
Although you fling them at my feet
Until none stays
That is not struck across with wounds:
Flowers and flowers
That you may break them utterly
As you have always done.

Sure happily
I still bring flowers, flowers,
Knowing how all
Are crumpled in your praise
And may not live
To speak a lesser thing.

TRANSLATIONS FROM THE SPANISH, "EL ROMANCERO"

I

Although you do your best to regard me
With an air seeming offended,
Never can you deny, when all's ended,
Calm eyes, that you *did* regard me.

However much you're at pains to
Offend me, by which I may suffer,
What offence is there can make up for
The great good he finds who attains you?
For though with mortal fear you reward me,
Until my sorry sense is plenished,
Never can you deny, when all's ended,
Calm eyes, that you did regard me.

Thinking thus to dismay me
You beheld me with disdain,
But instead of destroying the gain,
In fact with doubled good you paid me.
For though you show them how hardly
They keep off from leniency bended,
Never can you deny, when all's ended,
Calm eyes, that you did regard me.

II

Ah, little green eyes,
Ah, little eyes of mine,
Ah, Heaven be willing
That you think of me somewise.

The day of departure
You came full of grieving
And to see I was leaving
The tears 'gan to start sure
With the heavy torture
Of sorrows unbrightened
When you lie down at night and
When there to you dreams rise,

Ah, Heaven be willing
That you think of me somewise.

Deep is my assurance
Of you, little green eyes,
That in truth you realize
Something of my durance
Eyes of hope's fair assurance
And good premonition
By virtue of whose condition
All green colors I prize.
Ah, Heaven be willing
That you think of me somewise.

Would God I might know you
To which quarter bended
And why comprehended
When sighings overflow you,
And if you must go through
Some certain despair,
For that you lose his care
Who was faithful always.
Ah, Heaven be willing
That you think of me these days.

Through never a moment
I've known how to live lest
All my thoughts but as one pressed
You-ward for their concernment.
May God send chastisement
If in this I belie me
And if it truth be
My own little green eyes.
Ah, Heaven be willing
That you think of me somewise.

III

Poplars of the meadow,
Fountains of Madrid,

Now I am absent from you
All are slandering me.

Each of you is telling
How evil my chance is
The wind among the branches,
The fountains in their welling
To every one telling
You were happy to see.
Now I am absent from you
All are slandering me.

With good right I may wonder
For that at my last leaving
The plants with sighs heaving
And the waters in tears were.
That you played double, never
Thought I this could be,
Now I am absent from you
All are slandering me.

There full in your presence
Music you sought to waken,
Later I'm forsaken
Since you are ware of my absence.
God, wilt Thou give me patience
Here while suffer I ye,
Now I am absent from you
All are slandering me.

IV

The day draweth nearer,
And morrow ends our meeting,
Ere they take thee sleeping
Be up—away, my treasure!

Soft, leave her breasts all unheeded,
Far hence though the master still remaineth!
For soon uptil our earth regaineth

The sun all embraces dividing.
N'er grew pleasure all unimpeded,
N'er was delight lest passion won,
And to the wise man the fit occasion
Has not yet refused a full measure:
Be up—away, my treasure!

If that my love thy bosom inflameth
With honest purpose and just intention,
To free me from my soul's contention
Give over joys the day shameth;
Who thee lameth he also me lameth,
And my good grace builds all in thy good grace;
Be up—away! Fear leaveth place,
That thou art here, no more unto pleasure,
Be up—away, my treasure!

Although thou with a sleep art wresting,
'Tis rightful thou bringst it close,
That of the favor one meeting shows
An hundred may hence be attesting.
'Tis fitting too thou shouldst be mindful
That the ease which we lose now, in kind, full
Many a promise holds for our leisure;
Ere they take thee sleeping;
Be up—away, my treasure!

HIC JACET

The coroner's merry little children
    Have such twinkling brown eyes.
Their father is not of gay men
    And their mother jocular in no wise,
Yet the coroner's merry little children
    Laugh so easily.

They laugh because they prosper.
    Fruit for them is upon all branches.

Lo! how they jibe at loss, for
   Kind heaven fills their little paunches!
It's the coroner's merry, merry children
   Who laugh so easily.

CONTEMPORANIA

The corner of a great rain
Steamy with the country
Has fallen upon my garden.

I go back and forth now
And the little leaves follow me
Talking of the great rain,
Of branches broken,
And the farmer's curses!

But I go back and forth
In this corner of a garden
And the green shoots follow me
Praising the great rain.

We are not curst together,
The leaves and I,
Framing devices, flower devices
And other ways of peopling
The barren country.
Truly it was a very great rain
That makes the little leaves follow me.

TO WISH MYSELF COURAGE

On the day when youth is no more upon me
I will write of the leaves and the moon in a tree top!
I will sing then the song, long in the making—
When the stress of youth is put away from me.

How can I ever be written out as men say?
Surely it is merely an interference with the long song—
This that I am now doing.

But when the spring of it is worn like the old moon
And the eaten leaves are lace upon the cold earth—
Then I will rise up in my great desire—
Long at the birth—and sing me the youth-song!

POEMS
1909–1917

THE USES OF POETRY

I've fond anticipation of a day
O'erfilled with pure diversion presently,
For I must read a lady poesy
The while we glide by many a leafy bay,

Hid deep in rushes, where at random play
The glossy black winged May-flies, or whence flee
Hush-throated nestlings in alarm,
Whom we have idly frighted with our boat's long sway.

For, lest o'ersaddened by such woes as spring
To rural peace from our meek onward trend,
What else more fit? We'll draw the light latch-string

And close the door of sense; then satiate wend,
On poesy's transforming giant wing,
To worlds afar whose fruits all anguish mend.

LOVE

Love is twain, it is not single,
Gold and silver mixed in one,
Passion 'tis and pain which mingle
Glist'ring then for aye undone.

Pain it is not; wondering pity
Dies or e'er the pang is fled:
Passion 'tis not, foul and gritty,
Born one instant, instant dead.

Love is twain, it is not single,
Gold and silver mixed in one,

Passion 'tis and pain which mingle
Glist'ring then for aye undone.

ON A PROPOSED TRIP SOUTH

They tell me on the morrow I must leave
This winter eyrie for a southern flight
And truth to tell I tremble with delight
At thought of such unheralded reprieve.

E'er have I known December in a weave
Of blanched crystal, when, thrice one short night
Packed full with magic, and O blissful sight!
N'er May so warmly doth for April grieve.

To in a breath's space wish the winter through
And lo, to see it fading! Where, oh, where
Is caract could endow this princely boon?

Yet I have found it and shall shortly view
The lush high grasses, shortly see in air
Gay birds and hear the bees make heavy droon.

AND THUS WITH ALL PRAISE

Wonderful creatures!
Why must I call you bride and mother?
Curst be the idle mockery and fashion lie of such names!
Be delight unto me rather!
Joy at the encounter!
Sorrow at the ends of things!
Be to me deeds of compassion:
Have these for name, none other.

MARTIN AND KATHERINE

Alone today I mounted that steep hill
On which the Wartburg stands. Here Luther dwelt
In a small room one year through, here he spelt
The German Bible out by God's good will.

The birds piped ti-ti-tu, and as I went
I thought how Katherine von Bora knelt
At Grimma, idle she, waiting to melt
Her surpliced heart in folds less straitly meant.

As now, it was March then: Lo, he'll fulfill
Today his weighty task! Sing for content
Ye birds! Pipe now! for now 'tis Love's wing's bent.
Work sleeps; love wakes; sing and the glad air thrill!

MISERICORDIA

I am frightened Master, quivering with fear
Half nude before the gloom bed, for one
Persephone the moon wrested and won
Against the black leaves and lo, she was here!

And she looked weary and foredone
With heaviness as seeming to have tried
Many welcomes who once more in her ride
Through the green host flees the pursuing sun.

But oh she was strange with me and not near,
Smooth browed as once, but glimpsed me up sliteyed
And vanished silent. There was bitter pride
Writ in her features! Come to me Master!

MIN SCHLEPPNER

Gaunt, my hope, horse-wise
He goes with wide, half-glazed eyes
That neither blink, turn aside nor blaze,
Fixed as we plough the cold haze.
Round me the ruinous light
Smothers out sight,
Surges billowing up, parts—!
To come rolling in again—starts
The wheel once more, a renewed weight.
But he—high, slow, heavy of gait
Sees!

I WILL SING A JOYOUS SONG

I will sing a joyous song
      To you, my Lady!
On a hill the wind is blowing!
Lady, Lady, we have stood upon the hill
      But now I'm far
And you are far from me
And yet the wind is all between us blowing.

I will sing to you, my Lady,
      Of the wind!
On a hill the wind is blowing!
Hand in hand we were and round us lay the valley.
      Now, I am far
And you are far from me
But still between the wind's a blowing, blowing.

Hear me sing to you, my Lady,
      In the wind!
On a hill the wind is blowing!
Down he went, the golden sun,
   And home went we.
      Though I am far

And you are far from me
The wind is blowing, blowing all between.

FOR VIOLA: DE GUSTIBUS

Belovéd you are
Caviar of Caviar
Of all I love you best
O my Japanese bird nest

No herring from Norway
Can touch you for flavor. Nay
Pimento itself
Is flat as an empty shelf
When compared to your piquancy
O quince of my despondency.

A MAN TO A WOMAN

Though you complain of me
That I build no marvel to your name;
That I have never grappled time to proclaim
You everlastingly;

Though no marble, however white it be,
Compels me to win your fame:
My soul is shapen as by a flame
In your identity.

IN SAN MARCO, VENEZIA

I for whom the world is a clear stream
Of Beauty's holding,—fashioned to reflect
Her loveliness; a hollow cave perfect
In echo, that her voice meet full esteem,

Around me here are arching walls gold-decked,
Of her grey children breathing forth their praise,
I am an outcast, too strange to but raise
One least harmonious whisper of respect.

I am wild, uncouth; before the dream
Thou givest me I stand weak in amaze,
Or dare I lift one hand to serve, it lays
All waste the very mesh I hold supreme.

SICILIAN EMIGRANT'S SONG

O—eh—lee! La—la!
    Donna! Donna!
Blue is the sky of Palermo;
Blue is the little bay;
And dost thou remember the orange and fig,
The lively sun and the sea-breeze at evening?
        Hey—la!
Donna! Donna! Maria!

O—eh—li! La—la!
    Donna! Donna!
Grey is the sky of this land.
Grey and green is the water.
I see no trees, dost thou? The wind
Is cold for the big woman there with the candle.
        Hey—la!
Donna! Donna! Maria!

O—eh—li! O—la!
    Donna! Donna!
I sang thee by the blue waters;
I sing thee here in the grey dawning.
Kiss, for I put down my guitar;
I'll sing thee more songs after the landing.
        O Jesu, I love thee!
Donna! Donna! Maria!

ON FIRST OPENING THE LYRIC YEAR

It is a certain satisfaction to overlook a cemetery,
All the little two-yard-long mounds that vary
So negligibly after all. I mean it brings on a mood
Of clear proportions. I remember once how I stood
Thinking, one summer's day, how good it must be to spend
Some thousand years there from beginning to the end,
There on the cool hillside. But with that feeling grew the dread
That I too would have to be like all the other dead.
That unpleasant sense which one has when one smothers,
Unhappy to leave so much behind merely to resemble others.
It's good no doubt to lie socially well ordered when one has so long to lie,
But for myself somehow this does not satisfy.

THE WANDERER: A ROCOCO STUDY
[First Version]

ADVENT

Even in the time when still I
Had no certain vision of her
She sprang from the nest as a young crow
At first flight circling the forest,
And I know now how then she showed me
Her mind, flying near the tree tops,
Reaching out and over toward the horizon.
I saw her eyes straining in the new distance
And as the woods fell from her flying,
Likewise they fell from me as I followed—
So that I knew (that time) what I must put from me
To hold myself ready for the high courses.

But one day crossing the ferry
With the great towers of Manhattan before me,
Out at the prow with the sea-wind blowing
I had been wearying many questions
Which she had put on to try me:

How shall I be a mirror to this modernity?
When in a rush, dragging
A blunt boat on the yielding river—
Suddenly I saw her! and she waved me
From the white wet in midst of her playing!
She cried me, "Haia! here I am son!
See how strong my little finger! Can I not swim well?
I can fly too!" and with that a great sea-gull
Went to the left, vanishing with a wild cry.
But in my mind all the persons of godhead
Followed after.

CLARITY

Come! cried my mind and by her might
That was upon us we flew above the river
Seeking her, grey gulls among the white—
In air speaking as she had willed it—
"I am given, cried I, now I know it!
I know now all my time is forespent!
For me one face is all the world!
For this day I have at last seen her,
In whom age in age is united—
Indifferent, out of sequence, marvelously!
Saving alone that one sequence
Which is the beauty of all the world, for surely
Either there, in the rolling smoke spheres below us,
Or here with us in the air intercircling,
Certainly somewhere here about us
I know she is revealing these things!"
And as gulls we flew and with soft cries
We beset speech flying, "It is she,
The mighty, recreating the whole world
And this the first day of wonders!
Attiring herself before me—
Taking shape before me for worship
As a red leaf fallen upon a stone!
She of whom I told you, that old queen,
Forgiveless, unreconcilable!
That high wanderer of byways

Walking imperious in beggary—
On her throat a single chain of the many
Rings from which most stones are fallen,
Wrists wearing a diminished state, whose ankles
Are bare! Toward the river! Is it she there?
And we swerved clamorously downward—
In her I will take my peace henceforth!"

BROADWAY

Then it was, as with the edge of a great wing
She struck!—from behind, in mid air
And instantly down the mists of my eyes
There came crowds walking—men as visions
With expressionless, animate faces;
Empty men with shell-thin bodies
Jostling close above the gutter,
Hasting nowhere! And then, for the first time,
I really scented the sweat of her presence
And turning saw her and—fell back sickened!
Ominous, old, painted—
With bright lips and eyes of the street sort—
Her might strapped in by a corset
To give her age youth, perfect
In that will to be young she had covered
Her godhead to go beside me.
Silent, her voice entered at my eyes
And my astonished thought followed her easily:
Well, do their eyes shine, their clothes fit?
These *live* I tell you. Old men with red cheeks,
Young men in gay suits! See them!
Dogged, quivering, impassive—
"Well—are these the ones you envied?"
At which I answered her, Marvelous old queen,
If I could only catch something of this day's
Air and sun into your service,
Those toilers after peace and after pleasure
That toil and pleasure drive, broken at all hours—
Would turn again worshippers at all hours!—
But she sniffed upon the words warily—

Yet I persisted, watching for an answer,—
To you, old harlot of greatest lusting—
Indiscriminate reveller in all ages—
Knower of all fires out of the bodies
Of all men that walked the night with lust at heart!
To you. O mighty, crafty prowler
After the youth of all cities, reeling drunk
With the sight of your archness! All the youth
That comes to you, you having the knowledge
Rather than to those uninitiate—
To you, marvelous old queen, give me,
Them and me, always a new marriage
Each hour of the day's high posting,
New grip upon that garment that brushed me
One time on beach, lawn, in forest!
May I be lifted still up and out of terror,
Up from the death living around me!
Torn up continually and carried
Whatever way the head of your whim is!
A bur upon those streaming tatters—
But with the fall of night she led me quietly away.

PATERSON — THE STRIKE

At the first peep of dawn she roused me
Trembling at those changes the night saw,
For brooding wretchedly in a corner
Of the room to which she had taken me—
Her old eyes glittering fiercely—
Go! she said and I hurried shivering
Out into the deserted streets of Paterson.

That night she came again, hovering
In rags within the filmy ceiling—
Great Queen, bless me with your tatters!
You are blest! Go on!

Hot for savagery,
I went sucking the air! Into the city,
Out again, baffled, on to the mountain!

Back into the city!
                    Nowhere
The subtle! Everywhere the electric!

A short bread-line before a hitherto empty tea shop:
No questions—all stood patiently,
Dominated by one idea: something
That carried them as they are always wanting to be carried,
But what is it, I asked those nearest me,
This thing heretofore unobtainable
That they seem so clever to have put on now?

Why since I have failed them can it be anything
But their own brood? Can it be anything but brutality?
On that at least they're united! That at least
Is their bean soup, their calm bread and a few luxuries!

But in me more sensitive, marvelous old queen,
It sank deep into the blood, that I rose upon
The tense air enjoying the dusty fight!
Heavy wrought drink were the low foreheads,
The flat heads with the unkempt black or blond hair!
Below the skirt the ugly legs of the young girls
Pistons too powerful for delicacy!
The women's wrists, the men's arms, red,
Used to heat and cold, to toss quartered beeves
And barrels and milk cans and crates of fruit!
Faces all knotted up like burls on oaks,
Grasping, fox snouted, thick lipped,
Sagging breasts and protruding stomachs,
Rasping voices, filthy habits with the hands.

Nowhere you! Everywhere the electric!

Ugly, venomous, gigantic!
Tossing me as a great father his helpless
Infant till it shriek with ecstasy
And its eyes roll and its tongue hangs out—!

I am at peace again, old queen, I listen clearer now.

ABROAD

Never, even in a dream
Have I winged so high nor so well
As with her, leading by the hand,
That first day on the Jersey mountains.
And never shall I forget
The trembling interest with which I heard
Her low voice in a thunder:
You are safe here, look child, look open-mouth!
The patch of road between precipitous bramble banks,
The tree in the wind, the white house, the sky!
Speak to them of these concerning me!
For never while you permit them to ignore me
In these shall the full of my freed voice
Come grappling the ear with intent!
At which I cried out with all the might I had,
Waken! O people, to the boughs green
With unripe fruit within you!
Waken to the myriad cinquefoil
In the waving grass of your minds!
Waken to the silent Phoebe nest
Under the eaves of your spirit!

But she stooping nearer the shifting hills
Spoke again, Look there! See them!
There in the oat-field with the horses!
The weight of the sky is upon them,
The great fire-flies in the evening of heaven
Beneath which all roof beams crumble!
There is none but the single roof beam,
There is no love bears against the great fire-flies!

At this I shouted again still more loudly
But my voice was a seed in the wind,
And she, the old one, laughing
Seized me and whirling about, bore back
To the city, upward, still laughing
Until the great towers stood above the meadow
Wheeling beneath, the little creeks, the mallows

That I picked as a boy, the Hackensack
So quiet, that looked so broad formerly:
The crawling trains, the cedar swamp upon the one side—
All so old, so familiar—so new now
To my marvelling eyes as we passed
Invisible.

SOOTHSAY

Eight days went by, eight days
Comforted by no nights, until finally:
Would you behold yourself old, beloved?
And I was pierced! yet I consented gladly
For I knew it could not be otherwise.
And she—Behold yourself old!
Sustained in strength, wielding might in gript surges.
Not bodying the sun in weak leaps
But holding way over rockish men
With fern free fingers on their little crags,
Their hollows, the new Atlas, to bear them
For pride and for mockery! Behold
Yourself old! Winding with slow might
A vine among oaks to the thin tops,
Leaving the leafless leaved,
Bearing purple clusters! Behold
Yourself old! Birds are behind you
In forest silent to the hills.
You are the wind coming that stills birds,
Shakes the leaves in booming polyphony—
Slow winning high way amid the knocking
Of boughs, evenly crescendo,
The din and bellow of the male wind!
Leap then from forest into foam!
Lash about from low into high flames
Tipping sound, the female chorus—
Linking all lions, all twitterings
To make them nothing! Behold yourself old.
And as I made to answer she continued,
A little wistfully, yet in a voice clear cut—
Good is my over lip and evil

My under lip to you henceforth,
For I have taken your soul between my two hands
And this shall be as it is spoken.

SAINT JAMES' GROVE

And so it came to that last day
When, she leading by the hand, we went out
Early in the morning, I heavy of heart
For I knew the novitiate was ended,
The ecstasy was over, the life begun.
In my woollen shirt and the pale blue necktie
My grandmother gave me, there I went
With the old queen right past the houses
Of my friends down the hill to the river
As on any usual day, any errand.
Alone, walking under trees,
I went with her, she with me, in her wild hair
By Santiago Grove and presently
She bent forward and knelt by the river,
The Passaic, that filthy river.
And there, dabbling her mad hands,
She called me close beside her.
Raising the black water, then in the cupped palm
She bathed our brows wailing and laughing:
River we are old, you and I,
We are old and in our state, beggars.
Lo the filth in our hair! our bodies stink!
Old friend, here I have brought you
The young soul you have long asked of me.
My arms in your depths, river,
Let us hold this child between us,
Let us make him yours and mine!
Such were her words spoken.
Stand forth river and give me
The old friend of my revels!
Give me the well-worn spirit
For here I have made a room for it
And I will return to you forthwith
The youth you have long wanted.

Stand forth river and give me
The old friend of my revels!
And the filthy Passaic consented!
Then she leaping up with a great cry—
Enter youth into this bulk!
Enter river into this young man!

Then the river began to enter my heart
Eddying back cool and limpid
Clear to the beginning of days!
But with the rebound it leaped again forward—
Muddy then black and shrunken
Till I felt the utter depth of its filthiness,
The vile breath of its degradation,
And sank down knowing this was me now.
But she lifted me and the water took a new tide
Again into the older experiences.
And so, backward and forward,
It tortured itself within me
Until time had been washed finally under,
And the river had found its level—
And its last motion had ceased
And I knew all—it became me.
And I knew this for double certain
For there I saw myself, whitely,
Being borne off under the water!
I could have shouted out in my agony
At the sight of myself departing
Forever, but I bit back my despair
For she had averted her eyes
By which I knew well enough of her thoughts
And so the last of me was taken.
Then she—Be mostly silent!
And turning to the river, spoke again:
For him and for me, river, the wandering,
But by you I leave, for happiness,
Deepest foliage, the thickest beeches
Though elsewhere they are all dying:
Tallest oaks and yellow birches
That dip leaves in you mourning

As now I dip my hair, immemorial
Of me, immemorial of him,
Immemorial of these our promises!
Here shall be a birds' paradise—
They sing to you rememb'ring my voice;
Here the most secluded spaces
For wide around, hallowed by a stench
To be our joint solitude and temple,
A memory of this clear marriage
And the child I have brought you in the late years!
Live river, live in luxuriance
Rememb'ring this our son,
In remembrance of me and my sorrow
And of the new wandering.

AT DAWN

The war of your great beauty is in all the skies,
Yet these receive no hurt! I see your name
Written upon their faces,
Yet the bowls of the stars will be refilled—and lit again,
And their peace will live continuous!

O marvelous! what new configuration will come next?
I am bewildered with multiplicity.

RENDEZVOUS

My song! It is time!
Wider! Bolder! Spread the arms!
Have done with finger pointing.
Open windows even for the cold
To come whistling in, blowing the curtains:
We have looked out through glass
Long enough, my song.

Now, knowing the wind's knack,
We can make little of daring:
Has not laughter in the house corners
Spoken of it—the blind horse:
Has not every chink whispered
How she rides biting its ears,
How she drives it in secret?

Therefore my song—bolder!
Let in the wind! Open the windows!
Embrace the companion
That is whistling, waiting
Impatiently to receive us!

TO THE OUTER WORLD

At peace here—I feel you about me.
Do not think that I disdain your fine clothing,
The distinction of your robes clinging about the shoulders,

The magnificence of your ruddy hair, the grace of your distinguished
    bearing
As you move athwart me—here keeping
Pace to your splendors with my heart beats!

Surely the air were bare indeed
Were I not reaching up into it continually
To feel you passing.

But mighty and many as you are
There is one I have never seen among you,
Some small passer it may be: it is she keeps me waiting.

When she comes—if she come—in the end,
I shall spring up beside her well at ease
And we will join you all wherever you may be circling.

LA FLOR

I had been reading what you have written of your idleness,
When I came upon certain worthier selections
From the month's work of our industrious versifiers—
Those who bring their ingenious tapestries to such soft perfection,
Borrowing majesty from a true likeness to natural splendor:
Tracery of branches etched upon a cold sky, a leaf, a flower.

"But what," I then said to myself, "of him who goes,
"Himself surpassing flowers, a flower in that peculiar way which the
    choice follows?"
For certainly they take their daring in words carrying splendor,
And certainly his verse is crimson when they speak of the rose.
So I come deliberately to the most exquisite praise
I have imagined of any living thing—which is now manifest.

OFFERING

As the hedges, clipt and even,
That parallel the common way—
And upon one side the hedges
And upon one side bare trees—
As these hedges bear the dried leaves
That have fallen from spent branches,—
Having caught them in mid air—
And hold them yet awhile
That they may not be so soon
Jostled about and tramped on—

The red, the yellow, the purple—blues—
So do my words catch and bear
Both leaves and flowers that are fallen—
In all places before the feet
Of the passing many—to bear them
Yet awhile before they are trodden.

A LA LUNE

Slowly rising, slowly strengthening moon,
Pardon us our fear in pride:
Pardon us our troubled quietnesses!

Aye, pardon us, O moon,
Round, bright upon the darkening!
Pardon us our little journeys endlessly repeated!

All halting tendernesses pardon us,
O high moon!
For you, nooning by night,
You having crept to the full,
You, O moon, must have understanding of these things.

THE REVELATION

I awoke happy, the house
Was strange, voices
Were across a gap
Through which a girl
Came and paused,
Reaching out to me—

Then I remembered
What I had dreamed—
A girl
One whom I knew well
Leaned on the door of my car
And stroked my hand—

I shall pass her on the street
We shall say trivial things
To each other
But I shall never cease
To search her eyes
For that quiet look—

TRANSITIONAL

First he said:
It is the woman in us
That makes us write—
Let us acknowledge it—
Men would be silent.
We are not men
Therefore we can speak
And be conscious
(of the two sides)
Unbent by the sensual
As befits accuracy.

I then said:
Dare you make this
Your propaganda?

And he answered:
Am I not I—here?

INVITATION

We live in this flat blue basin,
We and the meadow things, my townspeople,
And there beyond where the snow lies
In ochred patches float the smoke-grey towers.
Has it never struck you as curious
That we do not all leave this place?
Surely we are blest
With a noteworthy wisdom, my townspeople!
Let us be conscious and talk of these things.

AUX IMAGISTES

I think I have never been so exalted
As I am now by you,

O frost bitten blossoms,
That are unfolding your wings
From out the envious black branches.

Bloom quickly and make much of the sunshine.
The twigs conspire against you!
Hear them!
They hold you from behind!

You shall not take wing
Except wing by wing, brokenly,
And yet—
Even they
Shall not endure for ever.

PEACE

I grant you: peace is desirable. War being, in a figure,
its antithesis is wholly detestable to the lover of peace.

But there are lovers and lovers.

It is stupid to advocate peace in order to have me work
in a factory or a field or a mine or a quarry or a forest
or on the sea or at a desk or on the ice or at the sea's
bottom—unless I please to do these things.

To substitute for me a lesser war for another greater
is the hollowest mockery—to substitute war with fire by
war with mud is vilest deception. Either I must have
war or none.

Peace is noble only when it sends me out a tramp—
my peace made with the world—a lily of the field if you
will.

But who is there that advocates peace? I have seen
no true apostles. I have read of few. And it is notable
that these do not form societies—Tolstoi to the contrary.

Peace requires genius to be preached. It is a rare high thing—it is not subsidized—it also has its courage.

Pastorals and Self-Portraits

SELF-PORTRAIT 1

You lie packed,
Dark:
Turned sluggishly
By plough.
Wheels stir you—
Up behind them!
You tissue out
You drink light
And go in clouds!

PASTORAL 1
[First Version]

The old man who goes about
Gathering dog lime
Walks in the gutter
Without looking up
And his tread
Is more majestic than
That of the Episcopal minister
Approaching the pulpit
Of a Sunday.
Meanwhile
The little sparrows
Hop ingenuously
About the pavement
Quarreling
Over those things

That interest them
With sharp voices
But we who are wiser
Shut ourselves in
On either hand
And no one knows
Whether we think good
Or evil.
                    These things
Astonish me beyond words!

IDYL

Wine of the grey sky
Wine of happiness
Invisible rain
Driven down
You bathe me
And I am refreshed:

Yesterday
I was in the city
I stood before
The new station
Watching
The white clouds
Passing
The great Hermes
And flying,
Flying toward Greece.
I saw
The fluted columns
(Not ground
    Piece into piece
    But fitted with plaster)
I saw the frieze
Of acanthus:
All that has endured

Through the long days
And the long, long nights
And I thought
Of Phidias,
O wine of the grey sky,
Watching
As there passed
Clouds
White and formless—
Without word
Without sign
Above his Parthanon
Out toward India
And the sea!

SERAPH

I was here alone,
The lamp back of me
There under the beams—
The heat of the fire in my face.
I straightened and turned

There stood you!
Immobile,
Gleaming with light!
The miraculous vision
Flaming, flashing itself
Upon me, an acid
To quench thirst
Once for all.

That is why when
You came forward
With your excuses
Asking if you had
Frightened me

I seized you,
Held you eagerly in my arms

But it was gone.

PASTORAL 2

If I talk to things
Do not flatter yourself
That I am mad
Rather realize yourself
To be deaf and that
Of two evils, the plants
Being deaf likewise,
I choose that
Which proves by other
Attributes worthier
Of the distinction.

Hear me
You who listen without malice.
Hear me
You crusts of blue moss,
And black earth
In the twisted roots
Of the white tree!

Hear me, black trees
The wind
Howling in your branches!
Hear me
Long red-grass
Matted down
And standing in the wind!
Hear me
Driven leaves!
Hear me

Though you never tell
The cause of this terror
That strikes me back
Feverishly upon petty business:
Saving the sick,
Getting shelter, food
And delights for my dear family—
I long
To fling aside clothes
And crawl in naked
There among you
Cold as it is!

Hear me
For I am wise,
Wiser than you—
Though you have virtues
Greater than mine.
I will give you
A counsel for it further on
When I have said my fill.
—wiser than you
Though you have virtues
Greater than mine:
You do not drive yourselves,
It is the wind's knives
That battle at you
From the outside—
You do not generate
Your own poisons.

See!
(Take note of this
You who have eyes.)
See these futile colors
That keep me from the wind.

Do not think
It is fear of these

That holds me
From *you* likewise—
I would fling them by in a moment
And the roof menders there,
Peacefully hammering,
Would rush down
And carry me away—
Even so it would be
A wise thing to have done
Were it not
That this hide
I have drawn about myself
To shield me
Has bound me more subtly
Than you have imagined.

It is no good
To strip the bark
From the old tree
It will not be young again—
I have bound myself
Better than that!

Kiss the wind when it kills you
Lean your surfaces
Against the frost
With your whole heart—

You have taken the counsel
Before given.

SELF-PORTRAIT 2

It is raining.
Fall!
You whitelivered kill-joys
Fall!

You heavy bellied sluts,
Fall from the sky!
Fall onto the edged leaves,
Let the bayonettes of the grass
Receive you—
Drive you to the ground:
There be broken finally
—and your life ends!

As for me—?
Beat upon my head
And upon my shoulders
You frighten me but little.
Let your very eyes pop out
Against the feather I wear
And dance down the edge
Of my sombrero—!
I'll keep my way in spite of all.

Only the flowers
Are kind to them—
Lips opening upward.

IDYL

They say to me, "There is
A roaring god outside
Beating the trees!"
I go hurriedly
And find
Two unfortunates
Cowering in the wind.
I think of this
As I lie here, warm
Watching the blinding white
That was saffron
Change to steel blue
Behind shaking trees.

I raise my head and
Sight leaps twenty miles
To the bleak horizon,
"But my desires,"
I say to myself
"Are thirty years
Behind all this."

It is late.
My wife comes out
And tucks me in
Telling me
Not to hurry—
—Not to hurry!
She brings our baby
And puts him
In the bed beside me.
I move over
Into the cold sheets
To make room for him
And thinking
Of the freezing poor
I consider myself
Happy—
Then we kiss.

GRoTEsqUe

The city has tits in rows.
The country is in the main—male,
It butts me with blunt stub-horns,
Forces me to oppose it
Or be trampled.

The city is full of milk
And lies still for the most part.
These crack skulls

And spill brains
Against her stomach.

THE SHADOW

Soft as the bed in the earth
where a stone has lain—
so soft, so smooth and so cool
Spring closes me in
with her arms and her hands.

Rich as the smell
of new earth on a stone
that has lain breathing
the damp through its pores—
Spring closes me in
with her blossomy hair
brings dark to my eyes.

SLOW MOVEMENT

All those treasures that lie in the little bolted box whose tiny space is
Mightier than the room of the stars, being secret and filled with dreams:
All those treasures—I hold them in my hand—are straining continually
Against the sides and the lid and the two ends of the little box in which
    I guard them;
Crying that there is no sun come among them this great while and that
    they weary of shining;
Calling me to fold back the lid of the little box and to give them sleep
    finally.

But the night I am hiding from them, dear friend, is far more desperate
    than their night!
And so I take pity on them and pretend to have lost the key to the little
    house of my treasures,

For they would die of weariness were I to open it, and not be merely
    faint and sleepy
As they are now.

A CONFIDENCE

Today, dear friend, this grey day,
I have been explaining to a young man of the West Indies
How the leaves all fall from the little branches
And lie soon in crowds along the bare ground;
   How they lie
On all sides so thick that no man
May pass any way without touching them,
Or hearing at his feet a great crying-out!

But in no way at all could I have told him
This that I tell you so easily:
How having become wise as a flame with watching
Above the year since that time he lifted
   His young face
For a moment—that time of the first passing—
They lie exultant, pressing his footprints,
Melting away because of their passion!

METRIC FIGURE

Veils of clarity
have succeeded
veils of color
that wove
as the sea
sliding above
submerged whiteness.

Veils of clarity
reveal sand

glistening—
falling away
to an edge—
sliding
beneath the advancing ripples.

EPIGRAMME

Hast ever seen man
Dig gold in a manure heap?
Then open two eyes
For digging among these,
Our fellow townsmen,
I turn up this nugget.

STILLNESS

Heavy white rooves
of Rutherford
sloping west and east
under the fast darkening sky:

What have I to say to you
that you may whisper it to them
in the night?

Round you
is a great smouldering distance
on all sides
that engulfs you
in utter loneliness.

Lean above their beds tonight
snow covered rooves;
listen;
feel them stirring warmly within
and say—nothing.

DRINK

My whiskey is
a tough way of life:

The wild cherry
continually pressing back
peach orchards.

I am a penniless
rumsoak.

Where shall I have that solidity
which trees find
in the ground?

My stuff
is the feel of good legs
and a broad pelvis
under the gold hair ornaments
of skyscrapers.

A LOVE SONG: FIRST VERSION, 1915

What have I to say to you
When we shall meet?
Yet—
I lie here thinking of you.

The stain of love
Is upon the world.
Yellow, yellow, yellow,
It eats into the leaves,
Smears with saffron
The horned branches that lean
Heavily
Against a smooth purple sky.

There is no light—
Only a honey-thick stain
That drips from leaf to leaf
And limb to limb
Spoiling the colors
Of the whole world.

I am alone.
The weight of love
Has buoyed me up
Till my head
Knocks against the sky.

See me!
My hair is dripping with nectar—
Starlings carry it
On their black wings.
See, at last
My arms and my hands
Are lying idle.

How can I tell
If I shall ever love you again
As I do now?

NAKED

What fool would feel
His cheeks burn
Because of the snow?
Would he call it
By a name, give it
Breasts, features,
Bare limbs?
Would he call it
A woman?

(Surely then he would be
A fool.)

And see her,
Warmed with the cold,
Go upon the heads
Of creatures
Whose faces lean
To the ground?

Would he watch
The compassion of
Her eyes,
That look, now up
Now down,
To the turn of
The wind and
The turn of
The shivering minds
She touches—
Motionless—troubled?

I ask you—
I ask you, my townspeople,
What fool is this?

Would he forget
The sight of
His mother and
His wife
Because of her?—
Have his heart
Turned to ice
That will not soften?

What!
Would he see a thing
Lovelier than
A high-school girl,

With the skill
Of Venus
To stand naked—
Naked on the air?

Falling snow and
               you up there—waiting.

MARRIAGE

So different, this man
And this woman:
A stream flowing
In a field.

THE OLD WORSHIPPER

How times change, old friend,
And how little anything changes!

We used to collect butterflies
And insects in Kipp's woods—
Do you remember?
Now this wonderful collection
From the Amazon
Comes quite naturally
For you to weigh and to classify.

Quiet and unnoticed
The flower of your whole life
Has opened its perfect petals—
And none to witness, save one
Old worshipper!

THE YOUNG HOUSEWIFE

At ten A.M. the young housewife
moves about in negligee behind
the wooden walls of her husband's house.
I pass solitary in my car.

Then again she comes to the curb
to call the ice-man, fish-man, and stands
shy, uncorseted, tucking in
stray ends of hair, and I compare her
to a fallen leaf.

The noiseless wheels of my car
rush with a crackling sound over
dried leaves as I bow and pass smiling.

SPRING SONG

Having died
one is at great advantage
over his fellows—
one can pretend.

And so,
the smell of earth
being upon you too—
I pretend

there is something
temptingly foreign
some subtle difference,
one last amour

to be divided for
our death-necklaces, when
I would merely lie
hand in hand in the dirt with you.

FIRE SPIRIT

I am old.
You warm yourselves at these fires?
In the center of these flames
I sit, my teeth chatter!
Where shall I turn for comfort?

NIGHT

Houses—
the dark side silhouetted
on flashes of moonlight!

The air—full of
invisible snow!

At the end of the street—
chrysanthemums in
a lighted window:
white and pink globes
in clusters massed!
They grow clearer
nearer . . . nearer!
I will reach them! !
(if I continue)

The window
is full of flowers—
more than I imagined . . .

They are gone!

The flower girl
has switched off the light.

Moon-shine
street lamps in my face.
"What do I care!"

SICK AFRICAN

Wm. Yates, colored,
Lies in bed reading
The Bible—
And recovering from
A dose of epididymitis
Contracted while Grace
Was pregnant with
The twelve day old
Baby:
There sits Grace, laughing,
Too weak to stand.

CHINESE NIGHTINGALE

Long before dawn your light
Shone in the window, Sam Wu;
You were at your trade.

AL QUE QUIERE!
1917

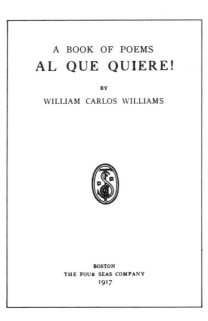

A BOOK OF POEMS

AL QUE QUIERE!

BY

WILLIAM CARLOS WILLIAMS

BOSTON
THE FOUR SEAS COMPANY
1917

SUB TERRA

Where shall I find you,
you my grotesque fellows
that I seek everywhere
to make up my band?
None, not one
with the earthy tastes I require;
the burrowing pride that rises
subtly as on a bush in May.

Where are you this day,
you my seven year locusts
with cased wings?
Ah my beauties how I long—!
That harvest
that shall be your advent—
thrusting up through the grass,
up under the weeds
answering me,
that will be satisfying!
The light shall leap and snap
that day as with a million lashes!

Oh, I have you; yes
you are about me in a sense:
playing under the blue pools
that are my windows,—
but they shut you out still,
there in the half light.
For the simple truth is
that though I see you clear enough
you are not there!

It is not that—it is you,
you I want!

—God, if I could fathom
the guts of shadows!

You to come with me
poking into negro houses
with their gloom and smell!
in among children
leaping around a dead dog!
Mimicking
onto the lawns of the rich!
You!
to go with me a-tip-toe,
head down under heaven,
nostrils lipping the wind!

PASTORAL

When I was younger
it was plain to me
I must make something of myself.
Older now
I walk back streets
admiring the houses
of the very poor:
roof out of line with sides
the yards cluttered
with old chicken wire, ashes,
furniture gone wrong;
the fences and outhouses
built of barrel-staves
and parts of boxes, all,
if I am fortunate,
smeared a bluish green
that properly weathered
pleases me best
of all colors.

No one
will believe this
of vast import to the nation.

CHICORY AND DAISIES

I

Lift your flowers
on bitter stems
chicory!
Lift them up
out of the scorched ground!
Bear no foliage
but give yourself
wholly to that!
Strain under them
you bitter stems
that no beast eats—
and scorn greyness!
Into the heat with them:
cool!
luxuriant! sky-blue!
The earth cracks and
is shriveled up;
the wind moans piteously;
the sky goes out
if you should fail.

II

I saw a child with daisies
for weaving into the hair
tear the stems
with her teeth!

METRIC FIGURE

There is a bird in the poplars!
It is the sun!
The leaves are little yellow fish
swimming in the river.
The bird skims above them,
day is on his wings.
Phoebus!
It is he that is making
the great gleam among the poplars!
It is his singing
outshines the noise
of leaves clashing in the wind.

WOMAN WALKING

An oblique cloud of purple smoke
across a milky silhouette
of house sides and tiny trees—
a little village—
that ends in a saw edge
of mist-covered trees
on a sheet of grey sky.

To the right, jutting in,
a dark crimson corner of roof.
To the left, half a tree:

    —what a blessing it is
to see you in the street again,
powerful woman,
coming with swinging haunches,
breasts straight forward,
supple shoulders, full arms
and strong, soft hands (I've felt them)
carrying the heavy basket.

I might well see you oftener!
And for a different reason
than the fresh eggs
you bring us so regularly.

Yes, you, young as I,
with boney brows,
kind grey eyes and a kind mouth;
you walking out toward me
from that dead hillside!
I might well see you oftener.

GULLS

My townspeople, beyond in the great world,
are many with whom it were far more
profitable for me to live than here with you.
These whirr about me calling, calling!
and for my own part I answer them, loud as I can,
but they, being free, pass!
I remain! Therefore, listen!
For you will not soon have another singer.

First I say this: You have seen
the strange birds, have you not, that sometimes
rest upon our river in winter?
Let them cause you to think well then of the storms
that drive many to shelter. These things
do not happen without reason.

And the next thing I say is this:
I saw an eagle once circling against the clouds
over one of our principal churches—
Easter, it was—a beautiful day!
three gulls came from above the river
and crossed slowly seaward!
Oh, I know you have your own hymns, I have heard them—

and because I knew they invoked some great protector
I could not be angry with you, no matter
how much they outraged true music—

You see, it is not necessary for us to leap at each other,
and, as I told you, in the end
the gulls moved seaward very quietly.

APPEAL

You who are so mighty,
crimson salamander,
hear me once more.
I lay among the half-burned sticks
at the edge of the fire.
The fiend was creeping in.
I felt the cold tips of fingers—

O crimson salamander!

Give me one little flame,
one!
that I may bind it
protectingly about the wrist
of him that flung me here,
here upon the very center!

This is my song.

IN HARBOR

Surely there, among the great docks, is peace, my mind;
there with the ships moored in the river.
Go out, timid child,
and snuggle in among the great ships talking so quietly.

Maybe you will even fall asleep near them and be
lifted into one of their laps, and in the morning—
There is always the morning in which to remember it all!
Of what are they gossiping? God knows.
And God knows it matters little for we cannot understand them.
Yet it is certainly of the sea, of that there can be no question.
It is a quiet sound. Rest! That's all I care for now.
The smell of them will put us to sleep presently.
Smell! It is the sea water mingling here into the river—
at least so it seems—perhaps it is something else—but what matter?
The sea water! It is quiet and smooth here!
How slowly they move, little by little trying
the hawsers that drop and groan with their agony.
Yes, it is certainly of the high sea they are talking.

WINTER SUNSET

Then I raised my head
and stared out over
the blue February waste
to the blue bank of hill
with stars on it
in strings and festoons—
but above that:
one opaque
stone of a cloud
just on the hill
left and right
as far as I could see;
and above that
a red streak, then
icy blue sky!

It was a fearful thing
to come into a man's heart
at that time; that stone
over the little blinking stars
they'd set there.

APOLOGY

Why do I write today?

The beauty of
the terrible faces
of our nonentities
stirs me to it:

colored women
day workers—
old and experienced—
returning home at dusk
in cast off clothing
faces like
old Florentine oak.

Also

the set pieces
of your faces stir me—
leading citizens—
but not
in the same way.

PASTORAL

The little sparrows
hop ingenuously
about the pavement
quarreling
with sharp voices
over those things
that interest them.
But we who are wiser
shut ourselves in
on either hand
and no one knows

whether we think good
or evil.
   Meanwhile,
the old man who goes about
gathering dog-lime
walks in the gutter
without looking up
and his tread
is more majestic than
that of the Episcopal minister
approaching the pulpit
of a Sunday.
   These things
astonish me beyond words.

LOVE SONG

Daisies are broken
petals are news of the day
stems lift to the grass tops
they catch on shoes
part in the middle
leave root and leaves secure.

Black branches
carry square leaves
to the wood's top.
They hold firm
break with a roar
show the white!

Your moods are slow
the shedding of leaves
and sure
the return in May!

We walked
in your father's grove

and saw the great oaks
lying with roots
ripped from the ground.

M. B.

Winter has spent this snow
out of envy, but spring is here!
He sits at the breakfast table
in his yellow hair
and disdains even the sun
walking outside
in spangled slippers:

He looks out: there is
a glare of lights
before a theater,—
a sparkling lady
passes quickly to
the seclusion of
her carriage.

                    Presently
under the dirty, wavy heaven
of a borrowed room he will make
reinhaled tobacco smoke
his clouds and try them
against the sky's limits!

TRACT

I will teach you my townspeople
how to perform a funeral—
for you have it over a troop
of artists—
unless one should scour the world—
you have the ground sense necessary.

See! the hearse leads.
I begin with a design for a hearse.
For Christ's sake not black—
nor white either—and not polished!
Let it be weathered—like a farm wagon—
with gilt wheels (this could be
applied fresh at small expense)
or no wheels at all:
a rough dray to drag over the ground.

Knock the glass out!
My God—glass, my townspeople!
For what purpose? Is it for the dead
to look out or for us to see
how well he is housed or to see
the flowers or the lack of them—
or what?
To keep the rain and snow from him?
He will have a heavier rain soon:
pebbles and dirt and what not.
Let there be no glass—
and no upholstery, phew!
and no little brass rollers
and small easy wheels on the bottom—
my townspeople what are you thinking of?

A rough plain hearse then
with gilt wheels and no top at all.
On this the coffin lies
by its own weight.

                    No wreaths please—
especially no hot house flowers.
Some common memento is better,
something he prized and is known by:
his old clothes—a few books perhaps—
God knows what! You realize
how we are about these things
my townspeople—
something will be found—anything

even flowers if he had come to that.
So much for the hearse.

For heaven's sake though see to the driver!
Take off the silk hat! In fact
that's no place at all for him—
up there unceremoniously
dragging our friend out to his own dignity!
Bring him down—bring him down!
Low and inconspicuous! I'd not have him ride
on the wagon at all—damn him—
the undertaker's understrapper!
Let him hold the reins
and walk at the side
and inconspicuously too!

Then briefly as to yourselves:
Walk behind—as they do in France,
seventh class, or if you ride
Hell take curtains! Go with some show
of inconvenience; sit openly—
to the weather as to grief.
Or do you think you can shut grief in?
What—from us? We who have perhaps
nothing to lose? Share with us
share with us—it will be money
in your pockets.
                                    Go now
I think you are ready.

PROMENADE

I

Well, mind, here we have
our little son beside us:
a little diversion before breakfast!

Come, we'll walk down the road
till the bacon will be frying.
We might better be idle?
A poem might come of it?
Oh, be useful. Save annoyance
to Flossie and besides—the wind!
It's cold. It blows our
old pants out! It makes us shiver!
See the heavy trees
shifting their weight before it.
Let us be trees, an old house,
a hill with grass on it!
The baby's arms are blue.
Come, move! Be quieted!

II

So. We'll sit here now
and throw pebbles into
this water-trickle.

            Splash the water up!
(Splash it up, Sonny!) Laugh!
Hit it there deep under the grass.
See it splash! Ah, mind,
see it splash! It is alive!
Throw pieces of broken leaves
into it. They'll pass through.
No! Yes—Just!

Away now for the cows! But—
It's cold!
It's getting dark.
It's going to rain.
No further!

III

Oh then, a wreath! Let's
refresh something they
used to write well of.

Two fern plumes. Strip them
to the mid-rib along one side.
Bind the tips with a grass stem.
Bend and intertwist the stalks
at the back. So!
Ah! now we are crowned!
Now we are a poet!
Quickly!
A bunch of little flowers
for Flossie—the little ones
only:
                    a red clover, one
blue heal-all, a sprig of
bone-set, one primrose,
a head of Indian tobacco, this
magenta speck and this
little lavender!
            Home now, my mind!—
Sonny's arms are icy, I tell you—
and have breakfast!

EL HOMBRE

It's a strange courage
you give me ancient star:

Shine alone in the sunrise
toward which you lend no part!

HERO

Fool,
put your adventures
into those things
which break ships—
not female flesh.

Let there pass
over the mind
the waters of
four oceans, the airs
of four skies!

Return hollow-bellied,
keen-eyed, hard!
A simple scar or two.

Little girls will come
bringing you
roses for your button-hole.

LIBERTAD! IGUALDAD! FRATERNIDAD!

You sullen pig of a man
you force me into the mud
with your stinking ash-cart!

Brother!
       —if we were rich
we'd stick our chests out
and hold our heads high!

It is dreams that have destroyed us.

There is no more pride
in horses or in rein holding.
We sit hunched together brooding
our fate.

       Well—
all things turn bitter in the end
whether you choose the right or
the left way
       and—
dreams are not a bad thing.

CANTHARA

The old black-man showed me
how he had been shocked
in his youth
by six women, dancing
a set-dance, stark naked below
the skirts raised round
their breasts:
                    bellies flung forward
knees flying!
                         —while
his gestures, against the
tiled wall of the dingy bath-room,
swished with ecstasy to
the familiar music of
                    his old emotion.

MUJER

Oh, black Persian cat!
Was not your life
already cursed with offspring?
We took you for rest to that old
Yankee farm,—so lonely
and with so many field mice
in the long grass—
and you return to us
in this condition—!

Oh, black Persian cat.

SUMMER SONG

Wanderer moon
smiling a

faintly ironical smile
at this
brilliant, dew-moistened
summer morning,—
a detached
sleepily indifferent
smile, a
wanderer's smile,—
if I should
buy a shirt
your color and
put on a necktie
sky-blue
where would they carry me?

LOVE SONG

Sweep the house clean,
hang fresh curtains
in the windows
put on a new dress
and come with me!
The elm is scattering
its little loaves
of sweet smells
from a white sky!

Who shall hear of us
in the time to come?
Let him say there was
a burst of fragrance
from black branches.

FOREIGN

Artsybashev is a Russian.
I am an American.

Let us wonder, my townspeople,
if Artsybashev tends his own fires
as I do, gets himself cursed
for the baby's failure to thrive,
loosens windows for the woman
who cleans his parlor—
or has he neat servants
and a quiet library, an
intellectual wife perhaps and
no children,—an apartment
somewhere in a back street or
lives alone or with his mother
or sister—

I wonder, my townspeople,
if Artsybashev looks upon
himself the more concernedly
or succeeds any better than I
in laying the world.

I wonder which is the bigger
fool in his own mind.

These are shining topics
my townspeople but—
hardly of great moment.

A PRELUDE

I know only the bare rocks of today.
In these lies my brown sea-weed,—
green quartz veins bent through the wet shale;
in these lie my pools left by the tide—
quiet, forgetting waves;
on these stiffen white star fish
on these I slip barefooted!

Whispers of the fishy air touch my body;
"Sisters," I say to them.

HISTORY

1

A wind might blow a lotus petal
over the pyramids—but not this wind.

Summer is a dried leaf.

Leaves stir this way then that
on the baked asphalt, the wheels
of motor cars rush over them,—
      gas smells mingle with leaf smells.

Oh, Sunday, day of worship! ! !

The steps to the Museum are high.
Worshippers pass in and out.
Nobody comes here today.
I come here to mingle faïence dug
from the tomb, turquoise-colored
necklaces and wind belched from the
stomach; delicately veined basins
of agate, cracked and discolored and
the stink of stale urine!

Enter! Elbow in at the door.
Men? Women?
Simpering, clay fetish-faces counting
through the turnstile.
               Ah!

2

This sarcophagus contained the body
of Uresh-Nai, priest to the goddess Mut,
Mother of All—

Run your finger against this edge!
—here went the chisel!—and think

of an arrogance endured six thousand years
without a flaw!

But love is an oil to embalm the body.
Love is a packet of spices, a strong-
smelling liquid to be squirted into
the thigh. No?
Love rubbed on a bald head will make
hair—and after? Love is
a lice comber!
            Gnats on dung!

"The chisel is in your hand, the block
is before you, cut as I shall dictate:
This is the coffin of Uresh-Nai,
priest to the Sky Goddess,—built
to endure forever!
            Carve the inside
with the image of my death in
little lines of figures three fingers high.
Put a lid on it cut with Mut bending over
the earth, for my headpiece, and in the year
to be chosen I shall rouse, the lid
shall be lifted and I will walk about
the temple where they have rested me
and eat the air of the place:

Ah—these walls are high! This
is in keeping."

3

The priest has passed into his tomb.
The stone has taken up his spirit!
Granite over flesh: who will deny
its advantages?

Your death?—water
spilled upon the ground—
though water will mount again into rose-leaves—

but you?—would hold life still,
even as a memory, when it is over.
Benevolence is rare.

Climb about this sarcophagus, read
what is writ for you in these figures
hard as the granite that has held them
with so soft a hand the while
your own flesh has been fifty times
through the guts of oxen,—read!
"I who am the one flesh say to you,
The rose-tree will have its donor
even though he give stingily.
The gift of some endures
ten years, the gift of some twenty
and the gift of some for the time a
great house rots and is torn down.
Some give for a thousand years to men of
one face, some for a thousand
to all men and some few to all men
while granite holds an edge against
the weather.
                    Judge then of love!"

4

"My flesh is turned to stone. I
have endured my summer. The flurry
of falling petals is ended. Lay
the finger upon this granite. I was
well desired and fully caressed
by many lovers but my flesh
withered swiftly and my heart was
never satisfied. Lay your hands
upon the granite as a lover lays his
hand upon the thigh and upon the
round breasts of her who is beside
him, for now I will not wither,
now I have thrown off secrecy, now
I have walked naked into the street,

now I have scattered my heavy beauty
in the open market.
Here I am with head high and a
burning heart eagerly awaiting
your caresses, whoever it may be,
for granite is not harder than
my love is open, runs loose among you!

I arrogant against death! I
who have endured! I worn against
the years!"

5

But it is five o'clock. Come!
Life is good—enjoy it!
A walk in the park while the day lasts.
I will go with you. Look! this
northern scenery is not the Nile, but—
these benches—the yellow and purple dusk—
the moon there—these tired people—
the lights on the water!

Are not these Jews and—Ethiopians?
The world is young, surely! Young
and colored like—a girl that has come upon
a lover! Will that do?

WINTER QUIET

Limb to limb, mouth to mouth
with the bleached grass
silver mist lies upon the back yards
among the outhouses.
                    The dwarf trees
pirouette awkwardly to it—
whirling round on one toe;
the big tree smiles and glances

                                        upward!
Tense with suppressed excitement
the fences watch where the ground
has humped an aching shoulder for
                            the ecstasy.

DAWN

Ecstatic bird songs pound
the hollow vastness of the sky
with metallic clinkings—
beating color up into it
at a far edge,—beating it, beating it
with rising, triumphant ardor,—
stirring it into warmth,
quickening in it a spreading change,—
bursting wildly against it as
dividing the horizon, a heavy sun
lifts himself—is lifted—
bit by bit above the edge
of things,—runs free at last
out into the open—! lumbering
glorified in full release upward—
                            songs cease.

GOOD NIGHT

In brilliant gas light
I turn the kitchen spigot
and watch the water plash
into the clean white sink.
On the grooved drain-board
to one side is
a glass filled with parsley—
crisped green.
                    Waiting

for the water to freshen—
I glance at the spotless floor—:
a pair of rubber sandals
lie side by side
under the wall-table
all is in order for the night.

Waiting, with a glass in my hand
—three girls in crimson satin
pass close before me on
the murmurous background of
the crowded opera—
                                    it is
memory playing the clown—
three vague, meaningless girls
full of smells and
the rustling sound of
cloth rubbing on cloth and
little slippers on carpet—
high-school French
spoken in a loud voice!

Parsley in a glass,
still and shining,
brings me back. I take my drink
and yawn deliciously.
I am ready for bed.

DANSE RUSSE

If I when my wife is sleeping
and the baby and Kathleen
are sleeping
and the sun is a flame-white disc
in silken mists
above shining trees,—
if I in my north room
dance naked, grotesquely

before my mirror
waving my shirt round my head
and singing softly to myself:
"I am lonely, lonely.
I was born to be lonely,
I am best so!"
If I admire my arms, my face,
my shoulders, flanks, buttocks
against the yellow drawn shades,—

Who shall say I am not
the happy genius of my household?

PORTRAIT OF A WOMAN IN BED

There's my things
drying in the corner:
that blue skirt
joined to the grey shirt—

I'm sick of trouble!
Lift the covers
if you want me
and you'll see
the rest of my clothes—
though it would be cold
lying with nothing on!

I won't work
and I've got no cash.
What are you going to do
about it?
—and no jewelry
(the crazy fools)

But I've my two eyes
and a smooth face
and here's this! look!
it's high!

There's brains and blood
in there—
my name's Robitza!
Corsets
can go to the devil—
and drawers along with them—
What do I care!

My two boys?
—they're keen!
Let the rich lady
care for them—
they'll beat the school
or
let them go to the gutter—
that ends trouble.

This house is empty
isn't it?
Then it's mine
because I need it.
Oh, I won't starve
while there's the Bible
to make them feed me.

Try to help me
if you want trouble
or leave me alone—
that ends trouble.

The county physician
is a damned fool
and you
can go to hell!

You could have closed the door
when you came in;
do it when you go out.
I'm tired.

VIRTUE

Now? Why—
whirlpools of
orange and purple flame
feather twists of chrome
on a green ground
funneling down upon
the steaming phallus-head
of the mad sun himself—
blackened crimson!

                              Now?

Why—
it is the smile of her
the smell of her
the vulgar inviting mouth of her!
It is—Oh, nothing new
nothing that lasts
an eternity, nothing worth
putting out to interest,
nothing—
but the fixing of an eye
concretely upon emptiness!

Come! here are—
cross-eyed men, a boy
with a patch, men walking
in their shirts, men in hats
dark men, a pale man
with little black moustaches
and a dirty white coat,
fat men with pudgy faces,
thin faces, crooked faces
slit eyes, grey eyes, black eyes
old men with dirty beards,
men in vests with
gold watch chains. Come!

CONQUEST
(Dedicated to F. W.)

Hard, chilly colors:
straw-grey, frost-grey
the grey of frozen ground:
and you, O Sun,
close above the horizon!
It is I holds you—
half against the sky
half against a black tree trunk
icily resplendent!

Lie there, blue city, mine at last—
rimming the banked blue-grey
and rise, indescribable smoky-yellow
into the overpowering white!

PORTRAIT OF A YOUNG MAN
WITH A BAD HEART

Have I seen her?
Only through the window
across the street.

If I go meeting her
on the corner
some damned fool
will go blabbing it
to the old man and
she'll get hell.
He's a queer old bastard!
Every time he sees me
you'd think
I wanted to kill him.
But I figure it out
it's best to let things
stay as they are—
for a while at least.

It's hard
giving up the thing
you want most
in the world, but with this
damned pump of mine
liable to give out . . .

She's a good kid
and I'd hate to hurt her
but if she can get over it—

it'd be the best thing.

KELLER GEGEN DOM

Witness, would you—
one more young man
in the evening of his love
hurrying to confession:
steps down a gutter
crosses a street
goes in at a doorway
opens for you—
like some great flower—
a room filled with lamplight;
or whirls himself
obediently to
the curl of a hill
some wind-dancing afternoon;
lies for you in
the futile darkness of
a wall, sets stars dancing
to the crack of a leaf—

and—leaning his head away—
snuffs (secretly)
the bitter powder from
his thumb's hollow,

takes your blessing and
goes home to bed?

Witness instead
whether you like it or not
a dark vinegar-smelling place
from which trickles
the chuckle of
beginning laughter.

It strikes midnight.

SMELL!

Oh strong-ridged and deeply hollowed
nose of mine! what will you not be smelling?
What tactless asses we are, you and I, boney nose,
always indiscriminate, always unashamed,
and now it is the souring flowers of the bedraggled
poplars: a festering pulp on the wet earth
beneath them. With what deep thirst
we quicken our desires
to that rank odor of a passing springtime!
Can you not be decent? Can you not reserve your ardors
for something less unlovely? What girl will care
for us, do you think, if we continue in these ways?
Must you taste everything? Must you know everything?
Must you have a part in everything?

BALLET

Are you not weary,
great gold cross
shining in the wind—
are you not weary
of seeing the stars
turning over you

and the sun
going to his rest
and you frozen with
a great lie
that leaves you
rigid as a knight
on a marble coffin?

—and you?
higher, still,
                    robin,
untwisting a song
from the bare
top-twigs,
are you not
weary of labor,
even the labor of
a song?

Come down—join me
for I am lonely.

First it will be
a quiet pace
to ease our stiffness
but as the west yellows
you will be ready!
Here in the middle
of the roadway
we will fling
ourselves round
with dust lilies
till we are bound in
their twining stems!
We will tear
their flowers
with arms flashing!

And when
the astonished stars

push aside
their curtains
they will see us
fall exhausted where
wheels and
the pounding feet
of horses
will crush forth
our laughter.

SYMPATHETIC PORTRAIT OF A CHILD

The murderer's little daughter
who is barely ten years old
jerks her shoulders
right and left
so as to catch a glimpse of me
without turning round.

Her skinny little arms
wrap themselves
this way then that
reversely about her body!
Nervously
she crushes her straw hat
about her eyes
and tilts her head
to deepen the shadow—
smiling excitedly!

As best as she can
she hides herself
in the full sunlight
her cordy legs writhing
beneath the little flowered dress
that leaves them bare
from mid-thigh to ankle—

Why has she chosen me
for the knife
that darts along her smile?

THE OGRE

Sweet child,
little girl with well-shaped legs
you cannot touch the thoughts
I put over and under and around you.
This is fortunate for they would
burn you to an ash otherwise.
Your petals would be quite curled up.

This is all beyond you—no doubt,
yet you do feel the brushings
of the fine needles;
the tentative lines of your whole body
prove it to me;
so does your fear of me,
your shyness;
likewise the toy baby cart
that you are pushing—
and besides, mother has begun
to dress your hair in a knot.
These are my excuses.

RIPOSTE

Love is like water or the air
my townspeople;
it cleanses, and dissipates evil gases.
It is like poetry too
and for the same reasons.

Love is so precious
my townspeople
that if I were you I would
have it under lock and key—
like the air or the Atlantic or
like poetry!

THE OLD MEN

Old men who have studied
every leg show
in the city
Old men cut from touch
by the perfumed music—
polished or fleeced skulls
that stand before
the whole theater
in silent attitudes
of attention,—
old men who have taken precedence
over young men
and even over dark-faced
husbands whose minds
are a street with arc-lights.
Solitary old men for whom
we find no excuses—
I bow my head in shame
for those who malign you.
Old men
the peaceful beer of impotence
be yours!

PASTORAL

If I say I have heard voices
who will believe me?

"None has dipped his hand
in the black waters of the sky
nor picked the yellow lilies
that sway on their clear stems
and no tree has waited
long enough nor still enough
to touch fingers with the moon."

I looked and there were little frogs
with puffed-out throats,
singing in the slime.

SPRING STRAINS

In a tissue-thin monotone of blue-grey buds
crowded erect with desire against
the sky—
        tense blue-grey twigs
slenderly anchoring them down, drawing
them in—

        two blue-grey birds chasing
a third struggle in circles, angles,
swift convergings to a point that bursts
instantly!

        Vibrant bowing limbs
pull downward, sucking in the sky
that bulges from behind, plastering itself
against them in packed rifts, rock blue
and dirty orange!

                                But—
(Hold hard, rigid jointed trees!)
the blinding and red-edged sun-blur—
creeping energy, concentrated
counterforce—welds sky, buds, trees,
rivets them in one puckering hold!

Sticks through! Pulls the whole
counter-pulling mass upward, to the right,
locks even the opaque, not yet defined
ground in a terrific drag that is
loosening the very tap-roots!

On a tissue-thin monotone of blue-grey buds
two blue-grey birds, chasing a third,
at full cry! Now they are
flung outward and up—disappearing suddenly!

TREES

Crooked, black tree
on your little grey-black hillock,
ridiculously raised one step toward
the infinite summits of the night:
even you the few grey stars
draw upward into a vague melody
of harsh threads.

Bent as you are from straining
against the bitter horizontals of
a north wind,—there below you
how easily the long yellow notes
of poplars flow upward in a descending
scale, each note secure in its own
posture—singularly woven.

All voices are blent willingly
against the heaving contra-bass
of the dark but you alone
warp yourself passionately to one side
in your eagerness.

A PORTRAIT IN GREYS

Will it never be possible
to separate you from your greyness?
Must you be always sinking backward
into your grey-brown landscapes—and trees
always in the distance, always against
a grey sky?
          Must I be always
moving counter to you? Is there no place
where we can be at peace together
and the motion of our drawing apart
be altogether taken up?
          I see myself
standing upon your shoulders touching
a grey, broken sky—
but you, weighted down with me,
yet gripping my ankles,—move
          laboriously on,
where it is level and undisturbed by colors.

INVITATION

You who had the sense
to choose me such a mother,
you who had the indifference
to create me,
you who went to some pains
to leave hands off me
in the formative stages,—
(I thank you most for that
perhaps)
               but you who
with an iron head, first,
fiercest and with strongest love
brutalized me into strength,
old dew-lap,—
I have reached the stage

where I am teaching myself
to laugh.

                    Come on,

take a walk with me.

DIVERTIMIENTO

Miserable little woman
in a brown coat—

                quit whining!

My hand for you!
We'll skip down the tin cornices
of Main Street
flicking the dull roof-line
with our toe-tips!
Hop clear of the bank! A
pin-wheel round the white flag-pole.

And I'll sing you the while
a thing to split your sides
about Johann Sebastian Bach,
the father of music, who had
three wives and twenty-two children.

JANUARY MORNING
Suite:

I

I have discovered that most of
the beauties of travel are due to
the strange hours we keep to see them:

the domes of the Church of
the Paulist Fathers in Weehawken
against a smoky dawn—the heart stirred—
are beautiful as Saint Peters
approached after years of anticipation.

II

Though the operation was postponed
I saw the tall probationers
in their tan uniforms
        hurrying to breakfast!

III

—and from basement entries
neatly coiffed, middle aged gentlemen
with orderly moustaches and
well-brushed coats

IV

—and the sun, dipping into the avenues
streaking the tops of
the irregular red houselets,
               and
the gay shadows dropping and dropping.

V

—and a young horse with a green bed-quilt
on his withers shaking his head:
bared teeth and nozzle high in the air!

VI

—and a semicircle of dirt-colored men
about a fire bursting from an old
ash can,

VII

       —and the worn,
blue car rails (like the sky!)
gleaming among the cobbles!

VIII

—and the rickety ferry-boat "Arden"!
What an object to be called "Arden"
among the great piers,—on the
ever new river!
                    "Put me a Touchstone
at the wheel, white gulls, and we'll
follow the ghost of the *Half Moon*
to the North West Passage—and through!
(at Albany!) for all that!"

IX

Exquisite brown waves—long
circlets of silver moving over you!
enough with crumbling ice crusts among you!
The sky has come down to you,
lighter than tiny bubbles, face to
face with you!
                    His spirit is
a white gull with delicate pink feet
and a snowy breast for you to
hold to your lips delicately!

X

The young doctor is dancing with happiness
in the sparkling wind, alone
at the prow of the ferry! He notices
the curdy barnacles and broken ice crusts
left at the slip's base by the low tide
and thinks of summer and green
shell-crusted ledges among
                    the emerald eel-grass!

XI

Who knows the Palisades as I do
knows the river breaks east from them

above the city—but they continue south
—under the sky—to bear a crest of
little peering houses that brighten
with dawn behind the moody
water-loving giants of Manhattan.

XII

Long yellow rushes bending
above the white snow patches;
purple and gold ribbon
of the distant wood:
                    what an angle
you make with each other as
you lie there in contemplation.

XIII

Work hard all your young days
and they'll find you too, some morning
staring up under
your chiffonier at its warped
bass-wood bottom and your soul—
out!
—among the little sparrows
behind the shutter.

XIV

—and the flapping flags are at
half mast for the dead admiral.

XV

All this—
            was for you, old woman.
I wanted to write a poem
that you would understand.
For what good is it to me
if you can't understand it?

But you got to try hard—
But—
Well, you know how
the young girls run giggling
on Park Avenue after dark
when they ought to be home in bed?
Well,
that's the way it is with me somehow.

TO A SOLITARY DISCIPLE

Rather notice, mon cher,
that the moon is
tilted above
the point of the steeple
than that its color
is shell-pink.

Rather observe
that it is early morning
than that the sky
is smooth
as a turquoise.

Rather grasp
how the dark
converging lines
of the steeple
meet at the pinnacle—
perceive how
its little ornament
tries to stop them—

See how it fails!
See how the converging lines
of the hexagonal spire
escape upward—
receding, dividing!

—sepals
that guard and contain
the flower!

Observe
how motionless
the eaten moon
lies in the protecting lines.

It is true:
in the light colors
of morning
brown-stone and slate
shine orange and dark blue.

But observe
the oppressive weight
of the squat edifice!
Observe
the jasmine lightness
of the moon.

DEDICATION FOR A PLOT OF GROUND

This plot of ground
facing the waters of this inlet
is dedicated to the living presence of
Emily Dickinson Wellcome
who was born in England; married;
lost her husband and with
her five year old son
sailed for New York in a two-master;
was driven to the Azores;
ran adrift on Fire Island shoal,
met her second husband
in a Brooklyn boarding house,
went with him to Puerto Rico
bore three more children, lost

her second husband, lived hard
for eight years in St. Thomas,
Puerto Rico, San Domingo, followed
the oldest son to New York,
lost her daughter, lost her "baby,"
seized the two boys of
the oldest son by the second marriage
mothered them—they being
motherless—fought for them
against the other grandmother
and the aunts, brought them here
summer after summer, defended
herself here against thieves,
storms, sun, fire,
against flies, against girls
that came smelling about, against
drought, against weeds, storm-tides,
neighbors, weasels that stole her chickens,
against the weakness of her own hands,
against the growing strength of
the boys, against wind, against
the stones, against trespassers,
against rents, against her own mind.

She grubbed this earth with her own hands,
domineered over this grass plot,
blackguarded her oldest son
into buying it, lived here fifteen years,
attained a final loneliness and—

If you can bring nothing to this place
but your carcass, keep out.

K. McB.

You exquisite chunk of mud
Kathleen—just like
any other chunk of mud!

—especially in April!
Curl up round their shoes
when they try to step on you,
spoil the polish!
I shall laugh till I am sick
at their amazement.
Do they expect the ground to be
always solid?
Give them the slip then;
let them sit in you;
soil their pants;
teach them a dignity
that is dignity, the dignity
of mud!

                    Lie basking in
the sun then—fast asleep!
Even become dust on occasion.

LOVE SONG

I lie here thinking of you:—

the stain of love
is upon the world!
Yellow, yellow, yellow
it eats into the leaves,
smears with saffron
the horned branches that lean
heavily
against a smooth purple sky!
There is no light
only a honey-thick stain
that drips from leaf to leaf
and limb to limb
spoiling the colors
of the whole world—

you far off there under
the wine-red selvage of the west!

THE WANDERER
A Rococo Study

A D V E N T

Even in the time when as yet
I had no certain knowledge of her
She sprang from the nest, a young crow,
Whose first flight circled the forest.
I know now how then she showed me
Her mind, reaching out to the horizon,
She close above the tree tops.
I saw her eyes straining at the new distance
And as the woods fell from her flying
Likewise they fell from me as I followed—
So that I strongly guessed all that I must put from me
To come through ready for the high courses.

But one day, crossing the ferry
With the great towers of Manhattan before me,
Out at the prow with the sea wind blowing,
I had been wearying many questions
Which she had put on to try me:
How shall I be a mirror to this modernity?
When lo! in a rush, dragging
A blunt boat on the yielding river—
Suddenly I saw her! And she waved me
From the white wet in midst of her playing!
She cried me, "Haia! Here I am, son!
See how strong my little finger is!
Can I not swim well?
I can fly too!" And with that a great sea-gull
Went to the left, vanishing with a wild cry—
But in my mind all the persons of godhead
Followed after.

CLARITY

"Come!" cried my mind and by her might
That was upon us we flew above the river
Seeking her, grey gulls among the white—
In the air speaking as she had willed it;
"I am given," cried I, "now I know it!
I know now all my time is forespent!
For me one face is all the world!
For I have seen her at last, this day,
In whom age in age is united—
Indifferent, out of sequence, marvelously!
Saving alone that one sequence
Which is the beauty of all the world, for surely
Either there in the rolling smoke spheres below us
Or here with us in the air intercircling,
Certainly somewhere here about us
I know she is revealing these things!"
And as gulls we flew and with soft cries
We seemed to speak, flying, "It is she
The mighty, recreating the whole world,
This is the first day of wonders!

She is attiring herself before me—
Taking shape before me for worship,
A red leaf that falls upon a stone!
It is she of whom I told you, old
Forgiveless, unreconcilable;
That high wanderer of by-ways
Walking imperious in beggary!
At her throat is loose gold, a single chain
From among many, on her bent fingers
Are rings from which the stones are fallen,
Her wrists wear a diminished state, her ankles
Are bare! Toward the river! Is it she there?"
And we swerved clamorously downward—
"I will take my peace in her henceforth!"

BROADWAY

It was then she struck—from behind,
In mid air, as with the edge of a great wing!
And instantly down the mists of my eyes
There came crowds walking—men as visions
With expressionless, animate faces;
Empty men with shell-thin bodies
Jostling close above the gutter,
Hasting—nowhere! And then for the first time
I really saw her, really scented the sweat
Of her presence and—fell back sickened!
Ominous, old, painted—
With bright lips, and lewd Jew's eyes
Her might strapped in by a corset
To give her age youth, perfect
In her will to be young she had covered
The godhead to go beside me.
Silent, her voice entered at my eyes
And my astonished thought followed her easily:
"Well, do their eyes shine, do their clothes fit?
These *live* I tell you! Old men with red cheeks,
Young men in gay suits! See them!
Dogged, quivering, impassive—
Well—are these the ones you envied?"
At which I answered her, "Marvelous old queen,
Grant me power to catch something of this day's
Air and sun into your service!
That these toilers after peace and after pleasure
May turn to you, worshippers at all hours!"
But she sniffed upon the words warily—
Yet I persisted, watching for an answer:
"To you, horrible old woman,
Who know all fires out of the bodies
Of all men that walk with lust at heart!
To you, O mighty, crafty prowler
After the youth of all cities, drunk
With the sight of thy archness! All the youth
That come to you, you having the knowledge
Rather than to those uninitiate—

To you, marvelous old queen, give me always
A new marriage—"
      But she laughed loudly—
"A new grip upon those garments that brushed me
In days gone by on beach, lawn, and in forest!
May I be lifted still, up and out of terror,
Up from before the death living around me—
Torn up continually and carried
Whatever way the head of your whim is,
A burr upon those streaming tatters—"
But the night had fallen, she stilled me
And led me away.

THE STRIKE

At the first peep of dawn she roused me!
I rose trembling at the change which the night saw!
For there, wretchedly brooding in a corner
From which her old eyes glittered fiercely—
"Go!" she said, and I hurried shivering
Out into the deserted streets of Paterson.
That night she came again, hovering
In rags within the filmy ceiling—
"Great Queen, bless me with thy tatters!"
"You are blest, go on!"
      Hot for savagery,
Sucking the air! I went into the city,
Out again, baffled onto the mountain!
Back into the city!
    Nowhere
The subtle! Everywhere the electric!

"A short bread-line before a hitherto empty tea shop:
No questions—all stood patiently,
Dominated by one idea: something
That carried them as they are always wanting to be carried,
'But what is it,' I asked those nearest me,
'This thing heretofore unobtainable
That they seem so clever to have put on now!'

"Why since I have failed them can it be anything but their
    own brood?
Can it be anything but brutality?
On that at least they're united! That at least
Is their bean soup, their calm bread and a few luxuries!

"But in me, more sensitive, marvelous old queen
It sank deep into the blood, that I rose upon
The tense air enjoying the dusty fight!
Heavy drink where the low, sloping foreheads
The flat skulls with the unkempt black or blond hair,
The ugly legs of the young girls, pistons
Too powerful for delicacy!
The women's wrists, the men's arms red
Used to heat and cold, to toss quartered beeves
And barrels, and milk-cans, and crates of fruit!

"Faces all knotted up like burls on oaks,
Grasping, fox-snouted, thick-lipped,
Sagging breasts and protruding stomachs,
Rasping voices, filthy habits with the hands.

"Nowhere you! Everywhere the electric!

"Ugly, venomous, gigantic!
Tossing me as a great father his helpless
Infant till it shriek with ecstasy
And its eyes roll and its tongue hangs out!—

"I am at peace again, old queen, I listen clearer now."

ABROAD

Never, even in a dream,
Have I winged so high nor so well
As with her, she leading me by the hand,
That first day on the Jersey mountains!
And never shall I forget
The trembling interest with which I heard
Her voice in a low thunder:

"You are safe here. Look child, look open-mouth!
The patch of road between the steep bramble banks;
The tree in the wind, the white house there, the sky!
Speak to men of these, concerning me!
For never while you permit them to ignore me
In these shall the full of my freed voice
Come grappling the ear with intent!
Never while the air's clear coolness
Is seized to be a coat for pettiness;
Never while richness of greenery
Stands a shield for prurient minds;
Never, permitting these things unchallenged
Shall my voice of leaves and varicolored bark come free
    through!"
At which, knowing her solitude,
I shouted over the country below me:
"Waken! my people, to the boughs green
With ripening fruit within you!
Waken to the myriad cinquefoil
In the waving grass of your minds!
Waken to the silent phoebe nest
Under the eaves of your spirit!"

But she, stooping nearer the shifting hills
Spoke again. "Look there! See them!
There in the oat field with the horses,
See them there! bowed by their passions
Crushed down, that had been raised as a roof beam!
The weight of the sky is upon them
Under which all roof beams crumble.
There is none but the single roof beam:
There is no love bears against the great firefly!"
At this I looked up at the sun
Then shouted again with all the might I had.
But my voice was a seed in the wind.
Then she, the old one, laughing
Seized me and whirling about bore back
To the city, upward, still laughing
Until the great towers stood above the marshland
Wheeling beneath: the little creeks, the mallows

That I picked as a boy, the Hackensack
So quiet that seemed so broad formerly:
The crawling trains, the cedar swamp on the one side—
All so old, so familiar—so new now
To my marveling eyes as we passed
Invisible.

SOOTHSAY

Eight days went by, eight days
Comforted by no nights, until finally:
"Would you behold yourself old, beloved?"
I was pierced, yet I consented gladly
For I knew it could not be otherwise.
And she—"Behold yourself old!
Sustained in strength, wielding might in gript surges!
Not bodying the sun in weak leaps
But holding way over rockish men
With fern-free fingers on their little crags,
Their hollows, the new Atlas, to bear them
For pride and for mockery! Behold
Yourself old! winding with slow might—
A vine among oaks—to the thin tops:
Leaving the leafless leaved,
Bearing purple clusters! Behold
Yourself old! birds are behind you.
You are the wind coming that stills birds,
Shakes the leaves in booming polyphony—
Slow winning high way amid the knocking
Of boughs, evenly crescendo,
The din and bellow of the male wind!
Leap then from forest into foam!
Lash about from low into high flames
Tipping sound, the female chorus—
Linking all lions, all twitterings
To make them nothing! Behold yourself old!"
As I made to answer she continued,
A little wistfully yet in a voice clear cut:
"Good is my over lip and evil
My under lip to you henceforth:

For I have taken your soul between my two hands
And this shall be as it is spoken."

ST. JAMES' GROVE

And so it came to that last day
When, she leading by the hand, we went out
Early in the morning, I heavy of heart
For I knew the novitiate was ended
The ecstasy was over, the life begun.

In my woolen shirt and the pale-blue necktie
My grandmother gave me, there I went
With the old queen right past the houses
Of my friends down the hill to the river
As on any usual day, any errand.
Alone, walking under trees,
I went with her, she with me in her wild hair,
By Santiago Grove and presently
She bent forward and knelt by the river,
The Passaic, that filthy river.
And there dabbling her mad hands,
She called me close beside her.
Raising the water then in the cupped palm
She bathed our brows wailing and laughing:
"River, we are old, you and I,
We are old and by bad luck, beggars.
Lo, the filth in our hair, our bodies stink!
Old friend, here I have brought you
The young soul you long asked of me.
Stand forth, river, and give me
The old friend of my revels!
Give me the well-worn spirit,
For here I have made a room for it,
And I will return to you forthwith
The youth you have long asked of me:
Stand forth, river, and give me
The old friend of my revels!"

And the filthy Passaic consented!

Then she, leaping up with a fierce cry:
"Enter, youth, into this bulk!
Enter, river, into this young man!"

Then the river began to enter my heart,
Eddying back cool and limpid
Into the crystal beginning of its days.
But with the rebound it leaped forward:
Muddy, then black and shrunken
Till I felt the utter depth of its rottenness
The vile breadth of its degradation
And dropped down knowing this was me now.
But she lifted me and the water took a new tide
Again into the older experiences,
And so, backward and forward,
It tortured itself within me
Until time had been washed finally under,
And the river had found its level
And its last motion had ceased
And I knew all—it became me.
And I knew this for double certain
For there, whitely, I saw myself
Being borne off under the water!
I could have shouted out in my agony
At the sight of myself departing
Forever—but I bit back my despair
For she had averted her eyes
By which I knew well what she was thinking—
And so the last of me was taken.

Then she, "Be mostly silent!"
And turning to the river, spoke again:
"For him and for me, river, the wandering,
But by you I leave for happiness
Deep foliage, the thickest beeches—
Though elsewhere they are all dying—
Tallest oaks and yellow birches
That dip their leaves in you, mourning,
As now I dip my hair, immemorial
Of me, immemorial of him

Immemorial of these our promises!
Here shall be a bird's paradise,
They sing to you remembering my voice:
Here the most secluded spaces
For miles around, hallowed by a stench
To be our joint solitude and temple;
In memory of this clear marriage
And the child I have brought you in the late years.
Live, river, live in luxuriance
Remembering this our son,
In remembrance of me and my sorrow
And of the new wandering!"

POEMS
1918–1921

LOVE SONG

You have come between me and the terrifying presence
of the moon, the stars, the sun and the earth
with all its crooked outgrowths. The desolation of life
has been darkened by your shadow, but toward me
your face has been a light, your hands have been
a soft rain, the voice from between your lips
a thing that carries me as the air carries a bird.
I have spread my arms out wide feeling you about me
and looked up and taken a deep breath! Deep,
deep! an April in every finger tip!

S H E

From your eyes, from among what you say,
tangled like a singing bird in a green tree,
you have entered and spread down through me all
so that I treasure my youth again and wish it
never to go from me—for it is not mine but yours
that I shall hold warmly, safely within me forever.

(*after a pause*)

S H E

Your love song halts and repeats.

H E

Your song is glib.

LE MÉDECIN MALGRÉ LUI

Oh I suppose I should
wash the walls of my office
polish the rust from
my instruments and keep them
definitely in order
build shelves in the laboratory
empty out the old stains
clean the bottles
and refill them, buy
another lens, put
my journals on edge instead of
letting them lie flat
in heaps—then begin
ten years back and
gradually
read them to date
cataloguing important
articles for ready reference.
I suppose I should
read the new books.
If to this I added
a bill at the tailor's
and at the cleaner's
grew a decent beard
and cultivated a look
of importance—
Who can tell? I might be
a credit to my Lady Happiness
and never think anything
but a white thought!

THE YOUNG LAUNDRYMAN

Ladies, I crave your indulgence for
My friend Wu Kee; young, agile, clear-eyed
And clean-limbed, his muscles ripple

Under the thin blue shirt; and his naked feet, in
Their straw sandals, lift at the heels, shift and
Find new postures continually.

Your husband's shirts to wash, please, for Wu Kee.

TO BE CLOSELY WRITTEN ON A SMALL PIECE
OF PAPER WHICH FOLDED INTO A
TIGHT LOZENGE WILL FIT
ANY GIRL'S LOCKET

Lo the leaves
Upon the new autumn grass—
Look at them well . . . !

STROLLER

I have seen the hills blue,
I have seen them purple;
And it is as hard to know
The words of a woman
As to straighten the crumpled branch
Of an old willow.

MAN IN A ROOM

Here, no woman, nor man besides,
Nor child, nor dog, nor bird, nor wasp,
Nor ditch-pool, nor green thing. Color of flower,
Blood-bright berry none, nor flame-rust
On leaf, nor pink gall-sting on stem, nor
Staring stone, *Ay de mi!*
No hawthorn's white thorn-tree here, nor lawn
Of buttercups, nor any counterpart:

Bed, book-backs, walls, floor,
Flat pictures, desk, clothes-box, litter
Of paper scrawls. So sit I here,
So stand, so walk about. Beside
The flower-white tree not so lonely I:
Torn petals, dew-wet, yellowed my bare ankles.

A CORONAL

New books of poetry will be written
New books and unheard of manuscripts
will come wrapped in brown paper
and many and many a time
the postman will bow
and sidle down the leaf-plastered steps
thumbing over other men's business.

But we ran ahead of it all.
One coming after
could have seen her footprints
in the wet and followed us
among the stark chestnuts.

Anemones sprang where she pressed
and cresses
stood green in the slender source—
And new books of poetry
will be written, leather-colored oakleaves
many and many a time.

TO MARK ANTHONY IN HEAVEN

This quiet morning light
reflected, how many times
from grass and trees and clouds
enters my north room

touching the walls with
grass and clouds and trees.
Anthony,
trees and grass and clouds.
Why did you follow
that beloved body
with your ships at Actium?
I hope it was because
you knew her inch by inch
from slanting feet upward
to the roots of her hair
and down again and that
you saw her
above the battle's fury—
clouds and trees and grass—

For then you are
listening in heaven.

IT IS A SMALL PLANT

It is a small plant
delicately branched and
tapering conically
to a point, each branch
and the peak a wire for
green pods, blind lanterns
starting upward from
the stalk each way to
a pair of prickly edged blue
flowerets: it is her regard,
a little plant without leaves,
a finished thing guarding
its secret. Blue eyes—
but there are twenty looks
in one, alike as forty flowers
on twenty stems—Blue eyes
a little closed upon a wish

achieved and half lost again,
stemming back, garlanded
with green sacks of
satisfaction gone to seed,
back to a straight stem—if
one looks into you, trumpets—!
No. It is the pale hollow of
desire itself counting
over and over the moneys of
a stale achievement. Three
small lavender imploring tips
below and above them two
slender colored arrows
of disdain with anthers
between them and
at the edge of the goblet
a white lip, to drink from—!
And summer lifts her look
forty times over, forty times
over—namelessly.

HEALALL

It is the daily love, grass high
they say that will cure her.
No good to reply: the sorrel never
has four leaves, if the clover
may—It is the hydraheaded pulpit,
but an impassioned one in this case,
purple, lined with white velvet
for a young priest—by what
lady's hand? Agh it is no pulpit
but a baying dog, a kennel of
purple dogs on one leash,
fangs bared—to keep away harm
and never caring for the place:
down the torn lane
where the cows pass,

under the appletree, nodding
against high tide or in the lea of
a pasture thistle, almost blue,
never far to seek, they say
it will cure her.

BUTTERANDEGGS

It is a posture for two multiplied
into a bouquet, a kneeling mother
washing the feet of her naked infant
before crossed mirrors, shoes of
different pairs, a chinaman laughing
at a nigger, a maple mingling leaves
with an elm, it is butter and eggs:
yellow slippers with orange bows to them,
chickens and pigs in a barnyard,
not too important—the little double
favors, you and I, a shirt
handed to a naked man by his
barelegged wife, scratch my back
for me, oh and empty the slopbucket
when you go down—and get me
that flower, I can't reach it.
A low greyleaved thing
growing in clusters, how else?—
with a swollen head—slippers for sale,
they put mirrors in those stores
to make it seem—Closely packed
in a bouquet but never quite succeeding
to be more than—a passageway to
something else.

THISTLE

They should have called the thistle—
well, it is that we, we love each other.

Our heads side by side have a purple
flamebed over them. We are one, we love
ourself. The cows do not eat us nor tread
on us. It is a little like the lichen on
the blackened stones, a foaming winecup
with thorns on the handle. They say
jackasses eat them. Yes, and reindeer
eat lichen, lick them from the stones.
And we would be eaten—as England ate
Scotland? No.
It is the color they must eat if
they would have us. That offers itself
but that alone. The rest is for asses
or—forbidden. Purple! Striped bellied
flies and the black papillios are the
color-led evangels. Ah but they come
for the honey only. And so—a thistle.

SPIRIT OF '76

Dear Miss Monroe: Provided you will allow me to use small letters at
the beginning of my lines, I submit the following excellent American
poem to you for publication in your paying magazine:

SPIRIT OF '76

Her father
built a bridge
over
the Chicago River
but she
built a bridge
over the moon.

This, as you will at once recognize, is an excellent poem and very
American. I sincerely hope that no prehistoric prosodic rules will bar it
from publication. Yours,

W. C. Williams

PORTRAIT OF A LADY

Your thighs are appletrees
whose blossoms touch the sky.
Which sky? The sky
where Watteau hung a lady's
slipper. Your knees
are a southern breeze—or
a gust of snow. Agh! what
sort of man was Fragonard?
—as if that answered
anything. Ah, yes—below
the knees, since the tune
drops that way, it is
one of those white summer days,
the tall grass of your ankles
flickers upon the shore—
Which shore?—
the sand clings to my lips—
Which shore?
Agh, petals maybe. How
should I know?
Which shore? Which shore?
I said petals from an appletree.

MARIANNE MOORE

Will not some dozen sacks of rags
observant of intelligence
conspire from their outlandish cellar
to evade the law?

Let them, stuffed up, appear
before her door at ten some night
and say : Marianne, save us!
Put us in a book of yours.

Then she would ask the fellow in
and give him cake

and warm him with her talk
before he must return to the dark street.

ST. FRANCIS EINSTEIN OF THE DAFFODILS
[*First Version*]

In March's black boat
Einstein and April
have come at the time in fashion
up out of the sea
through the rippling daffodils
in the foreyard of
the dead Statue of Liberty
whose stonearms
are powerless against them
the Venusremembering wavelets
breaking into laughter—

Sweet Land of Liberty,
at last, in the end of time,
Einstein has come by force of
complicated mathematics
among the tormented fruit trees
to buy freedom
for the daffodils
till the unchained orchards
shake their tufted flowers—
Yiddishe springtime!

At the time in fashion
Einstein has come
bringing April in his head
up from the sea
in Thomas March Jefferson's
black boat bringing
freedom under the dead
Statue of Liberty
to free the daffodils in
the water which sing:

Einstein has remembered us
Savior of the daffodils!

A twig for all the dead!
shout the dark maples
in the tearing wind, shaking
pom-poms of green flowers—
April Einstein has come
to liberate us
here among
the Venusremembering daffodils
Yiddishe springtime of the mind
and a great pool of rainwater
under
the blossomy peachtrees.

April Einstein
through the blossomy waters
rebellious, laughing
under liberty's dead arm
has come among the daffodils
shouting
that flowers and men
were created
relatively equal.
Oldfashioned knowledge is
dead under the blossoming peachtrees.

Einstein, tall as a violet
in the latticearbor corner
is tall as a blossomy
peartree! The shell
of the world is split
and from under the sea
Einstein has emerged
triumphant, St. Francis
of the daffodils!

O Samos, Samos
dead and buried. Lesbia is

a black cat in the freshturned
garden. All dead.
All flesh that they have sung
is long since rotten.
Sing of it no longer.
Sing of Einstein's
Yiddishe peachtrees, sing of
sleep among the cherryblossoms.
Sing of wise newspapers
that quote the great mathematician:
A little touch of
Einstein in the night—

Side by side the young and old
trees take the sun together,
the maples, green and red
according to their kind,
yellowbells and the
vermillion quinceflower together—
The tall peartree with
foetid blossoms
sways its high topbranches
with contrary motions and green
has come out of the wood
upon them also—

The mathematics grow complex:
there are both pinkflowered
and coralflowered peachtrees
in the bare chickenyard
of the old negro
with white hair who hides
poisoned fish-heads
here and there
where stray cats find them—
find them—find them.

O spring days, swift
and mutable, wind blowing
four ways, hot and cold.

Now the northeast wind,
moving in fogs, leaves the grass
cold and dripping. The night
is dark but in the night
the southeast wind approaches.
It is April and Einstein!
The owner of the orchard
lies in his bed
with the windows wide
and throws off his covers
one by one.

It is Einstein
out of complicated mathematics
among the daffodils—
spring winds blowing
four ways, hot and cold,
shaking the flowers!

TO THE SHADE OF PO CHÜ-I

The work is heavy . I see
bare branches laden with snow .
I try to comfort myself
with thought of your old age .
A girl passes, in a red tam,
the coat above her quick ankles
snow smeared from running and falling -
Of what shall I think now
save of death the bright dancer ?

THE CATS' MONTH

Your frosty hands
your withered face
the merciless February

of it all -
It is for cats !
Their musk
clings in the entries
to good ladies' houses .
I catch it sometimes
even in the open street
where deep snow lies .

DAYBREAK

Half a moon is flaming in the south
below clear little stars .
Vague shapes begin to stir among
the yellow-poppy street lamps .
Oblique masses of purple and black
lift themselves . Is it earth or sky ?
It is the beginning ! - again ?
Answer, answer ! Huntress who spreadest
vitreous dawn before dawn !

SOUR GRAPES

1921

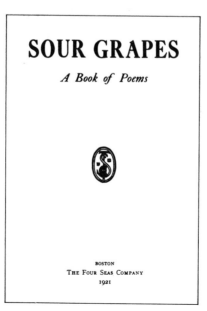

BOSTON
THE FOUR SEAS COMPANY
1921

THE LATE SINGER

Here it is spring again
and I still a young man!
I am late at my singing.
The sparrow with the black rain on his breast
has been at his cadenzas for two weeks past:
What is it that is dragging at my heart?
The grass by the back door
is stiff with sap.
The old maples are opening
their branches of brown and yellow moth-flowers.
A moon hangs in the blue
in the early afternoons over the marshes.
I am late at my singing.

MARCH

I

Winter is long in this climate
and spring—a matter of a few days
only,—a flower or two picked
from mud or from among wet leaves
or at best against treacherous
bitterness of wind, and sky shining
teasingly, then closing in black
and sudden, with fierce jaws.

II

March,
    you remind me of
the pyramids, our pyramids—

stript of the polished stone
that used to guard them!
                              March,
you are like Fra Angelico
at Fiesole, painting on plaster!

March,
      you are like a band of
young poets that have not learned
the blessedness of warmth
(or have forgotten it).
At any rate—
I am moved to write poetry
for the warmth there is in it
and for the loneliness—
a poem that shall have you
        in it March.

                    III

See!
      Ashur-ban-i-pal,
the archer king, on horse-back,
in blue and yellow enamel!
with drawn bow—facing lions
standing on their hind legs,
fangs bared! his shafts
bristling in their necks!

Sacred bulls—dragons
in embossed brickwork
marching—in four tiers—
along the sacred way to
Nebuchadnezzar's throne hall!
They shine in the sun,
they that have been marching—
marching under the dust of
ten thousand dirt years.

Now—
they are coming into bloom again!
See them!
marching still, bared by
the storms from my calendar
—winds that blow back the sand!
winds that enfilade dirt!
winds that by strange craft
have whipt up a black army
that by pick and shovel
bare a procession to
                 the god, Marduk!

Natives cursing and digging
for pay unearth dragons with
upright tails and sacred bulls
alternately—
         in four tiers—
lining the way to an old altar!
Natives digging at old walls—
digging me warmth—digging me sweet loneliness
high enamelled walls.

IV

My second spring—
passed in a monastery
with plaster walls—in Fiesole
on the hill above Florence.
My second spring—painted
a virgin—in a blue aureole
sitting on a three-legged stool,
arms crossed—
she is intently serious,
             and still
watching an angel
with colored wings
half kneeling before her—

and smiling—the angel's eyes
holding the eyes of Mary
as a snake's hold a bird's.
On the ground there are flowers,
trees are in leaf.

V

But! now for the battle!
Now for murder—now for the real thing!
My third springtime is approaching!
Winds!
lean, serious as a virgin,
seeking, seeking the flowers of March.

Seeking
flowers nowhere to be found,
they twine among the bare branches
in insatiable eagerness—
they whirl up the snow
seeking under it—
they—the winds—snakelike
roar among yellow reeds
seeking flowers—flowers.

I spring among them
seeking one flower
in which to warm myself!

I deride with all the ridicule
of misery—
my own starved misery.

Counter-cutting winds
    strike against me
refreshing their fury!

Come, good, cold fellows!
    Have we no flowers?
Defy then with even more

desperation than ever—being
   lean and frozen!

But though you are lean and frozen—
think of the blue bulls of Babylon.

Fling yourselves upon
   their empty roses—
      cut savagely!

But—
think of the painted monastery
   at Fiesole.

BERKET AND THE STARS

A day on the boulevards chosen out of ten years of
student poverty! One best day out of ten good ones.
Berket in high spirits—"Ha, oranges! Let's have one!"
And he made to snatch an orange from the vender's cart.

Now so clever was the deception, so nicely timed
to the full sweep of certain wave summits,
that the rumor of the thing has come down through
three generations—which is relatively forever!

A CELEBRATION

A middle-northern March, now as always—
gusts from the South broken against cold winds—
but from under, as if a slow hand lifted a tide,
it moves—not into April—into a second March,

the old skin of wind-clear scales dropping
upon the mold: this is the shadow projects the tree
upward causing the sun to shine in his sphere.

So we will put on our pink felt hat—new last year!
—newer this by virtue of brown eyes turning back
the seasons—and let us walk to the orchid-house,
see the flowers will take the prize tomorrow
at the Palace.
    Stop here, these are our oleanders.
When they are in bloom—
      You would waste words
It is clearer to me than if the pink
were on the branch. It would be a searching in
a colored cloud to reveal that which now, huskless,
shows the very reason for their being.

And these the orange-trees, in blossom—no need
to tell with this weight of perfume in the air.
If it were not so dark in this shed one could better
see the white.
    It is that very perfume
has drawn the darkness down among the leaves.
Do I speak clearly enough?
It is this darkness reveals that which darkness alone
loosens and sets spinning on waxen wings—
not the touch of a finger-tip, not the motion
of a sigh. A too heavy sweetness proves
its own caretaker.
And here are the orchids!
     Never having seen
such gaiety I will read these flowers for you:
This is an odd January, died—in Villon's time.
Snow, this is and this the stain of a violet
grew in that place the spring that foresaw its own doom.

And this, a certain July from Iceland:
a young woman of that place
breathed it toward the South. It took root there.
The color ran true but the plant is small.

This falling spray of snow-flakes is
a handful of dead Februaries

prayed into flower by Rafael Arévalo Martínez
of Guatemala.
                    Here's that old friend who
went by my side so many years: this full, fragile
head of veined lavender. Oh that April
that we first went with our stiff lusts
leaving the city behind, out to the green hill—
May, they said she was. A hand for all of us:
this branch of blue butterflies tied to this stem.

June is a yellow cup I'll not name; August
the over-heavy one. And here are—
russet and shiny, all but March. And March?
Ah, March—
                    Flowers are a tiresome pastime.
One has a wish to shake them from their pots
root and stem, for the sun to gnaw.

Walk out again into the cold and saunter home
to the fire. This day has blossomed long enough.
I have wiped out the red night and lit a blaze
instead which will at least warm our hands
and stir up the talk.
                    I think we have kept fair time.
Time is a green orchid.

APRIL

        If you had come away with me
        into another state
        we had been quiet together.
        But there the sun coming up
        out of the nothing beyond the lake was
        too low in the sky,
        there was too great a pushing
        against him,
        too much of sumac buds, pink

in the head
with the clear gum upon them,
too many opening hearts of lilac leaves,
too many, too many swollen
limp poplar tassels on the
bare branches!
It was too strong in the air.
I had no rest against that
springtime!
The pounding of the hoofs on the
raw sods
stayed with me half through the night.
I awoke smiling but tired.

A GOODNIGHT

Go to sleep—though of course you will not—
to tideless waves thundering slantwise against
strong embankments, rattle and swish of spray
dashed thirty feet high, caught by the lake wind,
scattered and strewn broadcast in over the steady
car rails! Sleep, sleep! Gulls' cries in a wind-gust
broken by the wind; calculating wings set above
the field of waves breaking.
Go to sleep to the lunge between foam-crests,
refuse churned in the recoil. Food! Food!
Offal! Offal! that holds them in the air, wave-white
for the one purpose, feather upon feather, the wild
chill in their eyes, the hoarseness in their voices—
sleep, sleep . . .

Gentlefooted crowds are treading out your lullaby.
Their arms nudge, they brush shoulders,
hitch this way then that, mass and surge at the crossings—
lullaby, lullaby! The wild-fowl police whistles,
the enraged roar of the traffic, machine shrieks:
it is all to put you to sleep,

to soften your limbs in relaxed postures,
and that your head slip sidewise, and your hair loosen
and fall over your eyes and over your mouth,
brushing your lips wistfully that you may dream,
sleep and dream—

A black fungus springs out about lonely church doors—
sleep, sleep. The Night, coming down upon
the wet boulevard, would start you awake with his
message, to have in at your window. Pay no
heed to him. He storms at your sill with
cooings, with gesticulations, curses!
You will not let him in. He would keep you from sleeping.
He would have you sit under your desk lamp
brooding, pondering; he would have you
slide out the drawer, take up the ornamented dagger
and handle it. It is late, it is nineteen-nineteen—
go to sleep, his cries are a lullaby;
his jabbering is a sleep-well-my-baby; he is
a crackbrained messenger.

The maid waking you in the morning
when you are up and dressing,
the rustle of your clothes as you raise them—
it is the same tune.
At table the cold, greenish, split grapefruit, its juice
on the tongue, the clink of the spoon in
your coffee, the toast odors say it over and over.

The open street-door lets in the breath of
the morning wind from over the lake.
The bus coming to a halt grinds from its sullen brakes—
lullaby, lullaby. The crackle of a newspaper,
the movement of the troubled coat beside you—
sleep, sleep, sleep, sleep . . .
It is the sting of snow, the burning liquor of
the moonlight, the rush of rain in the gutters packed
with dead leaves: go to sleep, go to sleep.
And the night passes—and never passes—

OVERTURE TO A DANCE OF LOCOMOTIVES

Men with picked voices chant the names
of cities in a huge gallery: promises
that pull through descending stairways
to a deep rumbling.

                      The rubbing feet
of those coming to be carried quicken a
grey pavement into soft light that rocks
to and fro, under the domed ceiling,
across and across from pale
earthcolored walls of bare limestone.

Covertly the hands of a great clock
go round and round! Were they to
move quickly and at once the whole
secret would be out and the shuffling
of all ants be done forever.

A leaning pyramid of sunlight, narrowing
out at a high window, moves by the clock:
disaccordant hands straining out from
a center: inevitable postures infinitely
repeated—
two—twofour—twoeight!
Porters in red hats run on narrow platforms.
This way ma'am!
                      —important not to take
the wrong train!
                      Lights from the concrete
ceiling hang crooked but—
                              Poised horizontal
on glittering parallels the dingy cylinders
packed with a warm glow—inviting entry—
pull against the hour. But brakes can
hold a fixed posture till—
                              The whistle!

Not twoeight. Not twofour. Two!

Gliding windows. Colored cooks sweating
in a small kitchen. Taillights—

In time: twofour!
In time: twoeight!

—rivers are tunneled: trestles
cross oozy swampland: wheels repeating
the same gesture remain relatively
stationary: rails forever parallel
return on themselves infinitely.
The dance is sure.

ROMANCE MODERNE

Tracks of rain and light linger in
the spongy greens of a nature whose
flickering mountain—bulging nearer,
ebbing back into the sun
hollowing itself away to hold a lake,—
or brown stream rising and falling
at the roadside, turning about,
churning itself white, drawing
green in over it,—plunging glassy funnels
fall—

And—the other world—
the windshield a blunt barrier:
Talk to me. Sh! they would hear us.
—the backs of their heads facing us—
The stream continues its motion of
a hound running over rough ground.

Trees vanish—reappear—vanish:
detached dance of gnomes—as a talk
dodging remarks, glows and fades.
—The unseen power of words—
And now that a few of the moves

are clear the first desire is
to fling oneself out at the side into
the other dance, to other music.

Peer Gynt. Rip Van Winkle. Diana.
If I were young I would try a new alignment—
alight nimbly from the car, Good-bye!—
Childhood companions linked two and two
criss-cross: four, three, two, one.
Back into self, tentacles withdrawn.
Feel about in warm self-flesh.
Since childhood, since childhood!
Childhood is a toad in the garden, a
happy toad. All toads are happy
and belong in gardens. A toad to Diana!

Lean forward. Punch the steersman
behind the ear. Twirl the wheel!
Over the edge! Screams! Crash!
The end. I sit above my head—
a little removed—or
a thin wash of rain on the roadway
—I am never afraid when he is driving,—
interposes new direction,
rides us sidewise, unforseen
into the ditch! All threads cut!
Death! Black. The end. The very end—

I would sit separate weighing a
small red handful: the dirt of these parts,
sliding mists sheeting the alders
against the touch of fingers creeping
to mine. All stuff of the blind emotions.
But—stirred, the eye seizes
for the first time—The eye awake!—
anything, a dirt bank with green stars
of scrawny weed flattened upon it under
a weight of air—For the first time!—
or a yawning depth: Big!

Swim around in it, through it—
all directions and find
vitreous seawater stuff—
God how I love you!—or, as I say,
a plunge into the ditch. The end. I sit
examining my red handful. Balancing
—this—in and out—agh.

Love you? It's
a fire in the blood, willy-nilly!
It's the sun coming up in the morning.
Ha, but it's the grey moon too, already up
in the morning. You are slow.
Men are not friends where it concerns
a woman? Fighters. Playfellows.
White round thighs! Youth! Sighs—!
It's the fillip of novelty. It's—

Mountains. Elephants humping along
against the sky—indifferent to
light withdrawing its tattered shreds,
worn out with embraces. It's
the fillip of novelty. It's a fire in the blood.

Oh get a flannel shirt, white flannel
or pongee. You'd look so well!
I married you because I liked your nose.
I wanted you! I wanted you
in spite of all they'd say—

Rain and light, mountain and rain,
rain and river. Will you love me always?
—A car overturned and two crushed bodies
under it.—Always! Always!
And the white moon already up.
White. Clean. All the colors.
A good head, backed by the eye—awake!
backed by the emotions—blind—
River and mountain, light and rain—or

rain, rock, light, trees—divided:
rain-light counter rocks-trees or
trees counter rain-light-rocks or—

Myriads of counter processions
crossing and recrossing, regaining
the advantage, buying here, selling there
—You are sold cheap everywhere in town!—
lingering, touching fingers, withdrawing
gathering forces into blares, hummocks,
peaks and rivers—river meeting rock
—I wish that you were lying there dead
and I sitting here beside you.—
It's the grey moon—over and over.
It's the clay of these parts.

THE DESOLATE FIELD

Vast and grey, the sky
is a simulacrum
to all but him whose days
are vast and grey, and—
In the tall, dried grasses
a goat stirs
with nozzle searching the ground.
—my head is in the air
but who am I . . ?
And amazed my heart leaps
at the thought of love
vast and grey
yearning silently over me.

WILLOW POEM

It is a willow when summer is over,
a willow by the river

from which no leaf has fallen nor
bitten by the sun
turned orange or crimson.
The leaves cling and grow paler,
swing and grow paler
over the swirling waters of the river
as if loath to let go,
they are so cool, so drunk with
the swirl of the wind and of the river—
oblivious to winter,
the last to let go and fall
into the water and on the ground.

APPROACH OF WINTER

The half-stripped trees
struck by a wind together,
bending all,
the leaves flutter drily
and refuse to let go
or driven like hail
stream bitterly out to one side
and fall
where the salvias, hard carmine,—
like no leaf that ever was—
edge the bare garden.

JANUARY

Again I reply to the triple winds
running chromatic fifths of derision
outside my window:
               Play louder.
You will not succeed. I am
bound more to my sentences
the more you batter at me

to follow you.
And the wind,
as before, fingers perfectly
its derisive music.

BLIZZARD

Snow:
years of anger following
hours that float idly down—
the blizzard
drifts its weight
deeper and deeper for three days
or sixty years, eh? Then
the sun! a clutter of
yellow and blue flakes—
Hairy looking trees stand out
in long alleys
over a wild solitude.
The man turns and there—
his solitary track stretched out
upon the world.

TO WAKEN AN OLD LADY

Old age is
a flight of small
cheeping birds
skimming
bare trees
above a snow glaze.
Gaining and failing
they are buffeted
by a dark wind—
But what?
On harsh weedstalks

the flock has rested,
the snow
is covered with broken
seedhusks
and the wind tempered
by a shrill
piping of plenty.

WINTER TREES

All the complicated details
of the attiring and
the disattiring are completed!
A liquid moon
moves gently among
the long branches.
Thus having prepared their buds
against a sure winter
the wise trees
stand sleeping in the cold.

COMPLAINT

They call me and I go.
It is a frozen road
past midnight, a dust
of snow caught
in the rigid wheeltracks.
The door opens.
I smile, enter and
shake off the cold.
Here is a great woman
on her side in the bed.
She is sick,
perhaps vomiting,
perhaps laboring

to give birth to
a tenth child. Joy! Joy!
Night is a room
darkened for lovers,
through the jalousies the sun
has sent one gold needle!
I pick the hair from her eyes
and watch her misery
with compassion.

THE COLD NIGHT

It is cold. The white moon
is up among her scattered stars—
like the bare thighs of
the Police Sergeant's wife—among
her five children . . .
No answer. Pale shadows lie upon
the frosted grass. One answer:
It is midnight, it is still
and it is cold . . . !
White thighs of the sky! a
new answer out of the depths of
my male belly: In April . . .
In April I shall see again—In April!
the round and perfect thighs
of the Police Sergeant's wife
perfect still after many babies.
Oya!

SPRING STORM

The sky has given over
its bitterness.
Out of the dark change

all day long
rain falls and falls
as if it would never end.
Still the snow keeps
its hold on the ground.
But water, water
from a thousand runnels!
It collects swiftly,
dappled with black
cuts a way for itself
through green ice in the gutters.
Drop after drop it falls
from the withered grass-stems
of the overhanging embankment.

THE DELICACIES

The hostess, in pink satin and blond hair—dressed high—shone beautifully in her white slippers against the great silent bald head of her little-eyed husband!

Raising a glass of yellow Rhine wine in the narrow space just beyond the light-varnished woodwork and the decorative column between dining-room and hall, she smiled the smile of water tumbling from one ledge to another.

We began with a herring salad: delicately flavored saltiness in scallops of lettuce-leaves.

The little owl-eyed and thick-set lady with masses of grey hair has smooth pink cheeks without a wrinkle. She cannot be the daughter of the little red-faced fellow dancing about inviting lion-headed Wolff the druggist to play the piano! But she is. Wolff is a terrific smoker: if the telephone goes off at night—so his curled-haired wife whispers—he rises from bed but cannot answer till he has lighted a cigarette.

Sherry wine in little conical glasses, dull brownish yellow, and tomatoes stuffed with finely cut chicken and mayonnaise!

The tall Irishman in a Prince Albert and the usual striped trousers is going to sing for us. (The piano is in a little alcove with dark curtains.) The hostess's sister—ten years younger than she—in black net and velvet, has hair like some filmy haystack, cloudy about the eyes. She will play for her husband.

My wife is young, yes she is young and pretty when she cares to be— when she is interested in a discussion: it is the little dancing mayor's wife telling her of the Day Nursery in East Rutherford, 'cross the track, divided from us by the railroad—and disputes as to precedence. It is in this town the saloon flourishes, the saloon of my friend on the right whose wife has twice offended with chance words. Her English is atrocious! It is in this town that the saloon is situated, close to the railroad track, close as may be, this side being dry, dry, dry: two people listening on opposite sides of a wall!—The Day Nursery had sixty-five babies the week before last, so my wife's eyes shine and her cheeks are pink and I cannot see a blemish.

Ice-cream in the shape of flowers and domestic objects: a pipe for me since I do not smoke, a doll for you.

The figure of some great bulk of a woman disappearing into the kitchen with a quick look over the shoulder. My friend on the left who has spent the whole day in a car the like of which some old fellow would give to an actress: flower-holders, mirrors, curtains, plush seats—my friend on the left who is chairman of the Streets committee of the town council—and who has spent the whole day studying automobile fire-engines in neighboring towns in view of purchase,—my friend, at the Elks last week at the breaking-up hymn, signalled for them to let Bill— a familiar friend of the saloon-keeper—sing out all alone to the organ— and he did sing!

Salz-rolls, exquisite! and Rhine wine *ad libitum*. A masterly caviar sandwich.

The children flitting about above stairs. The councilman has just bought a National eight—some car!

For heaven's sake I mustn't forget the halves of green peppers stuffed with cream cheese and whole walnuts!

THURSDAY

I have had my dream—like others—
and it has come to nothing, so that
I remain now carelessly
with feet planted on the ground
and look up at the sky—
feeling my clothes about me,
the weight of my body in my shoes,
the rim of my hat, air passing in and out
at my nose—and decide to dream no more.

THE DARK DAY

A three-day-long rain from the east—
an interminable talking, talking
of no consequence—patter, patter, patter.
Hand in hand little winds
blow the thin streams aslant.
Warm. Distance cut off. Seclusion.
A few passers-by, drawn in upon themselves,
hurry from one place to another.
Winds of the white poppy! there is no escape!—
An interminable talking, talking,
talking . . . it has happened before.
Backward, backward, backward.

TIME THE HANGMAN

Poor old Abner, poor old white-haired nigger!
I remember when you were so strong
you hung yourself by a rope round the neck
in Doc Hollister's barn to prove you could beat
the faker in the circus—and it didn't kill you.
Now your face is in your hands, and your elbows
are on your knees, and you are silent and broken.

TO A FRIEND

Well, Lizzie Anderson! seventeen men—and
the baby hard to find a father for!

What will the good Father in Heaven say
to the local judge if he do not solve this problem?
A little two-pointed smile and—pouff!—
the law is changed into a mouthful of phrases.

THE GENTLE MAN

I feel the caress of my own fingers
on my own neck as I place my collar
and think pityingly
of the kind women I have known.

THE SOUGHING WIND

Some leaves hang late, some fall
before the first frost—so goes
the tale of winter branches and old bones.

SPRING

O my grey hairs!
You are truly white as plum blossoms.

PLAY

Subtle, clever brain, wiser than I am,
by what devious means do you contrive
to remain idle? Teach me, O master.

LINES

Leaves are greygreen,
the glass broken, bright green.

THE POOR

By constantly tormenting them
with reminders of the lice in
their children's hair, the
School Physician first
brought their hatred down on him.
But by this familiarity
they grew used to him, and so,
at last,
took him for their friend and adviser.

COMPLETE DESTRUCTION

It was an icy day.
We buried the cat,
then took her box
and set match to it

in the back yard.
Those fleas that escaped
earth and fire
died by the cold.

MEMORY OF APRIL

You say love is this, love is that:
Poplar tassels, willow tendrils
the wind and the rain comb,

tinkle and drip, tinkle and drip—
branches drifting apart. Hagh!
Love has not even visited this country.

EPITAPH

An old willow with hollow branches
slowly swayed his few high bright tendrils
and sang:

Love is a young green willow
shimmering at the bare wood's edge.

DAISY

The dayseye hugging the earth
in August, ha! Spring is
gone down in purple,
weeds stand high in the corn,
the rainbeaten furrow
is clotted with sorrel
and crabgrass, the
branch is black under
the heavy mass of the leaves—
The sun is upon a
slender green stem
ribbed lengthwise.
He lies on his back—
it is a woman also—
he regards his former
majesty and
round the yellow center,
split and creviced and done into
minute flowerheads, he sends out
his twenty rays—a little
and the wind is among them
to grow cool there!

One turns the thing over
in his hand and looks
at it from the rear: brownedged,
green and pointed scales
armor his yellow.

But turn and turn,
the crisp petals remain
brief, translucent, greenfastened,
barely touching at the edges:
blades of limpid seashell.

PRIMROSE

Yellow, yellow, yellow, yellow!
It is not a color.
It is summer!
It is the wind on a willow,
the lap of waves, the shadow
under a bush, a bird, a bluebird,
three herons, a dead hawk
rotting on a pole—
Clear yellow!
It is a piece of blue paper
in the grass or a threecluster of
green walnuts swaying, children
playing croquet or one boy
fishing, a man
swinging his pink fists
as he walks—
It is ladysthumb, forget-me-nots
in the ditch, moss under
the flange of the carrail, the
wavy lines in split rock, a
great oaktree—
It is a disinclination to be
five red petals or a rose, it is
a cluster of birdsbreast flowers

on a red stem six feet high,
four open yellow petals
above sepals curled
backward into reverse spikes—
Tufts of purple grass spot the
green meadow and clouds the sky.

QUEEN-ANNE'S-LACE

Her body is not so white as
anemone petals nor so smooth—nor
so remote a thing. It is a field
of the wild carrot taking
the field by force; the grass
does not raise above it.
Here is no question of whiteness,
white as can be, with a purple mole
at the center of each flower.
Each flower is a hand's span
of her whiteness. Wherever
his hand has lain there is
a tiny purple blemish. Each part
is a blossom under his touch
to which the fibres of her being
stem one by one, each to its end,
until the whole field is a
white desire, empty, a single stem,
a cluster, flower by flower,
a pious wish to whiteness gone over—
or nothing.

GREAT MULLEN

One leaves his leaves at home
being a mullen and sends up a lighthouse
to peer from: I will have my way,

yellow—A mast with a lantern, ten
fifty, a hundred, smaller and smaller
as they grow more—Liar, liar, liar!
You come from her! I can smell djer-kiss
on your clothes. Ha! you come to me,
you—I am a point of dew on a grass-stem.
Why are you sending heat down on me
from your lantern?—You are cowdung, a
dead stick with the bark off. She is
squirting on us both. She has had her
hand on you!—well?—She has defiled
ME.—Your leaves are dull, thick
and hairy.—Every hair on my body will
hold you off from me. You are a
dungcake, birdlime on a fencerail.—
I love you, straight, yellow
finger of God pointing to—her!
Liar, broken weed, dungcake, you have—
I am a cricket waving his antennae
and you are high, grey and straight. Ha!

WAITING

When I am alone I am happy.
The air is cool. The sky is
flecked and splashed and wound
with color. The crimson phalloi
of the sassafras leaves
hang crowded before me
in shoals on the heavy branches.
When I reach my doorstep
I am greeted by
the happy shrieks of my children
and my heart sinks.
I am crushed.

Are not my children as dear to me
as falling leaves or

must one become stupid
to grow older?
It seems much as if Sorrow
had tripped up my heels.
Let us see, let us see!
What did I plan to say to her
when it should happen to me
as it has happened now?

THE HUNTER

In the flashes and black shadows
of July
the days, locked in each other's arms,
seem still
so that squirrels and colored birds
go about at ease over
the branches and through the air.

Where will a shoulder split or
a forehead open and victory be?

Nowhere.
Both sides grow older.

And you may be sure
not one leaf will lift itself
from the ground
and become fast to a twig again.

ARRIVAL

And yet one arrives somehow,
finds himself loosening the hooks of
her dress
in a strange bedroom—
feels the autumn

dropping its silk and linen leaves
about her ankles.
The tawdry veined body emerges
twisted upon itself
like a winter wind . . . !

TO A FRIEND CONCERNING SEVERAL LADIES

You know there is not much
that I desire, a few chrysanthemums
half lying on the grass, yellow
and brown and white, the
talk of a few people, the trees,
an expanse of dried leaves perhaps
with ditches among them.

But there comes
between me and these things
a letter
or even a look—well placed,
you understand,
so that I am confused, twisted
four ways and—left flat,
unable to lift the food to
my own mouth:
Here is what they say: Come!
and come! and come! And if
I do not go I remain stale to
myself and if I go—
                          I have watched
the city from a distance at night
and wondered why I wrote no poem.
Come! yes,
the city is ablaze for you
and you stand and look at it.

And they are right. There is
no good in the world except out of

a woman and certain women alone
for certain things. But what if
I arrive like a turtle,
with my house on my back or
a fish ogling from under water?
It will not do. I must be
steaming with love, colored
like a flamingo. For what?
To have legs and a silly head
and to smell, pah! like a flamingo
that soils its own feathers behind.
Must I go home filled
with a bad poem?
And they say:
Who can answer these things
till he has tried? Your eyes
are half closed, you are a child,
oh, a sweet one, ready to play
but I will make a man of you and
with love on his shoulder—!

And in the marshes
the crickets run
on the sunny dike's top and
make burrows there, the water
reflects the reeds and the reeds
move on their stalks and rattle drily.

YOUTH AND BEAUTY

I bought a dishmop—
having no daughter—
for they had twisted
fine ribbons of shining copper
about white twine
and made a tousled head
of it, fastened it
upon a turned ash stick

slender at the neck
straight, tall—
when tied upright
on the brass wallbracket
to be a light for me
and naked
as a girl should seem
to her father.

THE THINKER

My wife's new pink slippers
have gay pompons.
There is not a spot or a stain
on their satin toes or their sides.
All night they lie together
under her bed's edge.
Shivering I catch sight of them
and smile, in the morning.
Later I watch them
descending the stair,
hurrying through the doors
and round the table,
moving stiffly
with a shake of their gay pompons!
And I talk to them
in my secret mind
out of pure happiness.

THE DISPUTANTS

Upon the table in their bowl
in violent disarray
of yellow sprays, green spikes
of leaves, red pointed petals
and curled heads of blue

and white among the litter
of the forks and crumbs and plates
the flowers remain composed.
Coolly their colloquy continues
above the coffee and loud talk
grown frail as vaudeville.

THE TULIP BED

The May sun—whom
all things imitate—
that glues small leaves to
the wooden trees
shone from the sky
through bluegauze clouds
upon the ground.
Under the leafy trees
where the suburban streets
lay crossed,
with houses on each corner,
tangled shadows had begun
to join
the roadway and the lawns.
With excellent precision
the tulip bed
inside the iron fence
upreared its gaudy
yellow, white and red,
rimmed round with grass,
reposedly.

THE BIRDS

The world begins again!
Not wholly insufflated
the blackbirds in the rain

upon the dead topbranches
of the living tree,
stuck fast to the low clouds,
notate the dawn.
Their shrill cries sound
announcing appetite
and drop among the bending roses
and the dripping grass.

THE NIGHTINGALES

My shoes as I lean
unlacing them
stand out upon
flat worsted flowers.

Nimbly the shadows
of my fingers play
unlacing
over shoes and flowers.

SPOUTS

In this world of
as fine a pair of breasts
as ever I saw
the fountain in
Madison Square
spouts up of water
a white tree
that dies and lives
as the rocking water
in the basin
turns from the stonerim
back upon the jet
and rising there
reflectively drops down again.

BLUEFLAGS

I stopped the car
to let the children down
where the streets end
in the sun
at the marsh edge
and the reeds begin
and there are small houses
facing the reeds
and the blue mist
in the distance
with grapevine trellises
with grape clusters
small as strawberries
on the vines
and ditches
running springwater
that continue the gutters
with willows over them.
The reeds begin
like water at a shore
their pointed petals waving
dark green and light.
But blueflags are blossoming
in the reeds
which the children pluck
chattering in the reeds
high over their heads
which they part
with bare arms to appear
with fists of flowers
till in the air
there comes the smell
of calamus
from wet, gummy stalks.

THE WIDOW'S LAMENT IN SPRINGTIME

Sorrow is my own yard
where the new grass
flames as it has flamed
often before but not
with the cold fire
that closes round me this year.
Thirtyfive years
I lived with my husband.
The plumtree is white today
with masses of flowers.
Masses of flowers
load the cherry branches
and color some bushes
yellow and some red
but the grief in my heart
is stronger than they
for though they were my joy
formerly, today I notice them
and turn away forgetting.
Today my son told me
that in the meadows,
at the edge of the heavy woods
in the distance, he saw
trees of white flowers.
I feel that I would like
to go there
and fall into those flowers
and sink into the marsh near them.

LIGHT HEARTED WILLIAM

Light hearted William twirled
his November moustaches
and, half dressed, looked
from the bedroom window
upon the spring weather.

Heigh-ya! sighed he gaily
leaning out to see
up and down the street
where a heavy sunlight
lay beyond some blue shadows.

Into the room he drew
his head again and laughed
to himself quietly
twirling his green moustaches.

PORTRAIT OF THE AUTHOR

The birches are mad with green points
the wood's edge is burning with their green,
burning, seething—No, no, no.
The birches are opening their leaves one
by one. Their delicate leaves unfold cold
and separate, one by one. Slender tassels
hang swaying from the delicate branch tips—
Oh, I cannot say it. There is no word.
Black is split at once into flowers. In
every bog and ditch, flares of
small fire, white flowers!—Agh,
the birches are mad, mad with their green.
The world is gone, torn into shreds
with this blessing. What have I left undone
that I should have undertaken?

O my brother, you redfaced, living man
ignorant, stupid whose feet are upon
this same dirt that I touch—and eat.
We are alone in this terror, alone,
face to face on this road, you and I,
wrapped by this flame!
Let the polished plows stay idle,
their gloss already on the black soil.
But that face of yours—!

Answer me. I will clutch you. I
will hug you, grip you. I will poke my face
into your face and force you to see me.
Take me in your arms, tell me the commonest
thing that is in your mind to say,
say anything. I will understand you—!
It is the madness of the birch leaves opening
cold, one by one.

My rooms will receive me. But my rooms
are no longer sweet spaces where comfort
is ready to wait on me with its crumbs.
A darkness has brushed them. The mass
of yellow tulips in the bowl is shrunken.
Every familiar object is changed and dwarfed.
I am shaken, broken against a might
that splits comfort, blows apart
my careful partitions, crushes my house
and leaves me—with shrinking heart
and startled, empty eyes—peering out
into a cold world.

In the spring I would drink! In the spring
I would be drunk and lie forgetting all things.
Your face! Give me your face, Yang Kue Fei!
your hands, your lips to drink!
Give me your wrists to drink—
I drag you, I am drowned in you, you
overwhelm me! Drink!
Save me! The shad bush is in the edge
of the clearing. The yards in a fury
of lilac blossoms are driving me mad with terror.
Drink and lie forgetting the world.

And coldly the birch leaves are opening one by one.
Coldly I observe them and wait for the end.
And it ends.

THE LONELY STREET

School is over. It is too hot
to walk at ease. At ease
in light frocks they walk the streets
to while the time away.
They have grown tall. They hold
pink flames in their right hands.
In white from head to foot,
with sidelong, idle look—
in yellow, floating stuff,
black sash and stockings—
touching their avid mouths
with pink sugar on a stick—
like a carnation each holds in her hand—
they mount the lonely street.

THE GREAT FIGURE

Among the rain
and lights
I saw the figure 5
in gold
on a red
firetruck
moving
tense
unheeded
to gong clangs
siren howls
and wheels rumbling
through the dark city.

SPRING AND ALL

1923

Spring and All

by

William Carlos Williams

If anything of moment results—so much the better. And so much the more likely will it be that no one will want to see it.

There is a constant barrier between the reader and his consciousness of immediate contact with the world. If there is an ocean it is here. Or rather, the whole world is between: Yesterday, tomorrow, Europe, Asia, Africa,—all things removed and impossible, the tower of the church at Seville, the Parthenon.

What do they mean when they say: "I do not like your poems; you have no faith whatever. You seem neither to have suffered nor, in fact, to have felt anything very deeply. There is nothing appealing in what you say but on the contrary the poems are positively repellent. They are heartless, cruel, they make fun of humanity. What in God's name do you mean? Are you a pagan? Have you no tolerance for human frailty? Rhyme you may perhaps take away but rhythm! why there is none in your work whatever. Is this what you call poetry? It is the very antithesis of poetry. It is antipoetry. It is the annihilation of life upon which you are bent. Poetry that used to go hand in hand with life, poetry that interpreted our deepest promptings, poetry that inspired, that led us forward to new discoveries, new depths of tolerance, new heights of exaltation. You moderns! it is the death of poetry that you are accomplishing. No. I cannot understand this work. You have not yet suffered a cruel blow from life. When you have suffered you will write differently"?

Perhaps this noble apostrophe means something terrible for me, I am not certain, but for the moment I interpret it to say: "You have robbed me. God, I am naked. What shall I do?"—By it they mean that when I have suffered (provided I have not done so as yet) I too shall run for cover; that I too shall seek refuge in fantasy. And mind you, I do not say that I will not. To decorate my age.

But today it is different.

The reader knows himself as he was twenty years ago and he has also in mind a vision of what he would be, some day. Oh, some day! But the thing he never knows and never dares to know is what he is at the exact moment that he is. And this moment is the only thing in which I am at all interested. Ergo, who cares for anything I do? And what do I care?

I love my fellow creature. Jesus, how I love him: endways, sideways, frontways and all the other ways—but he doesn't exist! Neither does she. I do, in a bastardly sort of way.

To whom then am I addressed? To the imagination.

In fact to return upon my theme for the time nearly all writing, up to the present, if not all art, has been especially designed to keep up the barrier between sense and the vaporous fringe which distracts the attention from its agonized approaches to the moment. It has been always a search for "the beautiful illusion." Very well. I am not in search of "the beautiful illusion."

And if when I pompously announce that I am addressed—To the imagination—you believe that I thus divorce myself from life and so defeat my own end, I reply: To refine, to clarify, to intensify that eternal moment in which we alone live there is but a single force—the imagination. This is its book. I myself invite you to read and to see.

In the imagination, we are from henceforth (so long as you read) locked in a fraternal embrace, the classic caress of author and reader. We are one. Whenever I say "I" I mean also "you." And so, together, as one, we shall begin.

CHAPTER 19

o meager times, so fat in everything imaginable! imagine the New World that rises to our windows from the sea on Mondays and on Saturdays— and on every other day of the week also. Imagine it in all its prismatic colorings, its counterpart in our souls—our souls that are great pianos whose strings, of honey and of steel, the divisions of the rainbow set twanging, loosing on the air great novels of adventure! Imagine the monster project of the moment: Tomorrow we the people of the United States are going to Europe armed to kill every man, woman and child in the area west of the Carpathian Mountains (also east) sparing none.

Imagine the sensation it will cause. First we shall kill them and then they, us. But we are careful to spare the Spanish bulls, the birds, rabbits, small deer and of course—the Russians. For the Russians we shall build a bridge from edge to edge of the Atlantic—having first been at pains to slaughter all Canadians and Mexicans on this side. Then, oh then, the great feature will take place.

Never mind; the great event may not exist, so there is no need to speak further of it. Kill! kill! the English, the Irish, the French, the Germans, the Italians and the rest: friends or enemies, it makes no difference, kill them all. The bridge is to be blown up when all Russia is upon it. And why?

Because we love them—all. That is the secret: a new sort of murder. We make leberwurst of them. Bratwurst. But why, since we are ourselves doomed to suffer the same annihilation?

If I could say what is in my mind in Sanscrit or even Latin I would do so. But I cannot. I speak for the integrity of the soul and the greatness of life's inanity; the formality of its boredom; the orthodoxy of its stupidity. Kill! kill! let there be fresh meat . . .

The imagination, intoxicated by prohibitions, rises to drunken heights to destroy the world. Let it rage, let it kill. The imagination is supreme. To it all our works forever, from the remotest past to the farthest future, have been, are and will be dedicated. To it alone we show our wit by having raised in its honor as monument not the least pebble. To it now we come to dedicate our secret project: the annihilation of every human creature on the face of the earth. This is something never before attempted. None to remain; nothing but the lower vertebrates, the mollusks, insects and plants. Then at last will the world be made anew. Houses crumble to ruin, cities disappear giving place to mounds of soil blown thither by the winds, small bushes and grass give way to trees which grow old and are succeeded by other trees for countless generations. A marvelous serenity broken only by bird and wild beast calls reigns over the entire sphere. Order and peace abound.

This final and self inflicted holocaust has been all for love, for sweetest love, that together the human race, yellow, black, brown, red and white, agglutinated into one enormous soul may be gratified with the sight and retire to the heaven of heavens content to rest on its laurels. There, soul of souls, watching its own horrid unity, it boils and digests itself within the tissues of the great Being of Eternity that we shall then have become. With what magnificent explosions and odors will not the day be accomplished as we, the Great One among all creatures, shall go about contemplating our self-prohibited desires as we promenade them before the inward review of our own bowels—et cetera, et cetera, et cetera . . . and it is spring—both in Latin and Turkish, in English and Dutch, in Japanese and Italian; it is spring by Stinking River where a magnolia tree, without leaves, before what was once a farmhouse, now a ramshackle home for millworkers, raises its straggling branches of ivorywhite flowers.

CHAPTER XIII

Thus, weary of life, in view of the great consummation which awaits us—tomorrow, we rush among our friends congratulating ourselves upon the joy soon to be. Thoughtless of evil we crush out the marrow of those about us with our heavy cars as we go happily from place to place. It seems that there is not time enough in which to speak the full of our exaltation. Only a day is left, one miserable day, before the world comes into its own. Let us hurry! Why bother for this man or that? In the offices of the great newspapers a mad joy reigns as they prepare the final extras. Rushing about, men bump each other into the whirring presses. How funny it seems. All thought of misery has left us. Why should we care? Children laughingly fling themselves under the wheels of the street cars, airplanes crash gaily to the earth. Someone has written a poem.

Oh life, bizarre fowl, what color are your wings? Green, blue, red, yellow, purple, white, brown, orange, black, grey? In the imagination, flying above the wreck of ten thousand million souls, I see you departing sadly for the land of plants and insects, already far out to sea. (Thank you, I know well what I am plagiarizing) Your great wings flap as you disappear in the distance over the pre-Columbian acres of floating weed.

The new cathedral overlooking the park, looked down from its towers today, with great eyes, and saw by the decorative lake a group of people staring curiously at the corpse of a suicide: Peaceful, dead young man, the money they have put into the stones has been spent to teach men of life's austerity. You died and teach us the same lesson. You seem a cathedral, celebrant of the spring which shivers for me among the long black trees.

CHAPTER VI

Now, in the imagination, all flesh, all human flesh has been dead upon the earth for ten million, billion years. The bird has turned into a stone within whose heart an egg, unlaid, remained hidden.

It is spring! but miracle of miracles a miraculous miracle has gradually taken place during these seemingly wasted eons. Through the orderly sequences of unmentionable time EVOLUTION HAS REPEATED ITSELF FROM THE BEGINNING.

Good God!

Every step once taken in the first advance of the human race, from the amoeba to the highest type of intelligence, has been duplicated, every step exactly paralleling the one that preceded in the dead ages gone by. A perfect plagiarism results. Everything is and is new. Only the imagination is undeceived.

At this point the entire complicated and laborious process begins to near a new day. (More of this in Chapter XIX) But for the moment everything is fresh, perfect, recreated.

In fact now, for the first time, everything IS new. Now at last the perfect effect is being witlessly discovered. The terms "veracity" "actuality" "real" "natural" "sincere" are being discussed at length, every word in the discussion being evolved from an identical discussion which took place the day before yesterday.

Yes, the imagination, drunk with prohibitions, has destroyed and recreated everything afresh in the likeness of that which it was. Now indeed men look about in amazement at each other with a full realization of the meaning of "art."

CHAPTER 2

It is spring: life again begins to assume its normal appearance as of "today." Only the imagination is undeceived. The volcanos are extinct. Coal is beginning to be dug again where the fern forests stood last night. (If an error is noted here, pay no attention to it.)

CHAPTER XIX

I realize that the chapters are rather quick in their sequence and that nothing much is contained in any one of them but no one should be surprised at this today.

THE TRADITIONALISTS OF PLAGIARISM

It is spring. That is to say, it is approaching THE BEGINNING.

In that huge and microscopic career of time, as it were a wild horse racing in an illimitable pampa under the stars, describing immense and microscopic circles with his hoofs on the solid turf, running without a stop for the millionth part of a second until he is aged and worn to a heap of skin, bones and ragged hoofs—In that majestic progress of life, that gives the exact impression of Phidias' frieze, the men and beasts of which, though they seem of the rigidity of marble are not so but move, with blinding rapidity, though we do not have the time to notice it, their legs advancing a millionth part of an inch every fifty thousand years— In that progress of life which seems stillness itself in the mass of its movements—at last SPRING is approaching.

In that colossal surge toward the finite and the capable life has now arrived for the second time at that exact moment when in the ages past the destruction of the species *Homo sapiens* occurred.

Now at last that process of miraculous verisimilitude, that great copying which evolution has followed, repeating move for move every move that it made in the past—is approaching the end.

Suddenly it is at an end. THE WORLD IS NEW.

I

By the road to the contagious hospital
under the surge of the blue
mottled clouds driven from the
northeast—a cold wind. Beyond, the
waste of broad, muddy fields
brown with dried weeds, standing and fallen

patches of standing water
the scattering of tall trees

All along the road the reddish
purplish, forked, upstanding, twiggy
stuff of bushes and small trees
with dead, brown leaves under them
leafless vines—

Lifeless in appearance, sluggish
dazed spring approaches—

They enter the new world naked,
cold, uncertain of all
save that they enter. All about them
the cold, familiar wind—

Now the grass, tomorrow
the stiff curl of wildcarrot leaf

One by one objects are defined—
It quickens: clarity, outline of leaf

But now the stark dignity of
entrance—Still, the profound change
has come upon them: rooted, they
grip down and begin to awaken

II

Pink confused with white
flowers and flowers reversed
take and spill the shaded flame
darting it back
into the lamp's horn

petals aslant darkened with mauve

red where in whorls
petal lays its glow upon petal
round flamegreen throats

petals radiant with transpiercing light
contending
                    above

the leaves
reaching up their modest green
from the pot's rim

and there, wholly dark, the pot
gay with rough moss.

A terrific confusion has taken place. No man knows whither to turn.
There is nothing! Emptiness stares us once more in the face. Whither?
To what end? Each asks the other. Has life its tail in its mouth or its
mouth in its tail? Why are we here? Dora Marsden's philosophic alge-
bra. Everywhere men look into each other's faces and ask the old unan-
swerable question: Whither? How? What? Why?

At any rate, now at last spring is here!

The rock has split, the egg has hatched, the prismatically plumed bird
of life has escaped from its cage. It spreads its wings and is perched now
on the peak of the huge African mountain Kilimanjaro.

Strange recompense, in the depths of our despair at the unfathom-
able mist into which all mankind is plunging, a curious force awakens. It

is HOPE long asleep, aroused once more. Wilson has taken an army of advisers and sailed for England. The ship has sunk. But the men are all good swimmers. They take the women on their shoulders and buoyed on by the inspiration of the moment they churn the free seas with their sinewy arms, like Ulysses, landing all along the European seaboard.

Yes, hope has awakened once more in men's hearts. It is the NEW! Let us go forward!

The imagination, freed from the handcuffs of "art," takes the lead! Her feet are bare and not too delicate. In fact those who come behind her have much to think of. Hm. Let it pass.

CHAPTER I

SAMUEL BUTLER

The great English divine, Sam Butler, is shouting from a platform, warning us as we pass: There are two who can invent some extraordinary thing to one who can properly employ that which has been made use of before.

Enheartened by this thought THE TRADITIONALISTS OF PLAGIARISM try to get hold of the mob. They seize those nearest them and shout into their ears: Tradition! The solidarity of life!

The fight is on: These men who have had the governing of the mob through all the repetitious years resent the new order. Who can answer them? One perhaps here and there but it is an impossible situation. If life were anything but a bird, if it were a man, a Greek or an Egyptian, but it is only a bird that has eyes and wings, a beak, talons and a cry that reaches to every rock's center, but without intelligence?—

The voice of the Delphic Oracle itself, what was it? A poisonous gas from a rock's cleft.

Those who led yesterday wish to hold their sway a while longer. It is not difficult to understand their mood. They have their great weapons to hand: "science," "philosophy" and most dangerous of all "art."

Meanwhile, SPRING, which has been approaching for several pages, is at last here.

—they ask us to return to the proven truths of tradition, even to the twice proven, the substantiality of which is known. Demuth and a few others do their best to point out the error, telling us that design is a function of the IMAGINATION, describing its movements, its colors— but it is a hard battle. I myself seek to enter the lists with these few notes jotted down in the midst of the action, under distracting circumstances—to remind myself (see p. 177, paragraph 6) of the truth.

III

The farmer in deep thought
is pacing through the rain
among his blank fields, with
hands in pockets,
in his head
the harvest already planted.
A cold wind ruffles the water
among the browned weeds.
On all sides
the world rolls coldly away:
black orchards
darkened by the March clouds—
leaving room for thought.
Down past the brushwood
bristling by
the rainsluiced wagonroad
looms the artist figure of
the farmer—composing
—antagonist

IV

The Easter stars are shining
above lights that are flashing—
coronal of the black—

Nobody
to say it—
Nobody to say: pinholes

Thither I would carry her

among the lights—

Burst it asunder
break through to the fifty words
necessary—

a crown for her head with
castles upon it, skyscrapers
filled with nut-chocolates—

dovetame winds—
stars of tinsel
from the great end of a cornucopia
of glass

So long as the sky is recognized as an association

is recognized in its function of accessory to vague words whose mean-
ing it is impossible to rediscover
its value can be nothing but mathematical certain limits of gravity and
density of air

The farmer and the fisherman who read their own lives there have a
practical corrective for—

they rediscover or replace demoded meanings to the religious terms

Among them, without expansion of imagination, there is the residual
contact between life and the imagination which is essential to freedom

The man of imagination who turns to art for release and fulfillment of his baby promises contends with the sky through layers of demoded words and shapes. Demoded, not because the essential vitality which begot them is laid waste—this cannot be so, a young man feels, since he feels it in himself—but because meanings have been lost through laziness or changes in the form of existence which have let words empty.

Bare handed the man contends with the sky, without experience of existence seeking to invent and design.

Crude symbolism is to associate emotions with natural phenomena such as anger with lightning, flowers with love it goes further and associates certain textures with

Such work is empty. It is very typical of almost all that is done by the writers who fill the pages every month of such a paper as. Everything that I have done in the past—except those parts which may be called excellent—by chance, have that quality about them.

It is typified by use of the word "like" or that "evocation" of the "image" which served us for a time. Its abuse is apparent. The insignificant "image" may be "evoked" never so ably and still mean nothing.

With all his faults Alfred Kreymborg never did this. That is why his work—escaping a common fault—still has value and will tomorrow have more.

Sandburg, when uninspired by intimacies of the eye and ear, runs into this empty symbolism. Such poets of promise as ruin themselves with it, though many have major sentimental faults besides.

Marianne Moore escapes. The incomprehensibility of her poems is witness to at what cost (she cleaves herself away) as it is also to the distance which the most are from a comprehension of the purpose of composition.

The better work men do is always done under stress and at great personal cost.

It is no different from the aristocratic compositions of the earlier times, The Homeric inventions

but

these occurred in different times, to this extent, that life had not yet sieved through its own multiformity. That aside, the work the two-thousand-year-old poet did and that we do are one piece. That is the vitality of the classics.

So then—Nothing is put down in the present book—except through weakness of the imagination—which is not intended as of a piece with the "nature" which Shakespeare mentions and which Hartley speaks of so completely in his "Adventures": it is the common thing which is anonymously about us.

Composition is in no essential an escape from life. In fact if it is so it is negligible to the point of insignificance. Whatever "life" the artist may be forced to lead has no relation to the vitality of his compositions. Such names as Homer, the blind; Scheherazade, who lived under threat— Their compositions have as their excellence an identity with life since they are as actual, as sappy as the leaf of the tree which never moves from one spot.

What I put down of value will have this value: an escape from crude symbolism, the annihilation of strained associations, complicated ritualistic forms designed to separate the work from "reality"—such as rhyme, meter as meter and not as the essential of the work, one of its words.

But this smacks too much of the nature of—This is all negative and appears to be boastful. It is not intended to be so. Rather the opposite.

The work will be in the realm of the imagination as plain as the sky is to a fisherman—A very clouded sentence. The word must be put down for itself, not as a symbol of nature but a part, cognizant of the whole— aware—civilized.

V

Black winds from the north
enter black hearts. Barred from

seclusion in lilies they strike
to destroy—

Beastly humanity
where the wind breaks it—

                       strident voices, heat
quickened, built of waves

Drunk with goats or pavements

Hate is of the night and the day
of flowers and rocks. Nothing
is gained by saying the night breeds
murder—It is the classical mistake

The day

All that enters in another person
all grass, all blackbirds flying
all azalea trees in flower
salt winds—

Sold to them men knock blindly together
splitting their heads open

That is why boxing matches and
Chinese poems are the same—That is why
Hartley praises Miss Wirt

There is nothing in the twist
of the wind but—dashes of cold rain

It is one with submarine vistas
purple and black fish turning
among undulant seaweed—

Black wind, I have poured my heart out
to you until I am sick of it—

Now I run my hand over you feeling
the play of your body—the quiver
of its strength—

The grief of the bowmen of Shu
moves nearer—There is
an approach with difficulty from
the dead—the winter casing of grief

How easy to slip
into the old mode, how hard to
cling firmly to the advance—

VI

No that is not it
nothing that I have done
nothing
I have done

is made up of
nothing
and the diphthong

ae

together with
the first person
singular
indicative

of the auxiliary
verb
to have

everything
I have done
is the same

if to do
is capable
of an
infinity of
combinations

involving the
moral
physical
and religious

codes

for everything
and nothing
are synonymous
when

energy *in vacuo*
has the power
of confusion

which only to
have done nothing
can make
perfect

The inevitable flux of the seeing eye toward measuring itself by the world it inhabits can only result in himself crushing humiliation unless the individual raise to some approximate co-extension with the universe. This is possible by aid of the imagination. Only through the agency of this force can a man feel himself moved largely with sympathetic pulses at work—

A work of the imagination which fails to release the senses in accordance with this major requisite—the sympathies, the intelligence in its selective world, fails at the elucidation, the alleviation which is—

In the composition, the artist does exactly what every eye must do with life, fix the particular with the universality of his own personality—Taught by the largeness of his imagination to feel every form which he sees moving within himself, he must prove the truth of this by expression.

The contraction which is felt.

All this being anterior to technique, that can have only a sequent value; but since all that appears to the senses on a work of art does so through

fixation by the imagination of the external as well as internal means of expression the essential nature of technique or transcription.

Only when this position is reached can life proper be said to begin since only then can a value be affixed to the forms and activities of which it consists.

Only then can the sense of frustration which ends. All composition defeated.

Only through the imagination is the advance of intelligence possible, to keep beside growing understanding.

Complete lack of imagination would be the same at the cost of intelligence, complete.

Even the most robust constitution has its limits, though the Roman feast with its reliance upon regurgitation to prolong it shows an active ingenuity, yet the powers of a man are so pitifully small, with the ocean to swallow—that at the end of the feast nothing would be left but suicide.

That or the imagination which in this case takes the form of humor, is known in that form—the release from physical necessity. Having eaten to the full we must acknowledge our insufficiency since we have not annihilated all food nor even the quantity of a good sized steer. However we have annihilated all eating: quite plainly we have no more appetite. This is to say that the imagination has removed us from the banal necessity of bursting ourselves—by acknowledging a new situation. We must acknowledge that the ocean we would drink is too vast—but at the same time we realize that extension in our case is not confined to the intestine only. The stomach is full, the ocean no fuller, both have the same quality of fullness. In that, then, one is equal to the other. Having eaten, the man has released his mind.

THIS catalogue might be increased to larger proportions without stimulating the sense.

In works of the imagination that which is taken for great good sense, so that it seems as if an accurate precept were discovered, is in reality not so, but vigor and accuracy of the imagination alone. In work such as Shakespeare's—

This leads to the discovery that has been made today—old catalogues aside—full of meat—

"the divine illusion has about it that inaccuracy which reveals that which I mean."

There is only "illusion" in art where ignorance of the bystander confuses imagination and its works with cruder processes. Truly men feel an enlargement before great or good work, an expansion but this is not, as so many believe today a "lie," a stupefaction, a kind of mesmerism, a thing to block out "life," bitter to the individual, by a "vision of beauty." It is a work of the imagination. It gives the feeling of completion by revealing the oneness of experience; it rouses rather than stupefies the intelligence by demonstrating the importance of personality, by showing the individual, depressed before it, that his life is valuable—when completed by the imagination. And then only. Such work elucidates—

Such a realization shows us the falseness of attempting to "copy" nature. The thing is equally silly when we try to "make" pictures—

But such a picture as that of Juan Gris, though I have not seen it in color, is important as marking more clearly than any I have seen what the modern trend is: the attempt is being made to separate things of the imagination from life, and obviously, by using the forms common to experience so as not to frighten the onlooker away but to invite him,

The rose is obsolete
but each petal ends in
an edge, the double facet
cementing the grooved
columns of air—The edge
cuts without cutting
meets—nothing—renews
itself in metal or porcelain—

whither? It ends—

But if it ends
the start is begun
so that to engage roses
becomes a geometry—

Sharper, neater, more cutting
figured in majolica—
the broken plate
glazed with a rose

Somewhere the sense
makes copper roses
steel roses—

The rose carried weight of love
but love is at an end—of roses

It is at the edge of the
petal that love waits

Crisp, worked to defeat
laboredness—fragile
plucked, moist, half-raised
cold, precise, touching

What

The place between the petal's
edge and the

From the petal's edge a line starts
that being of steel
infinitely fine, infinitely
rigid penetrates
the Milky Way
without contact—lifting
from it—neither hanging
nor pushing—

The fragility of the flower
unbruised
penetrates space

VIII

The sunlight in a
yellow plaque upon the
varnished floor

is full of a song
inflated to
fifty pounds pressure

at the faucet of
June that rings
the triangle of the air

pulling at the
anemones in
Persephone's cow pasture—

When from among
the steel rocks leaps
J. P. M.

who enjoyed
extraordinary privileges
among virginity

to solve the core
of whirling flywheels
by cutting

the Gordian knot
with a Veronese or
perhaps a Rubens—

whose cars are about
the finest on
the market today—

And so it comes
to motor cars—
which is the son

leaving off the g
of sunlight and grass—
Impossible

to say, impossible
to underestimate—
wind, earthquakes in

Manchuria, a
partridge
from dry leaves

   things with which he is familiar, simple things—at the same time to
detach them from ordinary experience to the imagination. Thus they are
still "real" they are the same things they would be if photographed or
painted by Monet, they are recognizable as the things touched by the
hands during the day, but in this painting they are seen to be in some
peculiar way—detached

   Here is a shutter, a bunch of grapes, a sheet of music, a picture of sea
and mountains (particularly fine) which the onlooker is not for a mo-
ment permitted to witness as an "illusion." One thing laps over on the

other, the cloud laps over on the shutter, the bunch of grapes is part of the handle of the guitar, the mountain and sea are obviously not "the mountain and sea," but a picture of the mountain and the sea. All drawn with admirable simplicity and excellent design—all a unity—

This was not necessary where the subject of art was not "reality" but related to the "gods"—by force or otherwise. There was no need of the "illusion" in such a case since there was none possible where a picture or a work represented simply the imaginative reality which existed in the mind of the onlooker. No special effort was necessary to cleave where the cleavage already existed.

I don't know what the Spanish see in their Velásquez and Goya but

Today where everything is being brought into sight the realism of art has bewildered us, confused us and forced us to re-invent in order to retain that which the older generations had without that effort.

Cézanne—

The only realism in art is of the imagination. It is only thus that the work escapes plagiarism after nature and becomes a creation

Invention of new forms to embody this reality of art, the one thing which art is, must occupy all serious minds concerned.

From the time of Poe in the U. S.—the first American poet had to be a man of great separation—with close identity with life. Poe could not have written a word without the violence of expulsive emotion combined with the in-driving force of a crudely repressive environment. Between the two his imagination was forced into being to keep him to that reality, completeness, sense of escape which is felt in his work—his topics. Typically American—accurately, even inevitably set in his time.

So, after this tedious diversion—whatever of dull you find among my work, put it down to criticism, not to poetry. You will not be mistaken— Who am I but my own critic? Surely in isolation one becomes a god—At least one becomes something of everything, which is not wholly godlike, yet a little so—in many things.

It is not necessary to count every flake of the truth that falls: it is necessary to dwell in the imagination if the truth is to be numbered. It is necessary to speak from the imagination—

The great furor about perspective in Holbein's day had as a consequence much fine drawing, it made coins defy gravity, standing on the table as if in the act of falling. To say this was lifelike must have been satisfying to the master, it gave depth, pungency.

But all the while the picture escaped notice—partly because of the perspective. Or if noticed it was for the most part because one could see "the birds pecking at the grapes" in it.

Meanwhile the birds were pecking at the grapes outside the window and in the next street Bauermeister Kummel was letting a gold coin slip from his fingers to the counting table.

The representation was perfect, it "said something one was used to hearing" but with verve, cleverly.

Thus perspective and clever drawing kept the picture continually under cover of the "beautiful illusion" until today, when even Anatole France trips, saying: "Art—all lies!"—today when we are beginning to discover the truth that in great works of the imagination A CREATIVE FORCE IS SHOWN AT WORK MAKING OBJECTS WHICH ALONE COMPLETE SCIENCE AND ALLOW INTELLIGENCE TO SURVIVE—his picture lives anew. It lives as pictures only can: by their power TO ESCAPE ILLUSION and stand between man and nature as saints once stood between man and the sky—their reality in such work, say, as that of Juan Gris

No man could suffer the fragmentary nature of his understanding of his own life—

Whitman's proposals are of the same piece with the modern trend toward imaginative understanding of life. The largeness which he interprets as his identity with the least and the greatest about him, his "democracy" represents the vigor of his imaginative life.

IX

What about all this writing?

O "Kiki"
O Miss Margaret Jarvis
The backhandspring

I: clean
    clean
    clean: yes . . New-York

Wrigley's, appendicitis, John Marin:
skyscraper soup—

Either that or a bullet!

Once
anything might have happened
You lay relaxed on my knees—
the starry night
spread out warm and blind
above the hospital—

Pah!

It is unclean
which is not straight to the mark—

In my life the furniture eats me

the chairs, the floor
the walls
which heard your sobs
drank up my emotion—
they which alone know everything

and snitched on us in the morning—

What to want?

Drunk we go forward surely
Not I

beds, beds, beds
elevators, fruit, night-tables
breasts to see, white and blue—
to hold in the hand, to nozzle

It is not onion soup
Your sobs soaked through the walls
breaking the hospital to pieces

Everything
—windows, chairs
obscenely drunk, spinning—
white, blue, orange
—hot with our passion

wild tears, desperate rejoinders
my legs, turning slowly
end over end in the air!

But what would you have?

All I said was:
there, you see, it is broken

stockings, shoes, hairpins
your bed, I wrapped myself round you—

I watched.

You sobbed, you beat your pillow
you tore your hair
you dug your nails into your sides

I was your nightgown
                    I   watched!

Clean is he alone
after whom stream

the broken pieces of the city—
flying apart at his approaches

but I merely
caress you curiously

fifteen years ago and you still
go about the city, they say
patching up sick school children

Understood in a practical way, without calling upon mystic agencies, of this or that order, it is that life becomes actual only when it is identified with ourselves. When we name it, life exists. To repeat physical experiences has no—

The only means he has to give value to life is to recognize it with the imagination and name it; this is so. To repeat and repeat the thing without naming it is only to dull the sense and results in frustration.

this makes the artist the prey of life. He is easy of attack.

I think often of my earlier work and what it has cost me not to have been clear. I acknowledge I have moved chaotically about refusing or rejecting most things, seldom accepting values or acknowledging anything.

because I early recognized the futility of acquisitive understanding and at the same time rejected religious dogmatism. My whole life has been spent (so far) in seeking to place a value upon experience and the objects of experience that would satisfy my sense of inclusiveness without redundancy—completeness, lack of frustration with the liberty of choice; the things which the pursuit of "art" offers—

But though I have felt "free" only in the presence of works of the imagination, knowing the quickening of the sense which came of it, and though this experience has held me firm at such times, yet being of a slow but accurate understanding, I have not always been able to complete the intellectual steps which would make me firm in the position.

So most of my life has been lived in hell—a hell of repression lit by flashes of inspiration, when a poem such as this or that would appear

What would have happened in a world similarly lit by the imagination

Oh yes, you are a writer! a phrase that has often damned me, to myself. I rejected it with heat but the stigma remained. Not a man, not an understanding but a WRITER. I was unable to recognize.

I do not forget with what heat too I condemned some poems of some contemporary praised because of their loveliness—

I find that I was somewhat mistaken—ungenerous

Life's processes are very simple. One or two moves are made and that is the end. The rest is repetitious.

The Improvisations—coming at a time when I was trying to remain firm at great cost—I had recourse to the expedient of letting life go completely in order to live in the world of my choice.

I let the imagination have its own way to see if it could save itself. Something very definite came of it. I found myself alleviated but most important I began there and then to revalue experience, to understand what I was at—

The virtue of the improvisations is their placement in a world of new values—

their fault is their dislocation of sense, often complete. But it is the best I could do under the circumstances. It was the best I could do and retain any value to experience at all.

Now I have come to a different condition. I find that the values there discovered can be extended. I find myself extending the understanding to the work of others and to other things—

I find that there is work to be done in the creation of new forms, new names for experience and that "beauty" is related not to "loveliness" but to a state in which reality plays a part

Such painting as that of Juan Gris, coming after the impressionists, the expressionists, Cézanne—and dealing severe strokes as well to the expressionists as to the impressionists group—points forward to what will prove the greatest painting yet produced.

—the illusion once dispensed with, painting has this problem before it: to replace not the forms but the reality of experience with its own—

up to now shapes and meanings but always the illusion relying on composition to give likeness to "nature"

now works of art cannot be left in this category of France's "lie," they must be real, not "realism" but reality itself—

they must give not the sense of frustration but a sense of completion, of actuality—It is not a matter of "representation"—much may be represented actually, but of separate existence.

enlargement—revivification of values,

X

The universality of things
draws me toward the candy
with melon flowers that open

about the edge of refuse
proclaiming without accent
the quality of the farmer's

shoulders and his daughter's
accidental skin, so sweet
with clover and the small

yellow cinquefoil in the
parched places. It is
this that engages the favorable

distortion of eyeglasses
that see everything and remain
related to mathematics—

in the most practical frame of
brown celluloid made to
represent tortoiseshell—

A letter from the man who
wants to start a new magazine
made of linen

and he owns a typewriter—
July 1, 1922
All this is for eyeglasses

to discover. But
they lie there with the gold
earpieces folded down

tranquilly Titicaca—

XI

In passing with my mind
on nothing in the world

but the right of way
I enjoy on the road by

virtue of the law—
I saw

an elderly man who
smiled and looked away

to the north past a house—
a woman in blue

who was laughing and
leaning forward to look up

into the man's half
averted face

and a boy of eight who was
looking at the middle of

the man's belly
at a watchchain—

The supreme importance
of this nameless spectacle

sped me by them
without a word—

Why bother where I went?
for I went spinning on the

four wheels of my car
along the wet road until

I saw a girl with one leg
over the rail of a balcony

When in the condition of imaginative suspense only will the writing
have reality, as explained partially in what precedes—Not to attempt, at
that time, to set values on the word being used, according to presup-
posed measures, but to write down that which happens at that time—

To perfect the ability to record at the moment when the consciousness
is enlarged by the sympathies and the unity of understanding which the
imagination gives, to practice skill in recording the force moving, then
to know it, in the largeness of its proportions—

It is the presence of a

This is not "fit" but a unification of experience

That is, the imagination is an actual force comparable to electricity or steam, it is not a plaything but a power that has been used from the first to raise the understanding of—it is, not necessary to resort to mysticism—In fact it is this which has kept back the knowledge I seek—

The value of the imagination to the writer consists in its ability to make words. Its unique power is to give created forms reality, actual existence

This separates

Writing is not a searching about in the daily experience for apt similes and pretty thoughts and images. I have experienced that to my sorrow. It is not a conscious recording of the day's experiences "freshly and with the appearance of reality"—This sort of thing is serious to the development of any ability in a man, it fastens him down, makes him a—It destroys, makes nature an accessory to the particular theory he is following, it blinds him to his world,—

The writer of imagination would find himself released from observing things for the purpose of writing them down later. He would be there to enjoy, to taste, to engage the free world, not a world which he carries like a bag of food, always fearful lest he drop something or someone get more than he.

A world detached from the necessity of recording it, sufficient to itself, removed from him (as it most certainly is) with which he has bitter and delicious relations and from which he is independent—moving at will from one thing to another—as he pleases, unbound—complete

and the unique proof of this is the work of the imagination not "like" anything but transfused with the same forces which transfuse the earth— at least one small part of them.

Nature is the hint to composition not because it is familiar to us and therefore the terms we apply to it have a least common denominator quality which gives them currency—but because it possesses the quality of independent existence, of reality which we feel in ourselves. It is not opposed to art but apposed to it.

I suppose Shakespeare's familiar aphorism about holding the mirror up to nature has done more harm in stabilizing the copyist tendency of the arts among us than—

the mistake in it (though we forget that it is not S. speaking but an imaginative character of his) is to have believed that the reflection of nature is nature. It is not. It is only a sham nature, a "lie."

Of course S. is the most conspicuous example desirable of the falseness of this very thing.

He holds no mirror up to nature but with his imagination rivals nature's composition with his own.

He himself become "nature"—continuing "its" marvels—if you will

I am often diverted with a recital which I have made for myself concerning Shakespeare: he was a comparatively uninformed man, quite according to the orthodox tradition, who lived from first to last a life of amusing regularity and simplicity, a house and wife in the suburbs, delightful children, a girl at court (whom he really never confused with his writing) and a café life which gave him with the freshness of discovery, the information upon which his imagination fed. London was full of the concentrates of science and adventure. He saw at "The Mermaid" everything he knew. He was not conspicuous there except for his spirits.

His form was presented to him by Marlowe, his stories were the common talk of his associates or else some compiler set them before him. His types were particularly quickened with life about him.

Feeling the force of life, in his peculiar intelligence, the great dome of his head, he had no need of anything but writing material to relieve himself of his thoughts. His very lack of scientific training loosened his power. He was unencumbered.

For S. to pretend to knowledge would have been ridiculous—no escape there—but that he possessed knowledge, and extraordinary knowledge, of the affairs which concerned him, as they concerned the others about him, was self-apparent to him. It was not apparent to the others.

His actual power was PURELY of the imagination. Not permitted to speak as W.S., in fact peculiarly barred from speaking so because of his lack of information, learning, not being able to rival his fellows in scientific training or adventure and at the same time being keen enough, imaginative enough, to know that there is no escape except in perfection, in excellence, in technical excellence—his buoyancy of imagination raised him NOT TO COPY them, not to holding the mirror up to them but to equal, to surpass them as a creator of knowledge, as a vigorous, living force above their heads.

His escape was not simulated but real. Hamlet no doubt was written about at the middle of his life.

He speaks authoritatively through invention, through characters, through design. The objects of his world were real to him because he could use them and use them with understanding to make his inventions—

The imagination is a—

The vermiculations of modern criticism of S. particularly amuse when the attempt is made to force the role of a Solon upon the creator of Richard 3d.

So I come again to my present day gyrations.

So it is with the other classics: their meaning and worth can only be studied and understood in the imagination—that which begot them only can give them life again, re-enkindle their perfection—

useless to study by rote or scientific research—. Useful for certain understanding to corroborate the imagination—

Yes, Anatole was a fool when he said: It is a lie.—That is it. If the actor simulates life it *is* a lie. But—but why continue without an audience?

The reason people marvel at works of art and say: How in Christ's name did he do it?—is that they know nothing of the physiology of the

nervous system and have never in their experience witnessed the larger
processes of the imagination.

It is a step over from the profitless engagements of the arithmetical.

XII

The red paper box
hinged with cloth

is lined
inside and out
with imitation
leather

It is the sun
the table
with dinner
on it for
these are the same

Its twoinch trays
have engineers
that convey glue
to airplanes

or for old ladies
that darn socks
paper clips
and red elastics—

What is the end
to insects
that suck gummed
labels?

for this is eternity
through its
dial we discover

transparent tissue
on a spool

But the stars
are round
cardboard
with a tin edge

and a ring
to fasten them
to a trunk
for the vacation—

XIII

Crustaceous
wedge
of sweaty kitchens
on rock
overtopping
thrusts of the sea

Waves of steel
from swarming backstreets
shell
of coral
inventing
electricity—

Lights
speckle
El Greco
lakes
in renaissance
twilight
with triphammers

which pulverize
nitrogen

of old pastures
to dodge
motorcars
with arms and legs—

The aggregate
is untamed
encapsulating
irritants
but
of agonized spires
knits
peace

where bridge stanchions
rest
certainly
piercing
left ventricles
with long
sunburnt fingers

XIV

Of death
the barber
the barber
talked to me

cutting my
life with
sleep to trim
my hair—

It's just
a moment
he said, we die
every night—

And of
the newest
ways to grow
hair on

bald death—
I told him
of the quartz
lamp

and of old men
with third
sets of teeth
to the cue

of an old man
who said
at the door—
Sunshine today!

for which
death shaves
him twice
a week

XV

The decay of cathedrals
is efflorescent
through the phenomenal
growth of movie houses

whose catholicity is
progress since
destruction and creation
are simultaneous

without sacrifice
of even the smallest

detail even to the
volcanic organ whose

woe is translatable
to joy if light becomes
darkness and darkness
light, as it will—

But schism which seems
adamant is diverted
from the perpendicular
by simply rotating the object

cleaving away the root of
disaster which it
seemed to foster. Thus
the movies are a moral force

Nightly the crowds
with the closeness and
universality of sand
witness the selfspittle

which used to be drowned
in incense and intoned
over by the supple-jointed
imagination of inoffensiveness

backed by biblical
rigidity made into passion plays
upon the altar to
attract the dynamic mob

whose female relative
sweeping grass Tolstoi
saw injected into
the Russian nobility

It is rarely understood how such plays as Shakespeare's were written—
or in fact how any work of value has been written, the practical bearing

of which is that only as the work was produced, in that way alone can it be understood

Fruitless for the academic tapeworm to hoard its excrementa in books. The cage—

The most of all writing has not even begun in the province from which alone it can draw sustenance.

There is not life in the stuff because it tries to be "like" life.

First must come the transposition of the faculties to the only world of reality that men know: the world of the imagination, wholly our own. From this world alone does the work gain power, its soil the only one whose chemistry is perfect to the purpose.

The exaltation men feel before a work of art is the feeling of reality they draw from it. It sets them up, places a value upon experience— (said that half a dozen times already)

XVI

O tongue
licking
the sore on
her netherlip

O toppled belly

O passionate cotton
stuck with
matted hair

elysian slobber
upon
the folded handkerchief

I can't die

—moaned the old
jaundiced woman
rolling her
saffron eyeballs

I can't die
I can't die

XVII

Our orchestra
is the cat's nuts—

Banjo jazz
with a nickelplated

amplifier to
soothe

the savage beast—
Get the rhythm

That sheet stuff
's a lot a cheese.

Man
gimme the key

and lemme loose—
I make 'em crazy

with my harmonies—
Shoot it Jimmy

Nobody
Nobody else

but me—
They can't copy it

XVIII

The pure products of America
go crazy—
mountain folk from Kentucky

or the ribbed north end of
Jersey
with its isolate lakes and

valleys, its deaf-mutes, thieves
old names
and promiscuity between

devil-may-care men who have taken
to railroading
out of sheer lust of adventure—

and young slatterns, bathed
in filth
from Monday to Saturday

to be tricked out that night
with gauds
from imaginations which have no

peasant traditions to give them
character
but flutter and flaunt

sheer rags—succumbing without
emotion
save numbed terror

under some hedge of choke-cherry
or viburnum—
which they cannot express—

Unless it be that marriage
perhaps
with a dash of Indian blood

will throw up a girl so desolate
so hemmed round
with disease or murder

that she'll be rescued by an
agent—
reared by the state and

sent out at fifteen to work in
some hard-pressed
house in the suburbs—

some doctor's family, some Elsie—
voluptuous water
expressing with broken

brain the truth about us—
her great
ungainly hips and flopping breasts

addressed to cheap
jewelry
and rich young men with fine eyes

as if the earth under our feet
were
an excrement of some sky

and we degraded prisoners
destined
to hunger until we eat filth

while the imagination strains
after deer
going by fields of goldenrod in

the stifling heat of September
Somehow
it seems to destroy us

It is only in isolate flecks that
something
is given off

No one
to witness
and adjust, no one to drive the car

   or better: prose has to do with the fact of an emotion; poetry has to do with the dynamization of emotion into a separate form. This is the force of imagination.

prose: statement of facts concerning emotions, intellectual states, data of all sorts—technical expositions, jargon, of all sorts—fictional and other—

poetry: new form dealt with as a reality in itself.

The form of prose is the accuracy of its subject matter—how best to expose the multiform phases of its material

   the form of poetry is related to the movements of the imagination revealed in words—or whatever it may be—

the cleavage is complete

   Why should I go further than I am able? Is it not enough for you that I am perfect?

   The cleavage goes through all the phases of experience. It is the jump from prose to the process of imagination that is the next great leap of the intelligence—from the simulations of present experience to the facts of the imagination—

the greatest characteristic of the present age is that it is stale—stale as literature—

   To enter a new world, and have there freedom of movement and newness.

I mean that there will always be prose painting, representative work, clever as may be in revealing new phases of emotional research presented on the surface.

But the jump from that to Cézanne or back to certain of the primitives is the impossible.

The primitives are not back in some remote age—they are not BEHIND experience. Work which bridges the gap between the rigidities of vulgar experience and the imagination is rare. It is new, immediate—It is so because it is actual, always real. It is experience dynamized into reality.

Time does not move. Only ignorance and stupidity move. Intelligence (force, power) stands still with time and forces change about itself—sifting the world for permanence, in the drift of nonentity.

Pío Baroja interested me once—

Baroja leaving the medical profession, some not important inspector's work in the north of Spain, opened a bakery in Madrid.

The isolation he speaks of, as a member of the so called intellectual class, influenced him to abandon his position and engage himself, as far as possible, in the intricacies of the design patterned by the social class— He sees no interest in isolation—

These gestures are the effort for self preservation or the preservation of some quality held in high esteem—

Here it seems to be that a man, starved in imagination, changes his milieu so that his food may be richer—The social class, without the power of expression, lives upon imaginative values.

I mean only to emphasize the split that goes down through the abstractions of art to the everyday exercises of the most primitive types—

there is a sharp division—the energizing force of imagination on one side—and the acquisitive—PROGRESSIVE force of the lump on the other

The social class with its religion, its faith, sincerity and all the other imaginative values is positive (yes)

the merchant, hibernating, unmagnetized—tends to drop away into the isolate, inactive particles—Religion is continued then as a form, art as a convention—

To the social, energized class—ebullient now in Russia the particles adhere because of the force of the imagination energizing them—

Anyhow the change of Baroja interested me

Among artists, or as they are sometimes called "men of imagination" "creators," etc. this force is recognized in a pure state—All this can be used to show the relationships between genius, hand labor, religion— etc. and the lack of feeling between artists and the middle class type—

The jump between fact and the imaginative reality

The study of all human activity is the delineation of the cresence and ebb of this force, shifting from class to class and location to location— rhythm: the wave rhythm of Shakespeare watching clowns and kings sliding into nothing

XIX

This is the time of year
when boys fifteen and seventeen
wear two horned lilac blossoms
in their caps—or over one ear

What is it that does this?

It is a certain sort—
drivers for grocers or taxidrivers
white and colored—

fellows that let their hair grow long
in a curve over one eye—

Horned purple

Dirty satyrs, it is
vulgarity raised to the last power

They have stolen them
broken the bushes apart
with a curse for the owner—

Lilacs—

They stand in the doorways
on the business streets with a sneer
on their faces

adorned with blossoms

Out of their sweet heads
dark kisses—rough faces

XX

The sea that encloses her young body
ula lu la lu
is the sea of many arms—

The blazing secrecy of noon is undone
and and and
the broken sand is the sound of love—

The flesh is firm that turns in the sea
O la la O
the sea that is cold with dead men's tears—

Deeply the wooing that penetrated
to the edge of the sea
returns in the plash of the waves—

a wink over the shoulder
large as the ocean—
with wave following wave to the edge

Oom barroom

It is the cold of the sea
broken upon the sand by the force
of the moon—

In the sea the young flesh playing
floats with the cries of far off men
who rise in the sea

with green arms
to homage again the fields over there
where the night is deep—

la lu la lu
but lips too few
assume the new—marruu

Underneath the sea where it is dark
there is no edge
so two—

XXI

one day in Paradise
a Gipsy

smiled
to see the blandness

of the leaves—
so many

so lascivious
and still

XXII

so much depends
upon

a red wheel
barrow

glazed with rain
water

beside the white
chickens

The fixed categories into which life is divided must always hold. These things are normal—essential to every activity. But they exist— but not as dead dissections.

The curriculum of knowledge cannot but be divided into the sciences, the thousand and one groups of data, scientific, philosophic or whatnot— as many as there exist in Shakespeare—things that make him appear the university of all ages.

But this is not the thing. In the galvanic category of—The same things exist, but in a different condition when energized by the imagination.

The whole field of education is affected—There is no end of detail that is without significance.

Education would begin by placing in the mind of the student the nature of knowledge—in the dead state and the nature of the force which may energize it.

This would clarify his field at once—He would then see the use of data

But at present knowledge is placed before a man as if it were a stair at the top of which a DEGREE is obtained which is superlative.

nothing could be more ridiculous. To data there is no end. There is proficiency in dissection and a knowledge of parts but in the use of knowledge—

It is the imagination that—

That is: life is absolutely simple. In any civilized society everyone should know EVERYTHING there is to know about life at once and always. There should never be permitted, confusion—

There are difficulties to life, under conditions there are impasses, life may prove impossible—But it must never be lost—as it is today—

I remember so distinctly the young Pole in Leipzig going with hushed breath to hear Wundt lecture—In this mass of intricate philosophic data what one of the listeners was able to maintain himself for the winking of an eyelash. Not one. The inundation of the intelligence by masses of complicated fact is not knowledge. There is no end—

And what is the fourth dimension? It is the endlessness of knowledge—

It is the imagination on which reality rides—It is the imagination—It is a cleavage through everything by a force that does not exist in the mass and therefore can never be discovered by its anatomization.

It is for this reason that I have always placed art first and esteemed it over science—in spite of everything.

Art is the pure effect of the force upon which science depends for its reality—Poetry

The effect of this realization upon life will be the emplacement of knowledge into a living current—which it has always sought—

In other times—men counted it a tragedy to be dislocated from sense—Today boys are sent with dullest faith to technical schools of all sorts—broken, bruised

few escape whole—slaughter. This is not civilization but stupidity—Before entering knowledge the integrity of the imagination—

The effect will be to give importance to the subdivisions of experience—which today are absolutely lost—There exists simply nothing.

Prose—When values are important, such—For example there is no use denying that prose and poetry are not by any means the same IN INTENTION. But then what is prose? There is no need for it to approach poetry except to be weakened.

With decent knowledge to hand we can tell what things are for

I expect to see values blossom. I expect to see prose be prose. Prose, relieved of extraneous, unrelated values must return to its only purpose: to clarity to enlighten the understanding. There is no form to prose but that which depends on clarity. If prose is not accurately adjusted to the exposition of facts it does not exist—Its form is that alone. To penetrate everywhere with enlightenment—

Poetry is something quite different. Poetry has to do with the crystallization of the imagination—the perfection of new forms as additions to nature—Prose may follow to enlighten but poetry—

Is what I have written prose? The only answer is that form in prose ends with the end of that which is being communicated—If the power to go on falters in the middle of a sentence—that is the end of the sentence—Or if a new phase enters at that point it is only stupidity to go on.

There is no confusion—only difficulties.

XXIII

The veritable night
of wires and stars

the moon is in
the oak tree's crotch

and sleepers in
the windows cough

athwart the round
and pointed leaves

and insects sting
while on the grass

the whitish moonlight
tearfully

assumes the attitudes
of afternoon—

But it is real
where peaches hang

recalling death's
long-promised symphony

whose tuneful wood
and stringish undergrowth

are ghosts existing
without being

save to come with juice
and pulp to assuage

the hungers which
the night reveals

so that now at last
the truth's aglow

with devilish peace
forestalling day

which dawns tomorrow
with dreadful reds

the heart to predicate
with mists that loved

the ocean and the fields—
Thus moonlight

is the perfect
human touch

XXIV

The leaves embrace
in the trees

it is a wordless
world

without personality
I do not

seek a path
I am still with

Gipsy lips pressed
to my own—

It is the kiss
of leaves

without being
poison ivy

or nettle, the kiss
of oak leaves—

He who has kissed
a leaf

need look no further—
I ascend

through
a canopy of leaves

and at the same time
I descend

for I do nothing
unusual—

I ride in my car
I think about

prehistoric caves
in the Pyrenees—

the cave of
Les Trois Frères

The nature of the difference between what is termed prose on the one hand and verse on the other is not to be discovered by a study of the metrical characteristics of the words as they occur in juxtaposition. It is ridiculous to say that verse grades off into prose as the rhythm becomes less and less pronounced, in fact, that verse differs from prose in that the meter is more pronounced, that the movement is more impassioned and that rhythmical prose, so called, occupies a middle place between prose and verse.

It is true that verse is likely to be more strongly stressed than what is termed prose, but to say that this is in any way indicative of the difference in nature of the two is surely to make the mistake of arguing from the particular to the general, to the effect that since an object has a certain character that therefore the force which gave it form will always reveal itself in that character.

Of course there is nothing to do but to differentiate prose from verse by the only effective means at hand, the external, surface appearance. But a counter proposal may be made, to wit: that verse is of such a nature that it may appear without metrical stress of any sort and that prose may be strongly stressed—in short that meter has nothing to do with the question whatever.

Of course it may be said that if the difference is felt and is not discoverable to the eye and ear then what about it anyway? Or it may be argued, that since there is according to my proposal no discoverable difference between prose and verse that in all probability none exists and that both are phases of the same thing.

Yet, quite plainly, there is a very marked difference between the two which may arise in the fact of a separate origin for each, each using similar modes for dis-similar purposes; verse falling most commonly into meter but not always, and prose going forward most often without meter but not always.

This at least serves to explain some of the best work I see today and explains some of the most noteworthy failures which I discover. I search for "something" in the writing which moves me in a certain way—It offers a suggestion as to why some work of Whitman's is bad poetry and some, in the same meter is prose.

The practical point would be to discover when a work is to be taken as coming from this source and when from that. When discovering a work it would be—If it is poetry it means this and only this—and if it is prose it means that and only that. Anything else is a confusion, silly and bad practice.

I believe this is possible as I believe in the main that Marianne Moore is of all American writers most constantly a poet—not because her lines are invariably full of imagery they are not, they are often diagrammatically informative, and not because she clips her work into certain shapes—her pieces are without meter most often—but I believe she is most constantly a poet in her work because the purpose of her work is invariably from the source from which poetry starts—that it is constantly from the purpose of poetry. And that it actually possesses this characteristic, as of that origin, to a more distinguishable degree when it eschews verse rhythms than when it does not. It has the purpose of poetry written into it and therefore it is poetry.

I believe it possible, even essential, that when poetry fails it does not become prose but bad poetry. The test of Marianne Moore would be that she writes sometimes good and sometimes bad poetry but always—with a single purpose out of a single fountain which is of the sort—

The practical point would be to discover—

I can go no further than to say that poetry feeds the imagination and prose the emotions, poetry liberates the words from their emotional implications, prose confirms them in it. Both move centrifugally or centripetally toward the intelligence.

Of course it must be understood that writing deals with words and words only and that all discussions of it deal with single words and their association in groups.

As far as I can discover there is no way but the one I have marked out which will satisfactorily deal with certain lines such as occur in some play of Shakespeare or in a poem of Marianne Moore's, let us say: Tomorrow will be the first of April—

Certainly there is an emotional content in this for anyone living in the northern temperate zone, but whether it is prose or poetry—taken by itself—who is going to say unless some mark is put on it by the intent conveyed by the words which surround it—

Either to write or to comprehend poetry the words must be recognized to be moving in a direction separate from the jostling or lack of it which occurs within the piece.

Marianne's words remain separate, each unwilling to group with the others except as they move in the one direction. This is even an important—or amusing—character of Miss Moore's work.

Her work puzzles me. It is not easy to quote convincingly.

XXV

Somebody dies every four minutes
in New York State—

To hell with you and your poetry—
You will rot and be blown

through the next solar system
with the rest of the gases—

What the hell do you know about it?

AXIOMS

Don't get killed

Careful Crossing Campaign
Cross Crossings Cautiously

THE HORSES   black
                        &
PRANCED   white

Outings in New York City

Ho for the open country

Don't stay shut up in hot rooms
Go to one of the Great Parks
Pelham Bay for example

It's on Long Island Sound
with bathing, boating
tennis, baseball, golf, etc.

Acres and acres of green grass
wonderful shade trees, rippling brooks

        Take the Pelham Bay Park Branch
        of the Lexington Ave. (East Side)
        Line and you are there in a few
        minutes

Interborough Rapid Transit Co.

XXVI

The crowd at the ball game
is moved uniformly

by a spirit of uselessness
which delights them—

all the exciting detail
of the chase

and the escape, the error
the flash of genius—

all to no end save beauty
the eternal—

So in detail they, the crowd,
are beautiful

for this
to be warned against

saluted and defied—
It is alive, venomous

it smiles grimly
its words cut—

The flashy female with her
mother, gets it—

The Jew gets it straight—it
is deadly, terrifying—

It is the Inquisition, the
Revolution

It is beauty itself
that lives

day by day in them
idly—

This is
the power of their faces

It is summer, it is the solstice
the crowd is

cheering, the crowd is laughing
in detail

permanently, seriously
without thought

The imagination uses the phraseology of science. It attacks, stirs, animates, is radio-active in all that can be touched by action. Words occur in liberation by virtue of its processes.

In description words adhere to certain objects, and have the effect on the sense of oysters, or barnacles.

But the imagination is wrongly understood when it is supposed to be a removal from reality in the sense of John of Gaunt's speech in Richard the Second: to imagine possession of that which is lost. It is rightly understood when John of Gaunt's words are related not to their sense as objects adherent to his son's welfare or otherwise but as a dance over the body of his condition accurately accompanying it. By this means of the understanding, the play written to be understood as a play, the author and reader are liberated to pirouette with the words which have sprung from the old facts of history, reunited in present passion.

To understand the words as so liberated is to understand poetry. That they move independently when set free is the mark of their value

Imagination is not to avoid reality, nor is it description nor an evocation of objects or situations, it is to say that poetry does not tamper with the world but moves it—It affirms reality most powerfully and therefore, since reality needs no personal support but exists free from human action, as proven by science in the indestructibility of matter and of force, it creates a new object, a play, a dance which is not a mirror up to nature but—

As birds' wings beat the solid air without which none could fly so words freed by the imagination affirm reality by their flight

Writing is likened to music. The object would be it seems to make poetry a pure art, like music. Painting too. Writing, as with certain of the modern Russians whose work I have seen, would use unoriented sounds in place of conventional words. The poem then would be completely liberated when there is identity of sound with something—perhaps the emotion.

I do not believe that writing is music. I do not believe writing would gain in quality or force by seeking to attain to the conditions of music.

I think the conditions of music are objects for the action of the writer's imagination just as a table or—

According to my present theme the writer of imagination would attain closest to the conditions of music not when his words are disassociated from natural objects and specified meanings but when they are liberated from the usual quality of that meaning by transposition into another medium, the imagination.

Sometimes I speak of imagination as a force, an electricity or a medium, a place. It is immaterial which: for whether it is the condition of a place or a dynamization its effect is the same: to free the world of fact from the impositions of "art" (see Hartley's last chapter) and to liberate the man to act in whatever direction his disposition leads.

The word is not liberated, therefore able to communicate release from the fixities which destroy it until it is accurately tuned to the fact which giving it reality, by its own reality establishes its own freedom from the necessity of a word, thus freeing it and dynamizing it at the same time.

XXVII

Black eyed susan
rich orange
round the purple core

the white daisy
is not
enough

Crowds are white
as farmers
who live poorly

But you
are rich
in savagery—

Arab
Indian
dark woman

POEMS
1922–1928

WILD ORCHARD

It is a broken country,
the rugged land is
green from end to end;
the autumn has not come.

Embanked above the orchard
the hillside is a wall
of motionless green trees,
the grass is green and red.

Five days the bare sky
has stood there day and night.
No bird, no sound.
Between the trees

stillness
and the early morning light.
The apple trees
are laden down with fruit.

Among blue leaves
the apples green and red
upon one tree stand out
most enshrined.

Still, ripe, heavy,
spherical and close,
they mark the hillside.
It is a formal grandeur,

a stateliness,
a signal of finality
and perfect ease.
Among the savage

aristocracy of rocks
one, risen as a tree,
has turned
from his repose.

PICTURE SHOWING

Picture showing
return of bodies
ZR–2 victims.

—Give you a nice
trip home
after you're dead.

—Christ, I'd rather
come home
steerage.

MY LUV

My luv
is like
a
greenglass
insulator
on
a blue sky.

THE BULL

It is in captivity—
ringed, haltered, chained

to a drag
the bull is godlike

Unlike the cows
he lives alone, nozzles
the sweet grass gingerly
to pass the time away

He kneels, lies down
and stretching out
a foreleg licks himself
about the hoof

then stays
with half-closed eyes,
Olympian commentary on
the bright passage of days.

—The round sun
smooths his lacquer
through
the glossy pinetrees

his substance hard
as ivory or glass—
through which the wind
yet plays—
                    Milkless

he nods
the hair between his horns
and eyes matted
with hyacinthine curls

THE JUNGLE

It is not the still weight
of the trees, the

breathless interior of the wood,
tangled with wrist-thick

vines, the flies, reptiles,
the forever fearful monkeys
screaming and running
in the branches—

                    but
a girl waiting
shy, brown, soft-eyed—
to guide you
                    Upstairs, sir.

FISH

It is the whales that drive
the small fish into the fiords.
I have seen forty or fifty
of them in the water at one time.
I have been in a little boat
when the water was boiling
on all sides of us
from them swimming underneath.

The noise of the herring
can be heard nearly a mile.
So thick in the water, they are,
you can't dip the oars in.
All silver!

And all those millions of fish
must be taken, each one, by hand.
The women and children
pull out a little piece
under the throat with their fingers
so that the brine gets inside.

I have seen thousands of barrels
packed with the fish on the shore.

In winter they set the gill-nets
for the cod. Hundreds of them
are caught each night.
In the morning the men
pull in the nets and fish
altogether in the boats.
Cod so big—I have seen—
that when a man held one up
above his head
the tail swept the ground.

Sardines, mackerel, anchovies
all of these. And in the rivers
trout and salmon. I have seen
a net set at the foot of a falls
and in the morning sixty trout in it.

But I guess there are not
such fish in Norway nowadays.

On the Lofoten Islands—
till I was twelve.
Not a tree or a shrub on them.
But in summer
with the sun never gone
the grass is higher than here.

The sun circles the horizon.
Between twelve and one at night
it is very low, near the sea,
to the north. Then
it rises a little, slowly,
till midday, then down again
and so for three months, getting
higher at first, then lower,
until it disappears—

In winter the snow is often
as deep as the ceiling of this room.

If you go there you will see
many Englishmen
near the falls and on the bridges
fishing, fishing.
They will stand there for hours
to catch the fish.

Near the shore
where the water is twenty feet or so
you can see the kingflounders
on the sand. They have
red spots on the side. Men come
in boats and stick them
with long pointed poles.

Have you seen how the Swedes drink tea?
So, in the saucer. They blow it
and turn it this way then that: so.

Tall, gaunt
great drooping nose, eyes dark-circled,
the voice slow and smiling:

I have seen boys stand
where the stream is narrow
a foot each side on two rocks
and grip the trout as they pass through.
They have a special way to hold them,
in the gills, so. The long
fingers arched like grapplehooks.

Then the impatient silence
while a little man said:

The English are great sportsmen.
At the winter resorts
where I stayed

they were always the first up
in the morning, the first
on with the skis.
I once saw a young Englishman
worth seventy million pounds—

You do not know the north.
—and you will see perhaps *huldra*
with long tails
and all blue, from the night,
and the *nekke*, half man and half fish.
When they see one of them
they know some boat will be lost.

HULA-HULA

I should like to come upon
some of the girls from
"Tangerine"
doing their stunt
naked
in their hair
on Brighton Beach
one of these fine mornings
that the horned sun
might laugh
and I see him
fresh from the seas
shake his broad shoulders

VIEW

The moon
ovoid
in the black press
sits

hugging his knees,
gone with thought
above
the ringed city.

WHEN FRESH, IT WAS SWEET

Balieff's actors from The Bat
in Moscow seem as if from the
center of the onion—the vision
predominates. Removed from the intimate
it is all intimate, closely observed
to be deftly translated to the stage—

The swiftness, fullness, delicacy
of their compositions dance with
the imaginations of peasants and
musicians, philosophers, and
gipsies—The keen eyes of humor
look from tall women's faces
gently; the *ensemble* is felt
above the detail; the music goes
free of the fact; the satire puts
a varicolored bridle on the donkey—
the old and the young
engage in the same pastimes—

Pantomime and gesture
woman or man—a power suffuses everything
gathering it altogether
uniting without brushing even the bloom—
The free air
welcomes them to itself, the footlights
obey as if it were some lost master—
The Americans of the audience
crumble, sweetness escapes their lips,
their straining comedians feel
a lightness that bids them play—

They are relieved of their lot
Jolson is entranced

To what is this that everybody
comes with gifts as of old they used
to bring gifts to shrines or altars?

Russian skill of dancing? No.
Dadaistic scenery? No. Excellent
as these things are. The whole
reveals these things.
The quaintness of Russian types,
the depth, sweetness, gaiety, color
of the Russian character? No.
The symmetry, reserve, force, tallness
of the woman? The diverse simpleness
and open humor of the men?
The sheer skill as singers, the
ingenuity of the managers, the composers,
the depth of tradition? No.

All these things existed before
the performance. Is it Balieff?
There are other Balieffs. All these things
are essential—But it is not that
which makes men ashamed and tender and
wistful and submissive—ready to learn:

    Katinka dances her polka
on the contracted stage of composition
Gaiety is formalized in her dress
and her make-up. Youth is in
the choice of the actress. Her father blinks
to the music
to show his joy in her dancing
The mother with severe face of renunciation
in a shawl—

It cannot be more than it is
without in a peasant's cottage
being mercenary to the landlord

who kills the splendor of national character
by his demands for rent, the filth of
stupidity which has no escape
—blend to make impossible
all that is not imagined by men who have
lived yet unsated
by life's endless profusion
and color
and rhythms, who seeing the brevity
of their transit through the spinning world
have resort to—
translation
  Here life's exquisite diversity
its tenderness
ardor of spirits
find that in which they may move—

All enters—Katinka dances
The father blinks
The mother severely stares
—hey-la!
we all laugh together—Life has us
by the arm.

Katinka dies by bending
her body down in a crouch about her knees
there she stays panting from
the exertion of dancing—

The parents relent in alarm

Katinka rebegins to dance—
Finis

FROM A BOOK

I would rather look down
into the face of
a bed of portulaca

than into the level
black eyes
of the virgin whom I love

Tra-la
tra-la
tra-la la la la

NEW ENGLAND

is a condition—
of bedrooms whose electricity

is brickish or made into
T beams—They dangle them

on wire cables to the tops
of Woolworth buildings

five and ten cents worth—
There they have bolted them

into place at masculine risk—
Or a boy with a rose under

the lintel of his cap
standing to have his picture

taken on the butt of a girder
with the city a mile down—

captured, lonely cock atop
iron girders wears rosepetal

smile—a thought of Indians
on chestnut branches

to end "walking on the air"

THE DRUNKARD

(This poem, recently recovered, was sent by me to my mother in the fall of 1923 accompanied by a letter in part as follows:

Dearest Mother: Here is a poem to set beside some of my "incomprehensible" latter work. I think you will like this one. It seems the sort of thing that I am going to do. Art is a curious command. We must do what we are bidden to do and can go only so far as the light permits. I am always earnest as you, if anyone, must know. But no doubt I puzzle you—as I do myself. Plenty of love from your son. W.)

You drunken
tottering
bum

by Christ
in spite of all
your filth

and sordidness
I envy
you

It is the very face
of love
itself

abandoned
in that powerless
committal

to despair

THE NEW CATHEDRAL OVERLOOKING THE PARK

The new cathedral overlooking the park
looked down from its tower
with great eyes today and saw
by the decorative lake a group of people

staring curiously at the corpse
of a suicide—Peaceful dead young man
the money they have put into the stones
has been spent to teach men of
life's austerity. You died
and teach us the same lesson.
You seem a cathedral, celebrant of
the naked spring that shivers for me
among the long black trees

AT NIGHT

The stars, that are small lights—
now that I know them foreign,
uninterfering, like nothing
in my life—I walk by their sparkle
relieved and comforted. Or when
the moon moves slowly up among them
with flat shine then the night
has a novel light in it—curved
curiously in a thin half-circle

HOW HAS THE WAY BEEN FOUND?

How has the way been found?
Among wires
running through smoke
walking through and over
oily, stained waters—?
On the highest airs

THE HERMAPHRODITIC TELEPHONES

Warm rains
wash away winter's
hermaphroditic telephones

whose demonic bells
piercing the torpid
ground

have filled with circular
purple and green
and blue anemones

the radiant nothing
of crystalline
spring.

FULL MOON
[*First Version*]

Blessed moon
noon
of night

that through the dark
bids Love
stay—

curious shapes
awake
to plague me

Is day near
shining girl?
Yes day!

the warm
the radiant
all fulfilling

day.

LAST WORDS OF MY GRANDMOTHER
[First Version]

She stayed over after
the summer people had gone
at her little shack
on the shore, an old woman

impossible to get on with
unless you left her alone
with her things—among them
the young grandson, nineteen

whom she had raised.
He endured her because
he was too lazy to work
too lazy to think and

had a soft spot for her
in his bright heart, also a
moustache, a girl, bed
and board out of the old lady

the sea before him
and a ukulele—The two
had remained on and on
into the cold weather.

Thanksgiving day
after the heavy dinner
at a good neighbor's table
Death touched the old lady

in her head—Home she must
go leaning heavily on the
boy who put her to bed and
gave her what she wanted—

water and Mother Eddy's
Science and Health and

forgot her for other things.
But she began to rave in the night.

In the morning after frying
an egg for her
he combed his whiskers
picked his pimples

and got busy with
a telegram for help—
Gimme something to eat
Gimme something to eat

I'm starving
they're starving me
was all I got out of
the dazed old woman

There were some dirty plates
and a glass of milk
beside her on a small table
near her stinking bed

Wrinkled and nearly blind
she lay and snored
rousing to cry
with anger in her tones—

They're starving me—
You won't move me
I'm all right—I won't go
to the hospital. No, no, no

Give me something to eat!—
Let me take you
to the hospital, I said,
and after you are well

you can do as you please—
She smiled her old smile:

Yes, you do what you please
first then I can do what I please—

Oh, oh, oh, she cried
as the ambulance men lifted her
to their stretcher on the floor—
Is this what you call

making me comfortable?—
Now her mind was clear
Oh you think you're awfully
smart, you young people,

she said to us, but I'll tell
you you don't know
anything—Then we started.
On the way

we passed a long row
of elms, she looked
a long while out of the
ambulance window and said—

What are all those
fuzzy looking things out there?
Trees? Well, I'm
tired of them.

IT IS A LIVING CORAL

a trouble

archaically fettered
to produce

E *Pluribus Unum* an
island

in the sea a Capitol
surmounted

by Armed Liberty—
painting

sculpture straddled by
a dome

eight million pounds
in weight

iron plates constructed
to expand

and contract with
variations

of temperature
the folding

and unfolding of a lily.
And Congress

authorized and the
Commission

was entrusted was
entrusted!

a sculptured group
Mars

in Roman mail placing
a wreath

of laurel on the brow
of Washington

Commerce Minerva
Thomas

Jefferson John Hancock
at

the table Mrs. Motte
presenting

Indian burning arrows
to Generals

Marion and Lee to fire
her mansion

and dislodge the British—
this scaleless

jumble is superb

and accurate in its
expression

of the thing they
would destroy—

Baptism of Poca-
hontas

with a little card
hanging

under it to tell
the persons

in the picture.

It climbs

it runs, it is Geo.
Shoup

of Idaho it wears
a beard

it fetches naked
Indian

women from a river
Trumbull

Varnum Henderson
Frances

Willard's corset is
absurd—

Banks White Columbus
stretched

in bed men felling trees

The Hon. Michael
C. Kerr

onetime Speaker of
the House

of Representatives
Perry

in a rowboat on Lake
Erie

changing ships the
dead

among the wreckage
sickly green

INTERESTS OF 1926

It is spring
and we walk up the filthysweet

worn wooden stairs
to it, close by the miniature
bright poplar leaves
at a grimy window
wading . . . over the boards
of the second floor . . .
in the clear smile of
the boyish husband
all compassion for
her injury . . . and
                    such is the
celebrated May

POEM

Daniel Boone, the father of Kentucky. Col. W. Crawford, the
martyr to Indian revenge. Simon Gerty, the White Savage.
Molly Finney, the beautiful Canadian Captive. Majors Samuel
and John McCullough, patriots and frontiersmen. Lewis Wet-
zel, the Indian killer. Simon Kenton, the intrepid pioneer.
Gen. George R. Clark, that heroic conqueror. Capt. Brady,
the great Indian fighter. Davy Crockett, the hero of the Alamo.
Gen. Sam Houston, the liberator of the Lone Star State. Kit
Carson, the celebrated plainsman and explorer. Gen. Custer,
the hero of Little Big Horn. Buffalo Bill, the tireless rider,
hunter and scout. Wild Bill, the lightning marksman. Cali-
fornia Joe, the scout. Texas Jack, the government scout and
hunter. Captain Jack, the poet scout. Gen. Crook, the con-
queror of the Apaches.

THE GAYEST OF BRIGHT FLOWERS

The gayest of bright flowers
                    (last year)

could not have foretold how she
the old potbellied woman

with hands on hips
would have this ravenhaired boy
digging furiously beside
the green willow, tossing
the yellow soil with his spade
hammering it cutting it down—

Not work, this but a private
assignation with Spring
the voluptuous conception of
a potful of tomatoes

STRUGGLE OF WINGS

Roundclouds occluding patches of the
sky rival steam bluntly towering,
slowspinning billows which rival
the resting snow, which rivals the sun

beaten out upon it, flashing
to a struggle (of wings) which
fills the still air—still
but cold—yet burning . . .

It is the snow risen upon itself, it is
winter pressed breast to breast
with its own whiteness, transparent
yet visible:

Together, with their pigeon's heads whose
stupid eyes deceive no one—
they hold up between them something
which wants to fall to the ground . . .

And there's the river with thin ice upon it
fanning out half over the black
water, the free middlewater racing under its
ripples that move crosswise on the stream

But the wings and bodies of the pigeonlike
creatures keep fluttering, turning together
hiding that which is between them. It seems
to rest not in their claws but upon their breasts—

It is a baby!
Now it is very clear (*) they're keeping the child
(naked in the air) warm and safe between them.
The eyes of the birds are fixed in

a bestial ecstasy. They strive together panting.
It is an antithesis of logic, very
theoretical. To his face the baby claps
the bearded face of Socrates . . .

Ho, ho! he's dropped it. It was a mask.
Now indeed the encounter throws aside all dissim-
ulation. The false birdheads drop back, arms
spring from the wingedges, all the parts

of two women become distinct, the anatomy
familiar and complete to the smallest detail:
A meaning plainly antipoetical . . . and
. . . all there is is won
                    (. . . . .

It is Poesy, born of a man and two women
Exit No. 4, the string from the windowshade
has a noose at the bottom, a noose? or
a ring—bound with a white cord, knotted
around the circumference in a design—
                              And all there is is won

And it is Inness on the meadows and fruit is
yellow ripening in windows every minute
growing brighter in the bulblight by the
cabbages and spuds—
                              And all there is is won

What are black 4 a.m.'s after all but black
4 a.m.'s like anything else: a tree

a fork, a leaf, a pane of glass—?
          And all there is is won

A relic of old decency, a "very personal friend"
          And all there is is won

      (Envoi

Pic, your crows feed at your window sill
asso, try and get near mine . . .
          And all there is is won
      (· · · · · · · ·

                  All
up and down the Rio Grande the sand is sand
on every hand (Grand chorus and finale)
      (· · · · · · · ·

Out of such drab trash as this
by a metamorphosis
bright as wallpaper or crayon
or where the sun casts ray on ray on
flowers in a dish, you shall weave
for Poesy a gaudy sleeve
a scarf, a cap and find him gloves
whiter than the backs of doves
         · · · ·

              Clothe him
richly, those who loathe him
will besmirch him fast enough.
A surcease to sombre stuff—
black's black, black's one thing
but he's not a blackbird. Bring
something else for him to wear.
See! he's young he has black hair!
Very well then, a red vest . . .

TREE

The tree is stiff, the branch
is arching, arching, arching
to the ground. Already its tip
reaches the hats of the passersby
children leap at it, hang on it—
bite on it. It is rotten, it
will be thick with blossoms in
the spring. Then it will break off
of its own weight or from the pulls
of the blossom seekers who will
ravish it. Freed of this disgrace
the tree will remain, stiffly upright

PATERSON

Before the grass is out the people are out
and bare twigs still whip the wind—
when there is nothing, in the pause between
snow and grass in the parks and at the street ends
—Say it, no ideas but in things—
nothing but the blank faces of the houses
and cylindrical trees
bent, forked by preconception and accident
split, furrowed, creased, mottled, stained
secret—into the body of the light—

These are the ideas, savage and tender
somewhat of the music, et cetera
of Paterson, that great philosopher—

From above, higher than the spires, higher
even than the office towers, from oozy fields
abandoned to grey beds of dead grass
black sumac, withered weed stalks
mud and thickets cluttered with dead leaves—
the river comes pouring in above the city

and crashes from the edge of the gorge
in a recoil of spray and rainbow mists—
—Say it, no ideas but in things—
and factories crystallized from its force,
like ice from spray upon the chimney rocks

.   .   .   .   .

Say it! No ideas but in things. Mr.
Paterson has gone away
to rest and write. Inside the bus one sees
his thoughts sitting and standing. His thoughts
alight and scatter—

Who are these people (how complex
this mathematic) among whom I see myself
in the regularly ordered plateglass of
his thoughts, glimmering before shoes and bicycles—?
They walk incommunicado, the
equation is beyond solution, yet
its sense is clear—that they may live
his thought is listed in the Telephone
Directory—

            and there's young Alex Shorn
whose dad the boot-black bought a house
and painted it inside
with seascapes of a pale green monochrome—
the infant Dionysus springing from
Apollo's arm—the floors oakgrained in
Balkan fashion—Hermes' nose, the body
of a gourmand, the lips of Cupid, the eyes
the black eyes of Venus' sister—

But who! who are these people? It is
his flesh making the traffic, cranking the car
buying the meat—
Defeated in achieving the solution they
fall back among cheap pictures, furniture
filled silk, cardboard shoes, bad dentistry

windows that will not open, poisonous gin
scurvy, toothache—

. . . . .

But never, in despair and anxiety
forget to drive wit in, in till it
discover that his thoughts are decorous and simple
and never forget that though his thoughts are decorous
and simple, the despair and anxiety

the grace and detail of
a dynamo—

Divine thought! Jacob fell backwards off the press
and broke his spine. What pathos, what mercy
of nurses (who keep birthday books)
and doctors who can't speak proper english—
is here correctly on a spotless bed
painless to the Nth power—the two legs
perfect without movement or sensation

Twice a month Paterson receives letters
from the Pope, his works are translated
into French, the clerks in the post office
ungum the rare stamps from his packages
and steal them for their children's albums

So in his high decorum he is wise

. . . . .

What wind and sun of children stamping the snow
stamping the snow and screaming drunkenly
The actual, florid detail of cheap carpet
amazingly upon the floor and paid for
as no portrait ever was—Canary singing
and geraniums in tin cans spreading their leaves
reflecting red upon the frost—
They are the divisions and imbalances

of his whole concept, made small by pity
and desire, they are—no ideas beside the facts—

MARCH IS A LIGHT

upon the dead grass
and houses, the wind
retains its edge, let it—
A light has cut it off
it blows bewilderedly
The grass shakes, the houses
seem, by the lack of foliage
about them, to turn
their angles forward into
the wind to let it pass—

YOUNG SYCAMORE

I must tell you
this young tree
whose round and firm trunk
between the wet

pavement and the gutter
(where water
is trickling) rises
bodily

into the air with
one undulant
thrust half its height—
and then

dividing and waning
sending out
young branches on
all sides—

hung with cocoons—
it thins
till nothing is left of it
but two

eccentric knotted
twigs
bending forward
hornlike at the top

LINES ON RECEIVING THE DIAL'S AWARD: 1927

In the common mind a corked bottle,
that Senate's egg, today the prohibition
we all feel has been a little lifted

The sick carpenter fished up another bottle,
empty, from his cellar
for me last week, an old ginflask—

What a beauty! a fat quartflask of
greenish glass, *The Father of His Country*
embossed upon one side of it
in glass letters capping the green profile
and on the other
A Little More Grape Captain Bragg

A noteworthy antithesis, that, to petty
thievery on a large scale: generous
out of the sand, good to hold and to see—

It approaches poetry and my delight
at having been even for a moment shored
against a degradation
ticked off daily round me like the newspapers

An old, empty bottle in my hand
I go through the motions of drinking,
drinking to *The Dial* and its courtesy

THE DEAD BABY

Sweep the house
    under the feet of the curious
    holiday seekers—
sweep under the table and the bed
    the baby is dead—

The mother's eyes where she sits
    by the window, unconscled—
have purple bags under them
    the father—
tall, wellspoken, pitiful
    is the abler of these two—

Sweep the house clean
    here is one who has gone up
    (though problematically)
to heaven, blindly
    by force of the facts—
a clean sweep
    is one way of expressing it—

Hurry up! any minute
    they will be bringing it
    from the hospital—
a white model of our lives
    a curiosity—
surrounded by fresh flowers

ALL THE FANCY THINGS

music and painting and all that
That's all they thought of
in Puerto Rico in the old Spanish
days when she was a girl

So that now
she doesn't know what to do

with herself alone
and growing old up here—

Green is green
but the tag ends
of older things, *ma chère*

must withstand rebuffs
from that which returns
to the beginnings—

Or what? a
clean air, high up, unoffended
by gross odors

BRILLIANT SAD SUN

L EE'S
 UNCH

Spaghetti   Oysters
a Specialty   Clams

and raw Winter's done
to a turn—Restaurant: Spring!
Ah, Madam, what good are your thoughts

romantic but true
beside this gaiety of the sun
and that huge appetite?

Look!
from a glass pitcher she serves
clear water to the white chickens.

What are your memories
beside that purity?
The empty pitcher dangling

from her grip
her coarse voice croaks
Bon jor'

And Patti, on her first concert tour
sang at your house in Mayaguez
and your brother was there

What beauty
beside your sadness—and
what sorrow

IMPROMPTU: THE SUCKERS

Take it out in vile whiskey, take it out
in lifting your skirts to show your silken
crotches; it is this that is intended.
You are it. Your pleas will always be denied.
You too will always go up with the two guys,
scapegoats to save the Republic and
especially the State of Massachusetts. The
Governor says so and you ain't supposed
to ask for details—

Your case has been reviewed by high-minded
and unprejudiced observers (like hell
they were!) the president of a great
university, the president of a noteworthy
technical school and a judge too old to sit
on the bench, men already rewarded for
their services to pedagogy and the enforcement
of arbitrary statutes. In other words
pimps to tradition—

Why in hell didn't they choose some other
kind of "unprejudiced adviser" for their
death council? instead of sticking to that

autocratic strain of Boston backwash, except
that the council was far from unprejudiced
but the product of a rejected, discredited
class long since outgrown except for use in
courts and school, and that they
wanted it so—

Why didn't they choose at least one decent
Jew or some fair-minded Negro or anybody
but such a triumvirate of inversion, the
New England aristocracy, bent on working off
a grudge against you, Americans, you
are the suckers, you are the ones who will
be going up on the eleventh to get the current
shot into you, for the glory of the state
and the perpetuation of abstract justice—

And all this in the face of the facts: that
the man who swore, and deceived the jury
willfully by so doing, that the bullets found
in the bodies of the deceased could be
identified as having been fired from the pistol
of one of the accused—later
acknowledged that he could not so identify
them; that the jurors now seven years after
the crime do not remember the details and
have wanted to forget them; that the
prosecution has never succeeded in
apprehending the accomplices nor in connecting
the prisoners with any of the loot stolen—

The case is perfect against you, all the
documents say so—in spite of the fact that
it is reasonably certain that you were not
at the scene of the crime, shown, quite as
convincingly as the accusing facts in the
court evidence, by better reasoning to have
been committed by someone else with whom
the loot can be connected and among whom the
accomplices can be found—

It's no use, you are Americans, just the dregs.
It's all you deserve. You've got the cash,
what the hell do you care? You've got
nothing to lose. You are inheritors of a great
tradition. My country right or wrong!
You do what you're told to do. You don't
answer back the way Tommy Jeff did or Ben
Frank or Georgie Washing. I'll say you
don't. You're civilized. You let your
betters tell you where you get off. Go
ahead—

But after all, the thing that swung heaviest
against you was that you were scared when
they copped you. Explain that you
nature's nobleman! For you know that every
American is innocent and at peace in his
own heart. He hasn't a damned thing to be
afraid of. He knows the government is for
him. Why, when a cop steps up and grabs
you at night you just laugh and think it's
a hell of a good joke—

This is what was intended from the first.
So take it out in your rotten whiskey and
silk underwear. That's what *you* get out of
it. But put it down in your memory that this
is the kind of stuff that they can't get away
with. It is there and it's loaded. No one
can understand what makes the present age
what it is. They are mystified by certain
insistences.

From: A Folded Skyscraper

1

HEMMED-IN MALES

The saloon is gone up the creek
with the black sand round its
mouth, it went floating like

a backhouse on the Mississippi in
flood time but it went up
the creek into Limbo from whence

only empty bottles ever return
and that's where George is
He's gone upstream to ask 'em

to let him in at the hole
in the wall where the W.C.T.U.
sits knitting elastic stockings

for varicose veins. Poor George
he's got a job now as janitor
in Lincoln School but the saloon

is gone forever with pictures
of Sullivan and Kilrain on
the walls and Pop Anson holding

a bat. Poor George, they've cut
out his pituitary gland and his
vas deferens is in the spittoon—

You can laugh at him without his
organs but that's the way with
a river when it wants to

drown you, it sucks you in and
you feel the old saloon sinking
under you and you say good-by

just as George did, good-by poetry
the black sand's got me, the old
days are over, there's no place

any more for me to go now
except home—

2

When I think how my grandmother flirted with me I often wonder
why I have not been attracted by women of her type. SHE was a devil
if there ever was one. When she'd move into a neighborhood she'd go
out and clean it up, tonguewise. She'd lay 'em out, male and female—
and then sit back in peace to her mysterious memories and awkward as-
pirations toward heaven and the hold she'd have still on the world and
its accessories. She buried the keg of elderberry wine under the side of
the house, and the stuff she'd eat, not to waste it, would make you
shudder. This was especially after she'd gone nearly blind and had
taken up Christian Science so that you couldn't trust her. Boy, them
was the days. And the rags she'd use to wipe the dishes on when she'd
have the family up to a meal in her shack on the shore over the Fourth.
Baby, I can still see Pop wiping his knife on the edge of the tablecloth—
or something, before he'd use it. But talk was her best weapon, she could
lay you an argument like a steel fence and you might try to get through
it for a day or a week or till doomsday and there she'd be still back of it
laughing at you. The only fault she confessed to was a lack of self-
assertion. She was right too. She liked no society, no gadding—except
on some wild pretext, such as a fascination with the bicycle at sixty. She
fell flat with the handle in one eye, but she did it, bloomers and all. Yet
she— The city stifled her, she could not wait for the spring. School or no
school (they suffered for it later) out she would yank the two grandkids
and off she'd track it for the shore, April to snowfall there she'd make
her stand. Nobody could budge her, not even old man Nolan who had
his wife eating out of his hand, big and burly as she was. He never got

the best of Emily. That was it, she had it. She wanted to be out, away, alone, in the air, by the sea, breathing it in. She'd lie in the water's edge every summer's day till she was eighty. Sometimes she'd be so weak, all alone there, she couldn't get up with her wet rags dragging on her. She'd turn blue with the effort to lift herself on her hands and knees, laughing self consciously the while but doing it, doing it— She'd envy the birds the cherries they'd eat, or she'd sit and watch them playing and go get crumbs to throw them, or half scrape a fish the boys would be too lazy to clean, disgusted with its smallness— Lord what a bed she'd sleep in! It would carry you away with what it had in it. When she'd come to kiss you, you'd want to but you'd go easy and there'd be a good smell out of her scalp and up her neck— She liked me, I'd stand up and fight her by the day trying to get her to have clean dish rags or whatever it would be—some moral issue. All she wanted was to be alone and to have her quiet way. She had it. And love. She wanted that, hot foot into the grave, you couldn't get her without it. Took my father up to the cemetery the night before he married and made him promise her things over the grave of his dead sister. God pardon her for it.

3

THE WINDS

flowing edge to edge
their clear edges meeting—
the winds of this northern March—
blow the bark from the trees
the soil from the field
the hair from the heads of
girls, the shirts from the backs
of the men, roofs from the
houses, the cross from the
church, clouds from the sky
the fur from the faces of
wild animals, crusts
from scabby eyes, scales from
the mind and husbands from wives

4

In my uncivilized, amputated country thinking (I exist in a matrix of confusion) tobacco fed, looking for the number on a house down by Guinea Hill, thinking of Horace's (Quintus Horatius Flaccus) dictum: No wine, no poetry; undrunk no poetry—drunk in the caboose of my coupe, looking out dizzy from the smoke—thinking of poetry—just before the lights came out on the wires and pulleys and the poles, like cactus flowers (in a desert) as I often have the habit of thinking—thinking of Ezra Pound, our greatest and rightest poet, how excellent he is in his self-deception—opposed with a laugh to my fervent, my fierce, anger to have a country—speaking of his work, deriding me, saying that in the end his artificial pearl will be longer to last than anything I have made with all my striving—writing the greatest American poems today, his pearl-like cantos, so purely American—his self-deception, thinking how right he is in his self-deception that he had found poetry in the *quattro cento* in Dante, in them all of those old countries—when as a fact he had found poetry—how right he is a United States poet—when he thinks he has found poetry in the Renaissance, in his self-deception—for he HAS found poetry, an artificial pearly *Pound*, exile,—he has welded his material, he has what he has discovered, he has taken what there at least is—driven from my country that I strive so wildly to possess, he has taken the false, the make shift—the thing that they here—made him take—not the thing I want, but the thing I want.—It is poetry, it is United States poetry—but he is deceived in thinking the medieval is the poetry, *he* is the making of the poetry, it is artificial pearly poetry because it is driven from being MY poetry—still I am right and still he is righter than I and still what I see exists and still he is right in doing poetry out of what is left—and still he is self-deceived—thinking of these things. And while I was thinking all this I seen this gink come running down the hill, on the concrete like a Marathon runner at the first mile, arunning by the front of my coupe without looking right nor left, in his cap, and went in at the horse entry of a lot with a kind of fence in front of it where there was a scrubby stick of a young wild cherry tree all growin' in among the boards—holdin' it up growin' from a pit a bird had—there when the fence was first built—and kept on running down the kind of a dirt road down the middle of the lot where there was only one half the gate made of slats about as high as a man and a couple of trees back in it, a sort of store-lot for a contractor, it looked like, with a lot of things laying around, half rusty on the white grass there was there and a lot of dried weeds sticking in the bottom of the fence, and there was a heap of cobble stones on one side of the road heaped up with gutter slabs like they used to use before they began to put 'em in of concrete—he ran right down this here road back toward a house way at the back of the lot that had a two-story shed in front of it so's a steam shovel could get under it, and there was a ladder up to the top window, and an old junk of a shovel-truck was out in front of the house with a horse shoe tacked over the step. He kept right on hopping it past the house and beyond it—so I was dizzy with the tobacco smoke inside the coupe and I turned the car around,—well this guy that I'm telling you about had went running down that driveway and me sitting there in my coupe with my cigar in one hand half dizzy with the smoke not knowing which way I was going looking for the number and getting ready to turn my bus around there—right on down into this here contractor's lot with a heap of old ashes on one side. Down beyond the two-story shed you could see an old concrete mixer— and right near the slat fence there was a pile of logs about ten feet long and about a foot and a half thick, a lot of junk like that all the way back on both sides the road with a stack of old boards, a post that had been painted red and with a hawser hole in the top stuck in the ground on one side— Well he kept right on running, hopping it along down the ruts under the shed, as I'm telling you, and went on through, past the two trees and everything, a whole row of dumpcarts standing there with the tail boards let down like a two year old's diapers hanging round the knees standing there with the poleshaft stuck in the ground, rusty look-ing, and there was a kind of rusty boiler like, leaning on a pile of junk back there, an awful heap of stuff in that lot and you could see there was a lot more junk back of the house, you could see it by the concrete mixer I was telling you about.

WINTER

Now the snow
lies on the ground
and more snow

is descending upon it—
Patches of red dirt
hold together
the old
snow patches

This is winter—
rosettes of
leather-green leaves
by the old fence
and bare trees
marking the sky—

This is winter
winter, winter
leather-green leaves
spearshaped
in the falling snow

THE MEN

Wherein is Moscow's dignity
more than Passaic's dignity?
A few men have added color better
to the canvas, that's all.

The river is the same
the bridges are the same
there is the same to be discovered
of the sun—

Look how cold, steelgrey
run the waters of the Passaic.
The Church-of-the-Polaks'
bulbous towers

kiss the sky just so sternly
so dreamily

as in Warsaw, as in Moscow—
Violet smoke rises

from the mill chimneys—Only,
the men are different who see it
draw it down in their minds
or might be different

The Atlantic City Convention

A Composition in Two Parts: Poem and Speech

1. THE WAITRESS

No wit (and none needed) but
the silence of her ways, grey eyes in
a depth of black lashes—
The eyes look and the look falls.

There is no way, no way. So close
one may feel the warmth of the cheek and yet there is
no way.

The benefits of poverty are a roughened skin
of the hands, the broken
knuckles, the stained wrists.

Serious. Not as the others.
All the rest are liars, all but you.
Wait on us.
Wait on us, the hair held back practically
by a net, close behind the ears, at the sides of
the head. But the eyes—
but the mouth, lightly (quickly)
touched with rouge.

The black dress makes the hair dark, strangely
enough, and the white dress makes it light.

There is a mole under the jaw, low under
the right ear—

     And what arms!

           The glassruby ring
on the fourth finger of the left hand.

          —and the movements
under the scant dress as the weight of the tray
makes the hips shift forward slightly in lifting
and beginning to walk—

The Nominating Committee presents the following
resolutions, etc. etc. etc. All those
in favor signify by saying, Aye. Contrariminded,
No.
   Carried.
      And aye, and aye, and aye!

And the way the bell-hop runs downstairs:
   ta tuck a
     ta tuck a
       ta tuck a
         ta tuck a
           ta tuck a
and the gulls in the open window screaming over the slow
break of the cold waves—

     O unlit candle with the soft white
plume, Sunbeam Finest Safety Matches all together in
a little box—

     And the reflections of both in
the mirror and the reflection of the hand, writing
writing—
     Speak to me of her!

     —and nobody else and nothing else
in the whole city, not an electric sign of shifting

colors, fourfoot daisies and acanthus fronds going from
red to orange, green to blue—forty feet across—

Wait on us, wait
on us with your momentary beauty to be enjoyed by
none of us. Neither by you, certainly,
                              nor by me.

2. THE CONSERVATION OF THE HUMAN SUB-SPECIES

Ladies and Gentlemen—
    etcetera, etcetera . . . . .
    It is generally believed, I take it, that we have always had and shall
always have for our needs an inexhaustible supply of this essential
material, in fact, that it is as common and available as seawater. But
before I enter upon a qualitative consideration of such resources let me
point out that, even quantitively, unless we conserve our wealth it is in
some danger of exhaustion. Let us not forget that as elsewhere through-
out nature the human fertilizing agent is in great measure scattered and
destroyed during the series of acts leading up to impregnation and that
therefore only the part of it can be considered to exist which has final
access to the ripe ovum . . . so hedged about by social and other
impedimenta that the quantity which does finally come into contact
with the mature egg is in many instances rapidly approaching the van-
ishing point.
    It is quite conceivable, my friends, unless we arm ourselves against
such an eventuality, that within a measurable span of years the sperm
on which we thus naïvely rely for our continuance may so diminish as
in the end completely to disappear from the earth. Or let me put it this
way. Suppose for some perverse reason our germinal supply while it
continues latent should become unavailable, as foreshadowed by the
increasing number of individuals of all classes and for a great variety
of reasons, who, from the psychologically lamed boy to the excessively
specialized commercial male machine or burntout athlete, are today
impotent. We must realize that a racial group may drop out—or has
dropped out—just due to a lack of the requisite male sperm in sufficient
bulk to keep abreast of the quantitative requirements. This is the stuff
on which the race is founded. It must be thought of seriously. Unless it

is fostered it can be lost and if so—the race ends. It is not within the scope of this discussion to say whether this would be of cosmic benefit or otherwise. My concern here tonight is not with that phase of the subject. The sperm may be lost in total bulk and so a major catastrophe arise, racial groups may vanish, etc., but that must be the preoccupation of a later day than ours. The thing of real present significance is not that such a gross occurrence may eventuate but lies rather among the finer subdivisions of the data under consideration. It is that, qualitatively certain vastly important strains of men may die out due to lack of the penetration of their highly specialized reproductive material into adequate receptors.

It is stupid in the last degree for us to speak with the reverence we do of certain categories of the dead and then turn about and persecute the living representatives of that class until in one way or another we drive them out of existence. There are special classes of men just as there are special types of the physical brain. And these types or classes require certain specialized living conditions for their prosperity, access to certain special forms of nourishment and stimulation, leave for certain unusual periods of incubation—or hibernation and, mark the point, certain facilities for breeding which will be favorable to them and special to their kind if what we admire is to be continued for human enjoyment and benefit.

Too strongly adverse social conditions in the gross are antagonistic to the development of the finer characteristics. Vigor can make a virtue of adversity but not without end. Unless at some stage of the game there be specially conceived tolerances, honors, advantages incorporated into the social-moral code for the favoring of the higher human types, these must die out in the environment—as would be the case with dogs, horses or whatever other living thing—and lower types prevail and usurp the field. I am not making a plea against "race suicide," I say just that unless we take precautions certain tremendous types will continue to disappear and the whole fabric of the race be reduced by that much (Washington had no children)—whereas were the sperm of perhaps some one man, or some group of men, well used the whole racial fabric would be lifted and inestimable benefits to the whole mass be engendered.

This is inescapable from the viewpoint of the Mendelian law. It is sound heredity, sound biology; furthermore it is sound psychology. It is an unrecognized fact that men and women have a sure instinct in these things. When in highly specialized types the normal mental status becomes drawn too fine—as it must frequently happen under a stress of heavy work—and we approach a point of impending disintegration but before the breakup occurs (in genius perhaps, but a breakup for all that and this applies to women as well as to men) there is always, I think, a violent desire on the part of the individual to go back to some racial contact. There is a desire on the part of a highly organized man to breed with peasant girls and for women of the same fiber to lust for the purely physical male. This is sound logic and of great psychic importance. The subject does not want to be socially responsible for the results of the encounter perhaps but there is no biologic need that he should be commensurate with the benefits gained.

And from the other side, it is well known that men of power and genius, even when quite old, have little difficulty in attracting women, who are moved also by an instinct which if permitted a certain acceleration would cause them to attach themselves, even to the point of maternity, to such men. Excellent mothers they might be to whom for life a distinguished father could be reasonably accountable. It is a potent theme and a sound deduction that the genius of a race does not come generated out of the air but legitimately or otherwise out of the bodies of men of genius. I mean that the actual anatomic brain of genius is in the germ plasm only of certain men and is from them only transmitted to the race and has been so transmitted, tolerantly, to healthy (or otherwise) female bodies. In a place such as England, where some good man is expected to come up from "the people" at all moments, it is only reasonable to believe that the germinal particles responsible for such a phenomenon were planted in "the people" by distinguished sires at some earlier date. It is certainly the plausible explanation for obscurely emergent men of understanding.

But if the completion of a thorough biologic sexual experience be denied men and women of eminence at the selective moment and unless a means for such legitimate or a tolerance for a similar illegitimate consummation be found, the full development of these individuals and their continuance as a type will be frustrated. Their work, rather, in a practical sense, will be affected, attenuated; to a great extent weakened. It will be as it is, let us say, with American painting as contrasted with the French where a better conception of the full male instinct is plainly shown upon the canvas.

A democracy of understanding has certain prerogatives which it will exercise: accessibility of sentiment, an appreciation for the material thrown up by the breakdown of discipline in the lower classes; but it has this glaring defect, that it cannot discover a satisfactory selective mechanism by which to discriminate in favor of the higher biologic types. Unless it find a way to learn from its lesser freedoms to gain a tolerance by which to liberate its more specialized members for a full fertilization of the mass the vulgus will grow more lacking in the seeds of these types as time passes, or the types themselves will depreciate in effectiveness.

In summary let me say: Men desire vigorous girls for their occasional consorts and do not include in this a wish to be socially bound to them. Girls desire distinguished men as sires for their children and do not (necessarily) expect to hold them in leash except as economic requisites make it important. The young of both sexes entering upon these experiences do so by bringing into play an extensive mesh of uninsulated impulses of the greatest fragility. One of their own kind cannot hope to loosen this fine fabric or to take it into account. It is simply smashed in the impact. But a girl (boy) finding a man (woman) of proper understanding and who has been trained to recognize just this frailty— I do not speak of dotards—would receive, and does receive, at his (her) hands such a satisfaction, such a combing of the nerves as she (he) could never hope to achieve through any other type of contact during her (his) lifetime otherwise.

I have touched upon some of the degenerative processes the race must suffer from its present-day maladjustments to instincts governing a proper use of the male sperm. The race has been formerly wiser. We are today living upon the fruits of past planting but we are draining the mass of these fruits while we are doing nothing of adequate wisdom to replace their seeds. The future will suffer from this lack of foresight which must be attributable to our present imperfect standards of social theory. There are other phases to the subject as there are other solutions to the difficulties than I have presented. The race has generated what it needs by obscure means when it has failed by others. Nevertheless, if there is not a proper basic understanding, in all possible clarity, of the normal sexual impulses, it is stupidity itself when they are blocked to refine the study of the effects. If the cause of the disability and its prevention lies in a proper understanding of and tolerance for the desire itself and only dissections of the pathology are attempted, then simple statement becomes subtle and analytic subtlety grows nearly asinine. The male sperm has been so encumbered by custom and the social conse-

quences of paternity that any contemplation of its cycle has of late be-
come almost pure morbidity and any attempt to raise the discussion to
a physiological level must seem itself perverse.

I thank you.

ON GAY WALLPAPER

The green-blue ground
is ruled with silver lines
to say the sun is shining

And on this moral sea
of grass or dreams lie flowers
or baskets of desires

Heaven knows what they are
between cerulean shapes
laid regularly round

Mat roses and tridentate
leaves of gold
threes, threes and threes

Three roses and three stems
the basket floating
standing in the horns of blue

Repeated to the ceiling
to the windows
where the day

Blows in
the scalloped curtains to
the sound of rain

THE LILY

The branching head of
tiger-lilies through the window
in the air—

A humming bird
is still on whirring wings
above the flowers—

By spotted petals curling back
and tongues that hang
the air is seen—

It's raining—
water's caught
among the curled-back petals

Caught and held
and there's a fly—
are blossoming

THE SOURCE

I

The slope of the heavy woods
pales and disappears
in the wall of mist that hides

the edge above whose peak
last night the moon—

But it is morning and a new light
marks other things
a pasture which begins

where silhouettes of scrub
and balsams stand uncertainly

On whose green three maples
are distinctly pressed
beside a red barn

with new shingles in the old
all cancelled by

A triple elm's inverted
lichen mottled
triple thighs from which

wisps of twigs
droop with sharp leaves

Which shake in the crotch
brushing the stained bark
fitfully

II

Beyond which lies
the profound detail of the woods
restless, distressed

soft underfoot
the low ferns

Mounting a rusty root
the pungent mold
globular fungi

water in an old
hoof print

Cow dung and in
the uneven aisles of
the trees

rock strewn a stone
half-green

A spring in whose depth
white sand bubbles
overflows

clear under late raspberries
and delicate-stemmed touch-me-nots

Where alders follow it marking
the low ground
the water is cast upon

a stair of uneven stones
with a rustling sound

An edge of bubbles stirs
swiftness is molded
speed grows

the profuse body advances
over the stones unchanged

THE DESCENT
OF WINTER

1928

No. 4   Autumn, 1928

THE
EXILE

EDITED BY EZRA POUND

4

In this Number

WILLIAM CARLOS WILLIAMS
ROBERT McALMON
ZUKOFSKY
COURNOS
RAKOSI
FALKOFF-KLIORIN

COVICI FRIEDE, *Publishers*
NEW YORK

9/27

*"What are these elations I have
at my own underwear?*

*I touch it and it is strange
upon a strange thigh."*

* * *

9/29

My bed is narrow
in a small room
at sea

The numbers are on
the wall
Arabic 1

Berth No. 2
was empty above me
the steward

took it apart
and removed
it

only the number
remains
· 2 ·

on an oval disc
of celluloid
tacked

to the white-enameled
woodwork
with

two bright nails
like stars
beside

the moon

9/30

There are no perfect waves—
Your writings are a sea
full of misspellings and
faulty sentences. Level. Troubled.

A center distant from the land
touched by the wings
of nearly silent birds
that never seem to rest—

This is the sadness of the sea—
waves like words, all broken—
a sameness of lifting and falling mood.

I lean watching the detail
of brittle crest, the delicate
imperfect foam, yellow weed
one piece like another—

There is no hope—if not a coral
island slowly forming
to wait for birds to drop
the seeds will make it habitable

10/9

and there's a little blackboy
in a doorway
scratching his wrists

The cap on his head
is red and blue
with a broad peak to it

and his mouth
is open, his tongue
between his teeth—

10/10

Monday
            the canna flaunts
its crimson head

crimson lying folded
crisply down upon

                              the invisible

darkly crimson heart
of this poor yard

the grass is long

                              October tenth
      1927

10/13   a beard . . . not of stone but particular hairs purpleblack . . .
lies upon his stale breast

10/21

In the dead weeds a rubbish heap
aflame: the orange flames
stream horizontal, windblown
they parallel the ground
waving up and down
the flamepoints alternating
the body streaked with loops

and purple stains while
the pale smoke, above
steadily continues eastward—

What chance have the old?
There are no duties for them
no places where they may sit
their knowledge is laughed at
they cannot see, they cannot hear.
A small bundle on the shoulders
weighs them down
one hand is put back under it
to hold it steady.
Their feet hurt, they are weak
they should not have to suffer
as younger people must and do
there should be a truce for them

10/22

that brilliant field
of rainwet orange
blanketed

by the red grass
and oilgreen bayberry

the last yarrow
on the gutter
white by the sandy
rainwater

and a white birch
with yellow leaves
and few
and loosely hung

and a young dog
jumped out
of the old barrel

10/23   I will make a big, serious portrait of my time. The brown and creamwhite block of Mexican onyx has a poorly executed replica of the Aztec calendar on one of its dicefacets the central circle being a broad-nosed face with projected hanging tongue the sun perhaps though why the tongue is out I do not know unless to taste or gasp in the heat, its own heat, to say it's hot and is the sun. Puebla, Mexico, Calendario Azteca, four words are roughly engraved in the four corners where the circle leaves spaces on the square diceface this is America some years after the original, the art of writing is to do work so excellent that by its excellence it repels all idiots but idiots are like leaves and excellence of any sort is a tree when the leaves fall the tree is naked and the wind thrashes it till it howls it cannot get a book published it can only get poems into certain magazines that are suppressed because because waving waving waving waving waving waving tic tack tic tock tadick there is not excellence without the vibrant rhythm of a poem and poems are small and tied and gasping, they eat gasoline, they all ate gasoline and died, they died of—there is a hole in the wood and all I say brings to mind the rock shingles of Cherbourg, on the new houses they have put cheap tile which overlaps but the old roofs had flat stone sides steep but of stones fitted together and that is love there is no portrait without that has not turned to prose love is my hero who does not live, a man, but speaks of it every day

1. continued (the great law)

What is he saying? That love was never made for man and woman to crack between them and so he loves and loves his sons and loves as he pleases. But there is a great law over him which—is as it is. The wind blowing, the mud spots on the polished surface, the face reflected in the glass which as you advance the features disappear leaving only the hat and as you draw back the features return, the tip of the nose, the projection over the eyebrows, the cheek bones and the bulge of the lips the chin last.

2

I remember, she said, we had little silver plaques with a chain on it to hang over the necks of the bottles, whiskey, brandy or whatever it was. And a box of some kind of wood, not for the kitchen but a pretty box. Inside it was lined with something like yes, pewter, all inside and there was a cover of metal too with a little knob on it, all inside the wooden box. You would open the outer cover and inside was the lid. When you would take that off you would see the tea with a silver spoon for taking it out. But now, here are the roses—three opening. Out of love. For she loves them and so they are there. They are not a picture. Holbein never saw pink thorns in such a light. Nor did Masaccio. The petals are delicate, it is a question if they will open at all and not drop, loosing at one edge and falling tomorrow all in a heap. All around the roses there is today, machinery leaning upon the stem, an aeroplane is upon one leaf where a worm lies curled. Soppy it seems and enormous, it seems to hold up the sky for it has no size at all. We eat beside it—beside the three roses that she loves. And an oak tree grows out of my shoulders. Its roots are my arms and my legs. The air is a field. Yellow and red grass are writing their signature everywhere.

10/27   And Coolidge said let there be imitation brass filigree fire fenders behind insured plateglass windows and yellow pine booths with the molasses-candygrain in the wood instead of the oldtime cake-like whitepine boards always cut thick their faces! the white porcelain trough is no doubt made of some certain blanched clay baked and glazed but how they do it, how they shape it soft and have it hold its shape for the oven I don't know nor how the cloth is woven, the grey and the black with the orange and green strips wound together diagonally across the grain artificial pneumothorax their faces! the stripe of shadow along the pavement edge, the brownstone steeple low among the office buildings dark windows with a white wooden cross upon them, lights like fuchsias, lights like bleeding hearts lights like columbines, cherry-red danger and applegreen safety. Any hat in this window $2.00 barred windows, wavy opaque glass, a block of brownstone at the edge of the sidewalk crudely stippled on top for a footstep to a carriage, lights with sharp bright spikes, stick out round them their faces! STOP in black letters surrounded by a red glow, letters with each bulb a seed in the shaft of the L of the A lights on the river streaking the restless water lights upon pools of rainwater by the roadside a great pool of light full of overhanging sparks into whose lower edge a house looms its center marked by one yellow window-bright their faces!

10/28   born, September 15, 1927, 2nd child, wt. 6 lbs. 2 ozs. The hero is Dolores Marie Pischak, the place Fairfield, in my own state, my own county, its largest city, my own time. This is her portrait: O future worlds, this is her portrait—order be God damned. Fairfield is the place where the October marigolds go over into the empty lot with dead grass like Polish children's hair and the nauseous, the stupefying monotony of decency is dead, unkindled even by art or anything—dead: by God because Fairfield is alive, coming strong. Oh blessed love you are here in this golden air, this honey and dew sunshine, ambering the houses to jewels. Order—is dead. Here a goose flaps his wings by a fence, a white goose, women talk from second-story windows to a neighbor on the ground, the tops of the straggling backyard poplars have been left with a tail of twigs and on the bare trunk a pulley with a line in it is tied. A cop whizzes by on his sidecar cycle, the bank to the river is cinders where dry leaves drift. The cinders are eating forward over the green grass below, closer and closer to the river bank, children are in the gutters violently at play over a dam of mud, old women with seamed faces lean on the crooked front gates. Where is Pischak's place? I don't know. I tink it's up there at the corner. What you want?—

Here one drinks good beer. Don't tell my husband. I stopped there yesterday, really good. I was practically alone, yes.

Some streets paved, some dirt down the center. A Jew has a clothing store and looks at you wondering what he can sell. And you feel he has these people sized up. A nasty feeling. Unattached. When he gets his he'll burn it up and clear out in a day. And they do not suspect how nicely he has measured them. They need stuff. He sells it. Who's that guy I wonder. Never seen him around here before. Looks like a doctor.

That's the feeling of Fairfield. An old farm house in long tangled trees, leaning over it. A dell with a pretty stream in it below the little garden and fifty feet beyond, the board fence of the Ajax Aniline Dye Works with red and purple refuse dribbling out ragged and oily under the lower fence boards. No house is like another. Small, wooden, a garden at the back, all ruined by the year. Man leaning smoking from a window. And the dirt, dry dust. No grass, or grass in patches, hedged with sticks and a line of cord or wire or grass, a jewel, a garden embanked, all in a twenty-foot square, crowded with incident, a small terrace of begonias, a sanded path, pinks, roses in a dozen rococo beds.

Knock and walk in: The bar. Not a soul. In the back room the kitchen. Immaculate, the enameled table featured. The mother nursing her from a nearly empty breast. She lies and sucks. Black hair, pencilled down the top flat and silky smooth, the palmsized face asleep, the mother at a point of vantage where under an inside window raised two inches she can govern the street entrance.

Who's that?
A woman. Oh that old woman from next door.

The father, young, energetic, enormous. Unsmiling, big headed, a nervous twitch to his head and a momentary intense squint to his eyes. She watches the door. He is in shirt sleeves. Restless, goes in and out. Talks fast, manages the old woman begging help for a bruised hand. A man who might be a general or president of a corporation, or president of the states. Runs a bootleg saloon. Great!

This is the world. Here one breathes and the dignity of man holds on. "Here I shall live. Why not now? Why do I wait?"

Katharin, 9, sheepish, shy—adoring in response to gentleness so that her eyes almost weep for sentimental gratitude, has jaundice, leans on his knee. Follows him with her eyes. Her hair is straight and blond.

On the main river road, a grey board fence over which a grove of trees stick up. Oaks, maples, poplars and old fruit trees. Belmont Park, Magyar Home. For rent for picnics. Peace is here—rest, assurance, life hangs on.

Oh, blessed love, among insults, brawls, yelling, kicks, brutality— here the old dignity of life holds on—defying the law, defying monotony.

She lies in her mother's arms and sucks. The dream passes over her, dirt streets, a white goose flapping its wings and passes. Boys, wrestling, kicking a half-inflated football. A grey motheaten squirrel pauses at a picket fence where tomato vines, almost spent, hang on stakes.

Oh, blessed love—the dream engulfs her. She opens her eyes on the troubled bosom of the mother who is nursing the babe and watching the door. And watching the eye of the man. Talking English, a stream of Magyar, Polish what? to the tall man coming and going.

Oh, blessed love where are you there, pleasure driven out, order triumphant, one house like another, grass cut to pay lovelessly. Bored we turn to cars to take us to "the country" to "nature" to breathe her good air. Jesus Christ. To nature. It's about time, for most of us. She is holding the baby. Her eye under the window, watching. Her hair is bobbed halfshort. It stands straight down about her ears. You, you sit and have it waved and ordered. Fine. I'm glad of it. And nothing to do but play cards and whisper. Jesus Christ. Whisper of the high-school girl that had a baby and how smart her mama was to pretend in a flash of genius that it was hers. Jesus Christ. Or let us take a run up to the White Mountains or Lake Mohonk. Not Bethlehem (New Hampshire) any more, the Jews have ruined that like lice all over the lawns. Horrible to see. The dirty things. Eating everywhere. Parasites.

And so order, seclusion, the good of it all.

But in Fairfield men are peaceful and do as they please—and learn the necessity and the profit of order—and Dolores Marie Pischak was born.

10/28

On hot days
the sewing machine
whirling

in the next room
in the kitchen

and men at the bar
talking of the strike
and cash

10/28   a flash of juncos in the field of grey locust saplings with a white sun powdery upon them and a large rusty can wedged in the crotch of one of them, for the winter, human fruit, and on the polished straws of the dead grass a scroll of crimson paper—not yet rained on

10/28

in this strong light
the leafless beechtree
shines like a cloud

it seems to glow
of itself
with a soft stript light
of love
over the brittle
grass

But there are
on second look
a few yellow leaves
still shaking

far apart

just one here one there
trembling vividly

10/29

The justice of poverty
   its shame its dirt
are one with the meanness
   of love

its organ in a tarpaulin
   the green birds
the fat sleepy horse
   the old men

the grinder sourfaced
   hat over eyes
the beggar smiling all open
   the lantern out

and the popular tunes—
   sold to the least bidder
for a nickel
   two cents or

          nothing at all or even
           against the desire
          forced on us

10/30

        To freight cars in the air

        all the slow
          clank, clank
          clank, clank
        moving above the treetops

        the
          wha,   wha
        of the hoarse whistle

          pah,   pah,   pah
          pah, pah, pah, pah, pah

          piece and piece
          piece and piece
        moving still trippingly
        through the morningmist

        long after the engine
        has fought by
                 and disappeared

        in silence
             to the left

11/1   Introduction
in almost all verse you read, mine or anybody's else, the figures used and
the general impression of the things spoken of is vague "you could say
it better in prose" especially good prose, say the prose of Hemingway.
The truth of the object is somehow hazed over, dulled. So nobody would
go to see a play in verse if

the salvias, the rusty hydrangeas, the ragged cannas

there's too often no observation in it, in poetry. It is a soft second light
of dreaming. The sagas were not like that they seem to have been made
on the spot. The little Greek I have read—and in translation—is not like
that. Marlowe, Chaucer, el Cid, Shakespeare where he is homely, uncul-
tured, a shrewd guesser is not like that. Where he puts it over about
some woman he knew or a prince or Falstaff. The good poetry is where
the vividness comes up "true" like in prose but better. That's poetry.
Dante was wrestling with Italian, his vividness comes from his escape
from Latin. Don Quixote. I don't know about the Russians or the French.

> and the late, high growing red rose
> it is their time
> of a small garden

poetry should strive for nothing else, this vividness alone, *per se*, for it-
self. The realization of this has its own internal fire that is "like" noth-
ing. Therefore the bastardy of the simile. That thing, the vividness
which is poetry by itself, makes the poem. There is no need to explain
or compare. Make it and it *is* a poem. This is modern, not the saga.
There are no sagas—only trees now, animals, engines: There's that.

11/1   I won't have to powder my nose tonight 'cause Billie's gonna
take me home in his car—

> The moon, the dried weeds
> and the Pleiades—
>
> Seven feet tall
> the dark, dried weedstalks
> make a part of the night
> a red lace
> on the blue milky sky
>
> Write—
> by a small lamp
>
> the Pleiades are almost
> nameless

and the moon is tilted
and halfgone

And in runningpants and
with ecstatic, æsthetic faces
on the illumined
signboard are leaping
over printed hurdles and
"¼ of their energy comes from bread"

two
gigantic highschool boys
ten feet tall

11/2

Dahlias—
　　What a red
　　　and yellow and white
　mirror to the sun, round
　　　　and petaled
　　　is this she holds?
　　　with a red face
　all in black
　　　and grey hair
　　　sticking out
　from under the bonnet brim
Is this Washington Avenue Mr. please
　　　or do I have to
　　　cross the track?

11/2

A MORNING IMAGINATION OF RUSSIA

The earth and the sky were very close
When the sun rose it rose in his heart
It bathed the red cold world of
the dawn so that the chill was his own
The mists were sleep and sleep began
to fade from his eyes, below him in the

garden a few flowers were lying forward
on the intense green grass where
in the opalescent shadows oak leaves
were pressed hard down upon it in patches
by the night rain. There were no cities
between him and his desires
his hatreds and his loves were without walls
without rooms, without elevators
without files, delays of veiled murderers
muffled thieves, the tailings of
tedious, dead pavements, the walls
against desire save only for him who can pay
high, there were no cities—he was
without money—

                Cities had faded richly
into foreign countries, stolen from Russia—
the richness of her cities—

Scattered wealth was close to his heart
he felt it uncertainly beating at
that moment in his wrists, scattered
wealth—but there was not much at hand

Cities are full of light, fine clothes
delicacies for the table, variety,
novelty—fashion: all spent for this.
Never to be like that again:
the frame that was. It tickled his
imagination. But it passed in a rising calm

Tan dar a dei! Tan dar a dei!

He was singing. Two miserable peasants
very lazy and foolish
seemed to have walked out from his own
feet and were walking away with wooden rakes
under the six nearly bare poplars, up the hill

There go my feet.

He stood still in the window forgetting
to shave—

The very old past was refound
redirected. It had wandered into himself
The world was himself, these were
his own eyes that were seeing, his own mind
that was straining to comprehend, his own
hands that would be touching other hands
They were his own!
His own, feeble, uncertain. He would go
out to pick herbs, he graduate of
the old university. He would go out
and ask that old woman, in the little
village by the lake, to show him wild
ginger. He himself would not know the plant.

A horse was stepping up the dirt road
under his window

He decided not to shave. Like those two
that he knew now, as he had never
known them formerly. A city, fashion
had been between—

Nothing between now.

He would go to the soviet unshaven. This
was the day—and listen. Listen. That
was all he did, listen to them, weigh
for them. He was turning into
a pair of scales, the scales in the
zodiac.

    But closer, he was himself
the scales. The local soviet. They could
weigh. If it was not too late. He felt
uncertain many days. But all were uncertain
together and he must weigh for them out
of himself.

He took a small pair of scissors
from the shelf and clipped his nails
carefully. He himself served the fire.

We have cut out the cancer but
who knows? perhaps the patient will die.
The patient is anybody, anything
worthless that I desire, my hands
to have it—instead of the feeling
that there is a piece of glazed paper
between me and the paper—invisible
but tough running through the legal
processes of possession—a city, that
we could possess—

It's in art, it's in
the French school.

What we lacked was
everything. It is the middle of
everything. Not to have.

We have little now but
we have that. We are convalescents. Very
feeble. Our hands shake. We need a
transfusion. No one will give it to us,
they are afraid of infection. I do not
blame them. We have paid heavily. But we
have gotten—touch. The eyes and the ears
down on it. Close.

11/6   Russia is every country, here he must live, this for that, loss
for gain. Dolores Marie Pischak. "New York is a blight on my heart,
lost, a street full of lights fading to a bonfire—in order to see their hats
of wool on their heads, their lips to open and a word to come out. To
open my mouth and a word to come out, my word. Grown like grass, to
be like a stone. I pick it. It is poor. It must be so. There are no rich.
The richness is everywhere, belongs to everyone and it is hard to get.
And loss, loss, loss. Cut off from my kind—if any exist. To get that,

everything is lost. So he carries them and gets—himself and has nothing to do with himself. He also gets their lice.

Romance, decoration, fullness—are lost in touch, sight, a word, to bite an apple. Henry Ford has asked Chas. Sheeler to go to Detroit and photograph everything. Carte blanche. Sheeler! That's rich. Shakespeare had that mean ability to fuse himself with everyone which nobodies have, to be anything at any time, fluid, a nameless fellow whom nobody noticed—much, and *that* is what made him the great dramatist. Because he was nobody and was fluid and accessible. He took the print and reversed the film, as it went in so it came out. Certainly he never repeated himself since he did nothing but repeat what he heard and nobody ever hears the same words twice the same. Homekeeping youth had ever homely wit, Sheeler and Shakespeare should be on this Soviet. Mediæval England, Soviet Russia.

It is a pure literary adjustment. The supremacy of England is purely a matter of style. Officially they are realists, such as the treaty with Italy to divide Abyssinia. Realists—it is the tactical spread of realism that is the Soviets. Imperial Russia was romanticist, strabismic, atavistic. Style. He does not blame the other countries. They fear what he sees. He sees tribes of lawyers tripping each other up entirely off the ground and falling on pillows full of softly jumbled words from goose backs.

I know a good print when I see it. I know when it is good and why it is good. It is the neck of a man, the nose of a woman. It is the same Shakespeare. It is a photograph by Sheeler. It is. It is the thing where it is. So. That's the mine out of which riches have always been drawn. The kings come and beg for it. But it is too simple. In the complexity, when we try to enrich ourselves—the richness is lost. Loss and gain go hand in hand. And hand in hand means my hand in a hand which is in it: a child's hand soft skinned, small, a little fist to hold gently, a woman's hand, a certain woman's hand, a man's hand. Thus hand in hand means several classes of things. But loss is one thing. It is lost. It is one big thing that is an orchestra playing. Time, that's what it buys. But the gain is scattered. It is everywhere but there is not much in any place. A city is merely a relocation of metals in a certain place.—He feels the richness, but a distressing feeling of loss is close upon it. He knows he must coordinate the villages for effectiveness in a flood, a famine.

The United States should be, in effect, a Soviet State. It is a Soviet State decayed away in a misconception of richness. The states, counties, cities, are anemic Soviets. As rabbits are cottontailed the office-workers in cotton running pants get in a hot car, ride in a hot tunnel and confine themselves in a hot office—to sell asphalt, the trade in tanned leather. The trade in everything. Things they've never seen, will never own and can never name. Not even an analogous name do they know. As a carter, knowing the parts of a wagon will know, know, touch, the parts of—a woman. Maybe typists have some special skill. The long legged down east boys make good stage dancers and acrobats. But when most of them are drunk nothing comes off but—"Nevada" had a line of cowboy songs.

11/7

    We must listen. Before
    she died she told them—
    I always liked to be well dressed
    I wanted to look nice—

    So she asked them to dress
    her well. They curled her hair . . .

    Now she fought
    She didn't want to go
    She didn't want to!

The perfect type of the man of action is the suicide.

11/8

    O river of my heart polluted
    and defamed I have compared you
    to that other lying in
    the red November grass
    beginning to be cleaned now
    from factory pollution

    Though at night a watchman
    must still prowl lest some paid hand
    open the waste sluices—

That river will be clean
before ever you will be

11/8   Out of her childhood she remembered, as one might remember Charlie Wordsworth's print shop in the rear of Bagellons, the hinged paperknife, the colored posters of horses (I'll bet it was for the races at Clifton where the High School now stands). Once Pop made a big kite, five feet tall maybe, with the horses' heads in the middle and it flew and I couldn't hold it without help. They fastened it to a post of the back porch at nightfall, real rope they had on it, and in the morning it was still there. She remembered the day the old man painted the mirror back of the bar: He took off his coat and laid the brushes and pans from his bag on one of the barroom tables. No one else was there but Jake who sat with his head in his hands except when someone came in for something or to telephone. Then he'd unlock the inside door and sit down again watching the old man. It was a big mirror. First he painted in a river coming in over from the door and curving down greenywhite nearly the whole length of it and very wide to fall in a falls into the edge of another river that ran all along the bottom all the way across, only a little of the water to be seen. Then he put in a blue sky all across the top with white clouds in it and under them a row of brown hills coming down to the upper river banks. Green trees he made with a big brush, just daubing it on, some of it even up top over the hills on the clouds, the trunks of the trees to be put in later. But down below, under the top river and all down the right side where it curved down to the falls he painted in the trunks first like narrow dark brown bottles. Then he drew in the houses, with white sides, three of them near the falls. "A good place to fish," Jake said. The roofs were red. On the other side of the falls, between the two rivers, the houses were brown, two of them on brown hills with trees all among them. Then, after the paint of the rivers was dry, he began to paint in little boats, above and below— She never saw the work finished, for the saloon had been sold and they moved away. The last thing she saw him do was paint in the boats, "Look out that boat up there don't go over those falls," Jake said. The rivers were painted flat on the glass, wonderful rivers where she wanted to be. Some day she wanted to go to that place and see it. Like the song she remembered in school and she always wanted them to sing when you could ask what song you wanted sung, "Come again soon and you

shall hear sung the tale of those green little islands." She always wanted
to hear the rest of it but there was never any more. They moved away.

11/10

        The shell flowers
        the wax grapes and peaches
        the fancy oak or mahogany tables
        the highbacked baronial hall chairs

        Or the girls' legs
        agile stanchions
        the breasts
        the pinheads—

        —Wore my bathing suit
        wet
        four hours after sundown.
        That's how. Yea?
        Easy to get
        hard to get rid of.

        Then unexpectedly
        a small house with a soaring oak
        leafless above it

        Someone should summarize these things
        in the interest of local
        government or how
        a spotted dog goes up a gutter—

        and in chalk crudely
        upon the railroad bridge support
        a woman rampant
        brandishing two rolling pins

11/11   A cat licking herself solves most of the problems of infection.
We wash too much and finally it kills us.

By writing he escaped from the world into the natural world of his mind. The unemployable world of his fine head was unnaturally useless in the gross exterior of his day—or any day. By writing he made this active. He melted himself into that grossness, and colored it with his powers. The proof that he was right and they passing, being that he continues always and naturally while their artificiality destroyed them. A man unable to employ himself in his world.

Therefore his seriousness and his accuracies, because it was not his play but the drama of his life. It is his anonymity that is baffling to nit-wits and so they want to find an involved explanation—to defeat the plainness of the evidence.

When he speaks of fools he is one; when of kings he is one, doubly so in misfortune.

He is a woman, a pimp, a prince Hal—

Such a man is a prime borrower and standardizer—No inventor. He lives because he sinks back, does not go forward, sinks back into the mass—

He is Hamlet plainer than a theory—and in everything.

You can't buy a life again after it's gone, that's the way I mean.

He drinks awful bad and he beat me up every single month while I was carrying this baby, pretty nearly every week.

(Shakespeare) a man stirred alive, all round *not* minus the intelligence but the intelligence subjugated—by misfortune in this case maybe—subjugated to the instinctive whole as it must be, but not minus it as in almost everything—not by cupidity that blights an island literature—but round, round, a round world *E pur si muove. That* has never sunk into literature as it has into geography, cosmology. Literature is still mediæval, formal, dogmatic, the scholars, the obstinate rationalists—

These things are easy and obvious but it is not easy to formulate them, and it is still harder to put them down briefly. Yet it must be possible since I have done it here and there.

Such must be the future: penetrant and simple—minus the scaffolding of the academic, which is a "lie" in that it is inessential to the purpose as to the design.

This will do away with the stupidity of little children at school, which is the incubus of modern life—and the defense of the economists and modern rationalists of literature. To keep them drilled.

The difficulty of modern styles is made by the fragmentary stupidity of modern life, its lacunæ of sense, loops, perversions of instinct, blankets, amputations, fulsomeness of instruction and multiplications of inanity. To avoid this, accuracy is driven to a hard road. To be plain is to be subverted since every term must be forged new, every word is tricked out of meaning, hanging with as many cheap traps as an altar.

The only human value of anything, writing included, is intense vision of the facts, add to that by saying the truth and action upon them,—clear into the machine of absurdity to a core that is covered.

God—Sure if it means sense. "God" is poetic for the unobtainable. Sense is hard to get but it can be got. Certainly that destroys "God," it destroys everything that interferes with simple clarity of apprehension.

11/16   The art of writing is all but lost (not the science which comes afterward and depends completely on the first) it is to make the stores of the mind available to the pen—Wide! That which locks up the mind is vicious.

Mr. Seraphim: They hate me. Police Protection. She was a flaming type of stupidity and its resourceful manner under Police Protection—the only normal: a type. One of the few places where the truth (demeaned) clings on.

11/13 TRAVELLING IN FAST COMPANY

As the ferry came into the slip there was a pause then a young fellow on a motorcycle shot out of the exit, looked right and left, sighted the hill, opened her up and took the grade at top speed. Right behind him came three others bunched and went roaring by, and behind them was a youngster travelling in fast company his eyes fastened on the others, and behind him an older guy sitting firm and with a face on him like a piece of wood ripped by without a quiver. And that brings it all up—Shakespeare—plays.

. . . Its hands stuck up in the air like prongs. Just sticking up in the air, fingers spread apart.

                                          Goethe was a rotten
dramatist . . .

11/20

        Even idiots grow old
          in a cap with the peak
        over his right ear
          cross-eyed
        shamble-footed
          minding the three goats
        behind the firehouse
          his face is deeper lined
        than last year
          and the rain comes down
        in gusts suddenly

11/22

        and hunters still return
        even through the city
        with their guns slung
        openly from the shoulder
        emptyhanded howbeit
        for the most part
            but aloof

as if from and truly from
another older world

11/24   If genius is profuse, never ending—stuck in the middle of a work is—the wrong track. Genius is the track, seen. Once seen it is impossible to keep from it. The superficial definitions, such as "genius is industry, genius is hard work, etc." are nonsense. It is to see the track, to smell it out, to know it inevitable—sense sticking out all round feeling, feeling, seeing—hearing touching. The rest is pure gravity (the earth pull).

Creations:—they are situations of the soul (Lear, Harpagon, Œdipus Rex, Electra) but so closely (subjectively) identified with life that they become people. They are offshoots of an intensely simple mind. It is no matter what we think, no matter what we are.

The drama is the identification of the character with the man himself (Shakespeare—and his sphere of knowledge, close to him). As it flares in himself the drama is completed and the back kick of it is the other characters, created as the reflex of the first, so the dramatist "lives," himself in his world. A poem is a soliloquy without the "living" in the world. So the dramatist "lives" the character. But to labor over the "construction" over the "technique" is to defeat, to tie up the drama itself. One cannot live after a prearranged pattern, it is all simply dead.

This is the thing (obvious and simple) that except through genius makes the theater a corpse. To intensely realize identity makes it live (borrowing stealing the form by feeling it—as an uninformed man must). A play is this primary realization coming up to intensity and then fading (futilely) in self. This *is* the technique, the unlearnable, it is the *natural* drama, which can't imagine situations in any other way than in association with the flesh—till it becomes living, it is so personal to a nothing, a nobody.

The painfully scrupulous verisimilitude which honesty affects—drill, discipline defeats its own ends in—

To be nothing and unaffected by the results, to unlock, and to flow (They believe that when they have the mold of technique made perfect

without a leak in it that the mind will be *drilled* to flow there whereas
the mind is locked the more tightly the more perfect the technique is
forged) (or it may flow, disencumbered by what it has learned, become
unconscious, provided the technique becomes mechanical, goes out of
the mind and so the mind (now it has been cut for life in this pattern))
can devote itself to that just as if it had learned it imitatively or not
at all.

To be nothing and unaffected by the results, to unlock and flow, un-
colored, smooth, carelessly—not cling to the unsolvable lumps of per-
sonality (yourself and your concessions, poems) concretions—

11/28

        I make really very little money.
        What of it?
        I prefer the grass with the rain on it
        the short grass before my headlights
        when I am turning the car—
        a degenerate trait, no doubt.
        It would ruin England.

12/2   The first snow was a white sand that made the white rocks
seem red.

The police are "the soldiers of the Duke." The great old names:
Gaynor, Healy—

12/9   Imagine a family of four grown men, one in bed with a sore
throat, one with fresh plaster dust on his pants, one who played base-
ball all last summer and one holding the basin, four young men and no
women but the mother with smallpox scars marring the bridge and the
end of her nose and dinner on the table, oil and meat bits and cuts of
green peppers, the range giving out a heat for coats on the backs of the
chairs to dry in.

Fairfield: Peoples Loan and Service, Money to Loan: and a young
man carrying a bowling ball in a khaki canvas case. The Midland and

a fern in the window before the inner oak and cut-glass screen. House
and sign painting in all its branches. Fairfield Bowling and Billiard
Academy. Architect John Gabrone Architect, U.S. Post Office, Fairfield,
N.J. Branch. Commercial Barber Shop. The New Cigarette Three Cas-
tles. Real Estate and Insurance. Motor Vehicle Agency. Commercial
Lunch. Fairfield Home Laundry, soft water washing.

12/15

What an image in the face of Almighty God is she
her hands in her slicker pockets, head bowed,
Tam pulled down, flat-backed, lanky-legged,
loose feet kicking the pebbles as she goes

12/18   Here by the watertank and the stone, mottled granite, big as
a rhinocerous head—cracked on one side—Damn families. My grand-
father was a business man, you know. He kept the ice house in Maya-
guez. They imported the ice. He kept it and sold it. My grandmother,
my mother's mother, would make syrups, strawberry and like that. He
would sell them also. But his half-brother Henriquez, there's plenty of
that in my family, would go there, to the ice house, and drink all day
long without paying anything, until the man my grandfather had there
complained. "You know Henriquez comes and drinks five or six glasses
of syrup and never pays anything." He did that. Just drank, lived at the
house, took anything he pleased. That's how, as my mother says, she
came to know Manuel Henriquez, her half-cousin, better than she did
her own brother who was away much of the time studying. Henriquez
would never work, help or do anything until my grandfather had to tell
him to stop. It was at about this time my grandfather died and this is
how my mother came to distrust and hate the Germans. All my grand-
father's friends were German, all but a few. "It was a man named Krug.
I suppose he may have been father's partner anyhow he was his best
friend, I don't know. When my father died, Krug came to my mother
and asked her if she had anything because my father owed some money.
She had an *hacienda* in the country that she had had since before she
was married, her own. She gave that. Then Krug came and said it was
all gone, that there was nothing left. After that, he turned his back on
the family (The skunk). It was the Spanish druggist Mestre who lent
my mother the money to buy a few things and sell them to make a little

business. He was a Catalan—they can't say Pepe, like a Castilian but he would call his wife, Papeeta. My mother would send to Paris for a half dozen fine shirts, but fine, fine shirts and a few things like that. My brother was in Paris studying. When Krug told my mother she must send for him, that there was nothing left, she wrote. He answered her that he would sweep the streets of Paris rather than leave. She would send him money she made on her little business. Sometimes, he told us afterward, he would keep a sou in his pocket two weeks so as not to say he hadn't any money. The students helped each other. Barclay, an Englishman, was one of his best friends. He helped him."

That's why my own mother's education ended abruptly. Sometimes she would copy out letters for my grandmother, child that she was, to send to Paris. When her brother returned a doctor he himself sent her to Paris to study painting. But he married and he began to have children and he never collected any money—he had a wife too. So finally he sent for my mother to go back to Santo Domingo where they were living then. Mother cried for three days then she had to go and leave it all. When she got there her brother told her about his friend, Blackwell. A fine fellow, the best in the world *"pero no es musicante."* Blackwell was in the States at the time of my mother's return from Paris having his teeth fixed.

When a little child would be bothersome they would tell her to go ask the maid for a little piece of *ten te aya.*

When my brother was happy he would sing, walking up and down kicking out his feet: *Si j'étais roi de Bayaussi-e, tu serais reine-e par ma foi!* You made me think right away of him.

POEMS
1929–1935

QUESTION AND ANSWER

What's wrong with American literature?
You ask me? How much do I get?

SIMPLEX SIGILUM VERI: A CATALOGUE
[First Version]

an american papermatch packet
closed, gilt with a panel insert,
the bank, a narrow building
black, in a blue sky, puffs of

white cloud, the small windows
in perspective, bright green grass
a sixinch metal tray, polished
bronze, holding a blue pencil

hexagonal, a bright gilt metal
butt catching the window light,
the dullred eraser well worn
down and a cheap brownenameled

pen holder rest on the brown
mottled crust of the stained blotter
by an oystershell smudged
with cigarette ash, a primrose plant

in a gold ringed saucer, flowerless,
surfaces of all sorts
bearing printed characters, bottles,
words printed on the backs of

two telephone directories
The Advertising Biographical

Calendar of Medicine, Wednesday 18
Thursday 19, Friday 20, papers

of various shades sticking out
from under others, throwing
the printing out of line: portrait
of all that which we have lost,

a truncated pyramid, bronzed
metal (probably the surface
only) to match the tray, to which
a square, hinged lid is fixed,

the inkstand, from whose
imagined top the Prince of Wales
having climbed up once with all
his might drove a golf ball

THE FLOWER

A petal, colorless and without form
the oblong towers lie

beyond the low hill and northward the great
bridge stanchions,

small in the distance, have appeared,
pinkish and incomplete—

It is the city,
approaching over the river. Nothing

of it is mine, but visibly
for all that it is petal of a flower—my own.

It is a flower through which the wind
combs the whitened grass and a black dog

with yellow legs stands eating from a
garbage barrel. One petal goes eight blocks

past two churches and a brick school beyond
the edge of the park where under trees

leafless now, women having nothing else to do
sit in summer—to the small house

in which I happen to have been born. Or
a heap of dirt, if you care

to say it, frozen and sunstreaked in
the January sun, returning.

Then they hand you—they who wish to God
you'd keep your fingers out of

their business—science or philosophy or
anything else they can find to throw off

to distract you. But Madame Lenine
is a benefactress when under her picture

in the papers she is quoted as saying:
Children should be especially protected

from religion. Another petal
reaches to San Diego, California where

a number of young men, New Yorkers most
of them, are kicking up the dust.

A flower, at its heart (the stamens, pistil,
etc.) is a naked woman, about 38, just

out of bed, worth looking at both for
her body and her mind and what she has seen

and done. She it was put me straight
about the city when I said, It

makes me ill to see them run up
a new bridge like that in a few months

and I can't find time even to get
a book written. They have the power,

that's all, she replied. That's what you all
want. If you can't get it, acknowledge

at least what it is. And they're not
going to give it to you. Quite right.

For years I've been tormented by
that miracle, the buildings all lit up—

unable to say anything much to the point
though it is the major sight

of this region. But foolish to rhapsodize over
strings of lights, the blaze of a power

in which I have not the least part.
Another petal reaches

into the past, to Puerto Rico
when my mother was a child bathing in a small

river and splashing water up on
the yucca leaves to see them roll back pearls.

The snow is hard on the pavements. This
is no more a romance than an allegory.

I plan one thing—that I could press
buttons to do the curing of or caring for

the sick that I do laboriously now by hand
for cash, to have the time

when I am fresh, in the morning, when
my mind is clear and burning—to write.

THE ATTIC WHICH IS DESIRE:

the unused tent
of

bare beams
beyond which

directly wait
the night

and day—
Here

from the street
by

```
*  *  *
*  S  *
*  O  *
*  D  *
*  A  *
*  *  *
```

ringed with
running lights

the darkened
pane

exactly
down the center

is
transfixed

THE MOON—

diving
through bedrooms
makes the car
ride upon the page
by virtue of
the law of sentences
Bulleting
through roofs
behind reedy trees
it is the night
waking to
smells of lechery

BIRDS AND FLOWERS

I

It is summer, winter, any
time—
no time at all—but delight

the springing up
of those secret flowers
the others imitate and so

become round
extraordinary in petalage
yellow, blue

fluted and globed
slendercrimson
moonshaped—

in clusters on a wall.
                    Come!
And just now

you will not come, your
ankles
carry you another way, as

thought grown old—or
older—in
your eyes fires them against

me—small flowers
birds flitting here and there
between twigs

                    II

What have I done
to drive you away? It is
winter, true enough, but

this day I love you.
This day
there is no time at all

more than in under
my ribs where anatomists
say the heart is—

And just today you
will not have me. Well,
tomorrow it may be snowing—

I'll keep after you, your
repulse of me is no more
than a rebuff to the weather—

If we make a desert of
ourselves—we make
a desert . . .

III

Nothing is lost! the white
shellwhite
glassy, linenwhite, crystalwhite
crocuses with orange centers
the purple crocus with
an orange center, the yellow
crocus with a yellow center—

That which was large but
seemed spent of
power to fill the world with
its wave of splendor is
overflowing again into every
corner—

Though the eye
turns inward, the mind
has spread its embrace—in
a wind that
roughs the stiff petals—
More! the particular flower is
blossoming . . .

CHILD AND VEGETABLES

The fire of the seed is in her pose
upon the clipped lawn, alone

before the old white house
framed in by great elms planted there

symmetrically. Exactly in the center
of this gently sloping scene,

behind her table of squash and green
corn in a pile, facing the road

she sits with feet one by the other
straight and closely pressed

and knees held close, her hands
decorously folded in her lap. Precise

and mild before the vegetables,
the mouth poised in an even smile

of invitation—to come and buy,
the eyes alone appear—half wakened.

These are the lines of a flower-bud's
tight petals, thoughtfully

designed, the vegetable offerings
in a rite. Mutely the smooth globes

of the squash, the cornucopias
of the corn, fresh green, so still,

so aptly made, the whole so full
of peace and symmetry . . .

resting contours of eagerness
and unrest—

Della Primavera Trasportata al Morale

APRIL

the beginning—or
what you will:
          the dress

in which the veritable winter
walks in Spring—

Loose it!
Let it fall (where it will)
—again

A live thing
the buds are upon it
the green shoot come between
the red flowerets
                    curled back

Under whose green veil
strain trunk and limbs of
the supporting trees—

Yellow! the arched stick
pinning the fragile foil
—in abundance
                    or
the bush before the rose
pointed with green

bent into form
upon the iron frame

wild onion
swifter than the grass

the grass thick
at the post's base

iris blades unsheathed—

BUY THIS PROPERTY

—the complexion of the impossible
                    (you'll say)

never realized—
At a desk in a hotel in front of a

machine a year
later—for a day or two—

(Quite so—)
Whereas the reality trembles

frankly
in that though it was like this

in part
it was deformed

even when at its utmost to
touch—as it did

and fill and give and take
—a kind

of rough drawing of flowers
and April

STOP : GO

—she
opened the door! nearly
six feet tall, and I . . .
wanted to found a new country—

For the rest, virgin negress
at the glass
in blue-glass Venetian beads—

a green truck
dragging a concrete mixer
passes
in the street—

the clatter and true sound
of verse—

—the wind is howling
the river, shining mud—

Moral
        it looses me

Moral
        it supports me

Moral
        it has never ceased
        to flow

Moral
        the faded evergreen

Moral
        I can laugh

Moral
        the redhead sat
        in bed with her legs
        crossed and talked
        rough stuff

Moral
        the door is open

Moral
        the tree moving diversely
        in all parts—

—the moral is love, bred of
the mind and eyes and hands—

        But in the cross-current

between what the hands reach
and the mind desires

and the eyes see
and see starvation, it is

useless to have it thought
that we are full—

But April is a thing
comes just the same—

and in it we see now
what then we did not know—

STOP : STOP

I believe
        in the sound patriotic and
        progressive Mulish policies
        and if elected—

I believe
        in a continuance of the pro-
        tective tariff because—

I believe
        that the country can't do
        too much—

I believe
        in honest law enforcement—
        and I also believe—

I believe
        in giving the farmer and
        land owner adequate protection

I believe

I believe

I believe
    in equality for the negro—

    THIS IS MY PLATFORM

    I believe in your love
    the first dandelion
    flower at the edge of—

taraaaaaaa!   taraaaaaaa!

—the fishman's bugle announces
the warm wind—

    reminiscent of the sea
    the plumtree flaunts
    its blossom-encrusted
    branches—

I believe
    Moving to three doors
    above—May 1st.

I believe
    ICE—and warehouse site

No parking between tree and corner

You would "kill me with kindness"
I love you too, but I love you
too—

Thus, in that light and in that
light only can I say—

Winter : Spring

abandoned to you. The world lost—
in you

Is not that devastating enough
for one century?

I believe

Spumoni	$1.00
French Vanilla	.70
Chocolate	.70
Strawberry	.70
Maple Walnut	.70
Coffee	.70
Tutti Frutti	.70
Pistachio	.70
Cherry Special	.70
Orange Ice	.70
Biscuit Tortoni	

               25c per portion

trees—seeming dead:
      the long years—

   tactus eruditus

Maple, I see you have
a squirrel in your crotch—

And you have a woodpecker
in your hole, Sycamore

—a fat blonde, in purple (no trucking
on this street)

POISON!

I believe

WOMAN'S WARD

PRIVATE

The soul, my God, shall rise up
—a tree
    But who are You?
in this mortal wind
that I at least can understand
having sinned willingly

The forms
of the emotions are crystalline,
geometric-faceted. So we recognize
only in the white heat of
understanding, when a flame
runs through the gap made
by learning, the shapes of things—
the ovoid sun, the pointed trees

lashing branches

The wind is fierce, lashing

the long-limbed trees whose
branches
wildly toss—

FULL MOON

Blessed moon
noon
of night

that through the dark
bids Love
stay—

curious shapes
awake
to plague me

Is day near
shining girl?
Yes, day!

the warm
the radiant
all fulfilling

day.

THE TREES

The trees—being trees
thrash and scream
guffaw and curse—
wholly abandoned
damning the race of men—

Christ, the bastards
haven't even sense enough
to stay out in the rain—

Wha ha ha ha

Wheeeeee
clacka tacka tacka
tacka tacka
wha ha ha ha ha
ha ha ha

knocking knees, buds
bursting from each pore
even the trunk's self
putting out leafheads—

Loose desire!
we naked cry to you—
"Do what you please."

You cannot!

—ghosts
sapped of strength

wailing at the gate
heartbreak at the bridgehead—
desire
dead in the heart

haw haw haw haw
—and memory broken

wheeeeee

There were never satyrs
never maenads
never eagle-headed gods—
These were men
from whose hands sprung
love
bursting the wood—

Trees their companions
—a cold wind winterlong
in the hollows of our flesh
icy with pleasure—

no part of us untouched

THE WIND INCREASES

The harried
earth is swept
        The trees
the tulip's bright
    tips
        sidle and
toss—

    Loose your love
to flow

Blow!

Good Christ what is
a poet—if any
       exists?

a man
whose words will
    bite
       their way
home—being actual
having the form
      of motion

At each twigtip

new

upon the tortured
body of thought

   gripping

the ground

a way
   to the last leaftip

THE BIRD'S COMPANION

As love
  that is
each day upon the twig
  which may die

  So springs your love
fresh up
  lusty for the sun
the bird's companion—

THE HOUSE

The house is yours
to wander in as you please—
Your breakfasts will be kept
ready for you until

you choose to arise!
This is the front room
where we stood penniless
by the hogshead of crockery.

This is the kitchen—
We have a new
hotwater heater and a new
gas-stove to please you

And the front stairs
have been freshly painted—
white risers
and the treads mahogany.

Come upstairs
to the bedroom—
Your bed awaits you—
the chiffonier waits—

the whole house
is waiting—for you
to walk in it at your pleasure—
It is yours.

THE SEA-ELEPHANT

Trundled from
the strangeness of the sea—
a kind of
heaven—

Ladies and Gentlemen!
the greatest
sea-monster ever exhibited
alive

the gigantic
sea-elephant! O wallow
of flesh where
are

there fish enough for
that
appetite stupidity
cannot lessen?

Sick
of April's smallness
the little
leaves—

Flesh has lief of you
enormous sea—
Speak!
Blouaugh! (feed

me) my
flesh is riven—

fish after fish into his maw
unswallowing

to let them glide down
gulching back
half spittle half
brine

the
troubled eyes—torn
from the sea.
(In

a practical voice) They
ought
to put it back where
it came from.

Gape.
Strange head—
told by old sailors—
rising

bearded
to the surface—and
the only
sense out of them

is that woman's
Yes
it's wonderful but they
ought to

put it
back into the sea where
it came from.
Blouaugh!

Swing—ride
walk

on wires—toss balls
stoop and

contort yourselves—
But I
am love. I am
from the sea—

Blouaugh!
there is no crime save
the too-heavy
body

the sea
held playfully—comes
to the surface
the water

boiling
about the head the cows
scattering
fish dripping from

the bounty
of . . . and Spring
they say
Spring is icummen in—

RAIN

As the rain falls
so does
          your love

bathe every
              open
object of the world—

In houses
the priceless dry
                rooms
of illicit love
where we live
hear the wash of the
                        rain—

There
        paintings
and fine
        metalware
woven stuffs—
all the whorishness
of our
        delight
sees
from its window

the spring wash
of your love
                the falling
rain—

The trees
are become
beasts fresh-risen
from the sea—
water

trickles
from the crevices of
their hides—

So my life is spent
                to keep out love
with which
she rains upon

        the world

of spring

      drips

so spreads

      the words

far apart to let in

         her love

And running in between

the drops

      the rain

is a kind physician

         the rain
of her thoughts over
the ocean
      every

where

      walking with
invisible swift feet
over

      the helpless
         waves—

Unworldly love
that has no hope
      of the world

      and that
cannot change the world
to its delight—

The rain
falls upon the earth
and grass and flowers
come
    perfectly

into form from its
                liquid

clearness

        But love is
unworldly

       and nothing
comes of it but love

following
and falling endlessly
from
    her thoughts

DEATH

He's dead

the dog won't have to
sleep on his potatoes
any more to keep them
from freezing

he's dead
the old bastard—
He's a bastard because

there's nothing
legitimate in him any

more
    he's dead

He's sick-dead

           he's
a godforsaken curio
without
any breath in it

He's nothing at all
    he's dead

Shrunken up to skin

    Put his head on
one chair and his
feet on another and
he'll lie there
like an acrobat—

Love's beaten. He
beat it. That's why
he's insufferable—

    because
he's here needing a
shave and making love
an inside howl
of anguish and defeat—

He's come out of the man
and he's let
the man go—
      the liar

Dead
    his eyes
rolled up out of
the light—a mockery

which
love cannot touch—

just bury it
and hide its face—
for shame.

THE BOTTICELLIAN TREES

The alphabet of
the trees

is fading in the
song of the leaves

the crossing
bars of the thin

letters that spelled
winter

and the cold
have been illumined

with
pointed green

by the rain and sun—
The strict simple

principles of
straight branches

are being modified
by pinched-out

ifs of color, devout
conditions

the smiles of love—

. . . . . .

until the stript
sentences

move as a woman's
limbs under cloth

and praise from secrecy
quick with desire

love's ascendancy
in summer—

In summer the song
sings itself

above the muffled words—

A MARRIAGE RITUAL

Above
the darkness of a river upon
winter's icy sky
dreams the silhouette of the city:

This is my own! a flower,
a fruit, an animal by itself—

It does not recognize me
and never will. Still, it is my own
and my heart goes out to it
dumbly—

but eloquently in
my own breast for you whom I love
—and cannot express what
my love is, how it varies, though
I waste it—

    It is
a river flowing through refuse
the dried sticks of weeds
and falling shell-ice lilac
from above as if with thoughts
of you—

This is my face and its moods
my moods, a riffled whiteness
shaken by the flow
that's constant in its swiftness
as a pool—

    A Polack in
the stinging wind, her arms
wrapped to her breast
comes shambling near. To look
at what? downstream. It is
an old-world flavor: the poor
the unthrifty, passionately biased
by what errors of conviction—

        Now a boy
is rolling a stout metal drum
up from below the river bank.
The woman and the boy, two
thievish figures, struggle with
the object . . . in this light!

        And still
there is one leafless tree
just at the water's edge and—

                my face
constant to you!

THE UNFROCKED PRIEST

1

When a man had gone
up
in Russia from a small
town
to the University
he
returned a hero—
people
bowed down to him—
his
ego, nourished by this,
mount-
ed to notable works.

2

Here
in the streets the kids
say
Hello Pete! to me—
What
can one be or
imagine?
Nothing is reverenced
nothing
looked up to. What
can
come of that sort of
dis-
respect for the under-
standing?

POEM

As the cat
climbed over
the top of

the jamcloset
first the right
forefoot

carefully
then the hind
stepped down

into the pit of
the empty
flowerpot

FLOWERS BY THE SEA
[*First Version*]

Over the flowery, sharp pasture's edge
unseen, the salt ocean lifts its form

flowers and sea
bring, each to each, a change

Chickory and daisies, tied, yet released
seem no longer flowers alone

but color and the movement—or the shapes
of quietness, whereas

the thought of the sea is circled and
sways peacefully upon its plantlike stem

SEA-TROUT AND BUTTERFISH

The contours and the shine
hold the eye—caught and lying

orange-finned and the two
half its size, pout-mouthed

beside it on the white dish—
Silver scales, the weight

quick tails
whipping the streams aslant—

The eye comes down eagerly
unravelled of the sea

separates this from that
and the fine fins' sharp spines

SUNDAY
[First Version]

Small barking sounds—
clatter of metal in a pan—
a high fretting voice
and a low voice, musical
as a string twanged—

The tempo is evenly drawn
give and take
A splash of water, the
ting a ring of
small pieces of metal jangling
the clap of a door—
A tune, nameless as Time—

Then the voices—
sound of feet barely moving—
Slowly—
And the bark, "What?"
"The same, the same, the—"
scrape of a chair
click a clickety tee—

"Over Labor Day they'll
be gone"
"Jersey City, he's the
engineer—" "Ya"
"Being out on the Erie R.R.
is quite convenient"

"No, I think they're—"
"I think *she* is. I think—"
"German-American"
"Of course the Govern—"
Very quiet
Stillness. A distant door
slammed. Amen.

A CRYSTAL MAZE

I

Hard, hard to learn—
that love, through bars and against
back strokes, is to make mine
each by his own gesture—the toss
of a cigarette—
giving, laying himself bare,
offering, watching
for its flash of certainty in
the confused onslaught—

—that any one is not one
but twenty—twelve men, two women

a hidden positive and a visible
deception—

Take it, black curls clustered in
the hollow of the neck, unwilling
to be released for less—
laying desperately with impeccable
composure an unnecessary
body clean to the eye—

And emerge curiously changed—
amazement in that loveliness
about the perfect breasts
Venus, her way, close sister to
the martyr—each his own way

One avidly sheathing the flesh—
one denying it. One loosed through
the gone brain of an old man—

Pity has no part in it—

Loosed to take its course, love
is the master—and the variable
certainty in the crosses of
uncertainty—
                 the flesh, therewith,
a quietness—
and quieted—standing asserted

II

Hard, hard to learn—
that love, against bars and
counter strokes is mine,
each by his own gesture—
the toss of a cigarette—
laying himself bare
offering, watching
for a flash of certainty
in the confused onslaught—

That one is not one
but—twelve, two women,
a hidden positive and
a visible deception—

Take it! black curls clustered
in the hollow of the neck
laying desperately with
impeccable composure
an uncalled for body clean
to the eye—

      and emerging
curiously changed—
amazement in that loveliness
about the perfect breasts—
the flesh thereto
a quietness and
quieted, standing asserted

READIE POME

Grace - face: hot - pot: lank - spank: meat - eat:
hash - cash: sell - well: old - sold: sink - wink: deep -
sleep: come - numb: dum - rum: some - bum.

TWO ASPECTS OF APRIL

1

Nothing is more certain than the flower—
and best, sometimes, are those
that start into blossom directly from
the harshness of bare gardens—the crocus
breaking through, narcissi heaving

a trampled place, and I saw once
jonquils, forgotten, buried under
a new driveway, covered with broken stone
but still unsuppressed, rising still
into a graceful flower-head—

2

—and after ten years they've finally
graded the field back of the high school
making it fit for athletic purposes—
They've even relocated the baseball cage
—not quite correctly since it makes
A short left field, but at least
something has been accomplished—April
is that way. It wakes up, gets
things done, about as well as they can
be done—after winter's dullness—
Good luck, 1932! It's your turn now.

THE COD HEAD

Miscellaneous weed
strands, stems, debris—
firmament

to fishes—
where the yellow feet
of gulls dabble—

oars whip
ships churn to bubbles—
at night wildly

agitate phospores-
cent midges—but by day
flaccid

moons in whose
discs sometimes a red cross
lives—four

fathom—the bottom skids
a mottle of green
sands backward—

amorphous waver-
ing rocks—three fathom
the vitreous

body through which—
small scudding fish deep
down—and

now a lulling lift
and fall—
red stars—a severed cod-

head between two
green stones—lifting
falling

THE RED LILY

To the bob-white's call
and drone of reaper

tumbling daisies in the sun—
one by one

about the smutting panels of
white doors

grey shingles slip and fall—
But you, a loveliness

of even lines
curving to the throat, the

crossroads is your home.
You are, upon

your steady stem
one trumpeted wide flower

slightly tilted
above a scale of buds—

Sometimes a farmer's wife
gathers an armful

for her pitcher on the porch—
Topping a stone wall

against the shale-ledge
a field full—

By the road, the river
the edge of the woods

—opening in the sun
closing with the dark—

everywhere
Red Lily

in your common cup
all beauty lies—

THIS FLORIDA: 1924

of which I am the sand—
one of the sands—in which
the turtle eggs are baking—

The people are running away
toward me, Hibiscus,
where I lie, sad,

by the stern
slaying palm trees—
(They're so much better

at a distance than they are
up close. Cocoanuts
aren't they?

or Royal palms?
They are so tall the wind
rips them to shreds)

—this frightened
frantic pilgrimage has left
my bungalows up here

lonely as the Lido in April
"Florida the Flowery!"
Well,

it's a kind of borrowed
pleasure after all (as at the movies)
to see them

tearing off to escape it
this winter
this winter that I feel

So—
already ten o'clock?
Vorwärts!

e-e i-i o-o u-u a-a
Shall I write it in iambs?
Cottages in a row

all radioed and showerbathed?
But I am sick of rime—
The whole damned town

is riming up one street
and down another, yet there is
the rime of her white teeth

the rime of glasses
at my plate, the ripple rime
the rime her fingers make—

And we thought to escape rime
by imitation of the senseless
unarrangement of wild things—

the stupidest rime of all—
Rather, Hibiscus,
let me examine

those varying shades
of orange, clear as an electric
bulb on fire

or powdery with sediment—
matt, the shades and textures
of a Cubist picture

the charm
of fish by Hartley; orange
of ale and lilies

orange of topaz, orange of red hair
orange of curaçoa
orange of the Tiber

turbid, orange of the bottom
rocks in Maine rivers
orange of mushrooms

of Cepes that Marshal loved
to cook in copper
pans, orange of the sun—

I shall do my pees, instead—
boiling them in test tubes
holding them to the light

dropping in the acid—
Peggy has a little albumen
in hers—

TO

a child (a boy) bouncing
a ball (a blue ball)—

He bounces it (a toy racket
in his hand) and runs

and catches it (with his
left hand) six floors

straight down—
which is the old back yard

IN THE 'SCONSET BUS

Upon the fallen
cheek

a gauzy down—
And on

the nape
—indecently

a mat
of yellow hair

stuck with
celluloid

pins
not quite

matching it
—that's

two shades
darker

at the roots
Hanging

from the ears
the hooks

piercing the
flesh—

gold and semi-
precious

stones—
And in her

lap the dog
(Youth)

resting
his head on

the ample
shoulder his

bright
mouth agape

pants restlessly
backward

OUR (AMERICAN) RAGCADEMICIANS

Oh what fools! what shattered fools we are,
What brainless, headless, bellywitted lumps.
Who are we? Are we? more than camels' humps.
What capon-fats, what zeros under par,
What empty wagons hitched up to a star,
What miscellany of what garbage dumps,
Upon what butcher's hens what naked rumps!
If this be not too flattering by far.

We had a prod to virtue, writing! once.
Where is it now? Sold out—to pimps, unsound,
Strictured. Give? God pardon us, no nerve,
No "cause." Or we would force them to renounce
Their panders' traffic; sanction Ezra Pound
And back him up, to give—what we deserve.

RHYMED ADDRESS: THE LOBSTER

Rhymed address to Carl Rakosi
acknowledging (with thanks)
the excellence of his poem—

The Lobster:

Superb light
and life which in
the mind seems

red even when we know
it must be
green—

luminosity of genius
which strikes
livening it

even to the ocean's
bed!
The sun

which makes
leaves of two colors
dark and bright

in every tree
flower tho' he may
lacks light

without that final
brilliance
for me

THE FLOWERS ALONE

I should have to be
Chaucer to describe
them—
        Loss keeps
me from such a
catalogue—

But!
        —low, the
violet, scentless as
it is here! higher,
the peartree in full
bloom through which
a light falls as
rain—

And that is gone—

Only, there remains—

Now!
   the cherry trees
white in all back
yards—
   And bare as
they are, the coral
peach trees melting
the harsh air—
    excellence
priceless beyond
all later
    fruit!

And now, driven, I
go, forced to
another day—

Whose yellow quilt
flapping in the
stupendous light—

Forsythia, quince
blossoms—

   and all
the living hybrids

THE LOCUST TREE IN FLOWER
[First Version]

Among
the leaves
bright

green
of wrist-thick
tree

and old
stiff broken
branch

ferncool
swaying
loosely strung—

come May
again
white blossom

clusters
hide
to spill

their sweets
almost
unnoticed

down
and quickly
fall

THE CENTENARIAN

I don't think we shall
any of us live as long as
has she, we haven't the
steady mind and strong heart—

Wush a deen a daddy O
There's whiskey in the jar!

I wish you could have seen
her yesterday
with her red cheeks and
snow-white hair
so cheerful and contented—
she was a picture—

We sang hymns for her.

She couldn't join us but
when we had done she raised
her hands and clapped them
softly together.

Then when I brought her
her whiskey and water I said
to her as we always do—

*Wush a deen a daddy O
There's whiskey in the jar!*

She couldn't say the first
part but she managed to
repeat at the end—

There's whiskey in the jar!

4TH OF JULY

I

The ship moves
but its smoke
moves with the wind
faster than the ship

—thick coils of it
through leafy trees

pressing
upon the river

II

The heat makes
this place of the woods
a room
in which two robins pain

crying
distractedly
over the plight of
their unhappy young

III

During the explosions
at dawn, the celebrations
I could hear
a native cuckoo

in the distance
as at dusk, before
I'd heard
a night hawk calling

SONG

The black-winged gull
of love is flying—
hurl of the waters'
futile might!

Tirelessly
his deft strokes plying
he skims free in the licking
waves' despite—

There is no lying
to his shrill mockery
of their torment
day or night.

A FOOT-NOTE

Walk on the delicate parts
of necessary mechanisms
and you will pretty soon have
neither food, clothing, nor
even Communism itself,
Comrades. Read good poetry!

SLUGGISHLY

or with a rush
the river flows—

and none
is unaffected—

     Think:
the clear stream

boiling at
the boat's wake

or—
    a stench
your choice is—

And respond?

       crapulous
—having eaten

fouling
the water grass

THE ENTITY

Antipoetic is the thing
flowers mostly in the spring
and when it dies it lives again
first the egg and then the hen

Or is this merely an unreason
flowerless the which we beg
antipoetic mocks the season
first the hen and then the egg

THE SUN BATHERS

A tramp thawing out
on a doorstep
against an east wall
Nov. 1, 1933:

a young man begrimed
and in an old
army coat
wriggling and scratching

while a fat negress
in a yellow-house window
nearby
leans out and yawns

into the fine weather

NANTUCKET

Flowers through the window
lavender and yellow

changed by white curtains—
Smell of cleanliness—

Sunshine of late afternoon—
On the glass tray

a glass pitcher, the tumbler
turned down, by which

a key is lying—And the
immaculate white bed

THIS IS JUST TO SAY

I have eaten
the plums
that were in
the icebox

and which
you were probably
saving
for breakfast

Forgive me
they were delicious
so sweet
and so cold

YOUNG WOMAN AT A WINDOW

While she sits
there

with tears on
her cheek

her cheek on
her hand

this little child
who robs her

knows nothing of
his theft

but rubs his
nose

YOUNG WOMAN AT A WINDOW

She sits with
tears on

her cheek
her cheek on

her hand
the child

in her lap
his nose

pressed
to the glass

TO A DEAD JOURNALIST

Behind that white brow
now the mind simply sleeps—
the eyes, closed, the
lips, the mouth,

the chin, no longer useful,
the prow of the nose.
But rumors of the news,
unrealizable,

cling still among those
silent, butted features, a
sort of wonder at
this scoop

come now, too late:
beneath the lucid ripples
to have found so monstrous
an obscurity.

AN EARLY MARTYR
AND OTHER POEMS

1935

AN EARLY MARTYR

and

Other Poems

BY

WILLIAM CARLOS WILLIAMS

ætate suæ

52 (in September)

NEW YORK
THE ALCESTIS PRESS
551 Fifth Avenue
1 9 3 5

AN EARLY MARTYR

Rather than permit him
to testify in court
Giving reasons
why he stole from
Exclusive stores
then sent post-cards
To the police
to come and arrest him
—if they could—
They railroaded him
to an asylum for
The criminally insane
without trial

The prophylactic to
madness
Having been denied him
he went close to
The edge out of
frustration and
Doggedness—

Inflexible, finally they
had to release him—
The institution was
"overcrowded"
They let him go
in the custody of
A relative on condition
that he remain
Out of the state—

They "cured" him all
right

But the set-up
he fought against
Remains—
and his youthful deed
Signalizing
the romantic period
Of a revolt
he served well
Is still good—

Let him be
a factory whistle
That keeps blaring—
Sense, sense, sense!
so long as there's
A mind to remember
and a voice to
carry it on—
Never give up
keep at it!
Unavoided, terrifying
to such bought
Courts as he thought
to trust to but they
Double-crossed him.

FLOWERS BY THE SEA

When over the flowery, sharp pasture's
edge, unseen, the salt ocean

lifts its form—chicory and daisies
tied, released, seem hardly flowers alone

but color and the movement—or the shape
perhaps—of restlessness, whereas

the sea is circled and sways
peacefully upon its plantlike stem

ITEM

This, with a face
like a mashed blood orange
that suddenly

would get eyes
and look up and scream
War! War!

clutching her
thick, ragged coat
A piece of hat

broken shoes
War! War!
stumbling for dread

at the young men
who with their gun-butts
shove her

sprawling—
a note
at the foot of the page

THE LOCUST TREE IN FLOWER

Among
of
green

stiff
old
bright

broken
branch
come

white
sweet
May

again

VIEW OF A LAKE

from a
highway below a face
of rock

too recently blasted
to be overgrown
with grass or fern:

Where a
waste of cinders
slopes down to

the railroad and
the lake
stand three children

beside the weed-grown
chassis
of a wrecked car

immobile in a line
facing the water
To the left a boy

in falling off
blue overalls
Next to him a girl

in a grimy frock
And another boy
They are intent

watching something
below—?
A section sign: 50

on an iron post
planted
by a narrow concrete

service hut
(to which runs
a sheaf of wires)

in the universal
cinders beaten
into crossing paths

to form the front yard
of a frame house
at the right

that looks
to have been flayed
Opposite

remains a sycamore
in leaf
Intently fixed

the three
with straight backs
ignore

the stalled traffic
all eyes
toward the water

TO A MEXICAN PIG-BANK

and a small
    flock

of clay
    sheep—

a shepherd
    behind

them—The
    pig

is painted
    yellow

with green
    ears

There's a
    slot

at the
        top—

Hair-pin
    wires

hold up the
    sheep

turning
    away—

The shepherd
    wears

a red
    blanket

on his left
shoulder

TO A POOR OLD WOMAN

munching a plum on
the street a paper bag
of them in her hand

They taste good to her
They taste good
to her. They taste
good to her

You can see it by
the way she gives herself
to the one half
sucked out in her hand

Comforted
a solace of ripe plums
seeming to fill the air
They taste good to her

THE SADNESS OF THE SEA

This is the sadness of the sea—
waves like words, all broken—
a sameness of lifting and falling mood.

I lean watching the detail
of brittle crest, the delicate
imperfect foam, yellow weed
one piece like another—

There is no hope—if not a coral
island slowly forming

to wait for birds to drop
the seeds will make it habitable

LATE FOR SUMMER WEATHER

He has on
an old light grey Fedora
She a black beret

He a dirty sweater
She an old blue coat
that fits her tight

Grey flapping pants
Red skirt and
broken down black pumps

Fat Lost Ambling
nowhere through
the upper town they kick

their way through
heaps of
fallen maple leaves

still green—and
crisp as dollar bills
Nothing to do. Hot cha!

PROLETARIAN PORTRAIT

A big young bareheaded woman
in an apron

Her hair slicked back standing
on the street

One stockinged foot toeing
the sidewalk

Her shoe in her hand. Looking
intently into it

She pulls out the paper insole
to find the nail

That has been hurting her

TREE AND SKY

Again
the bare brush of
the half-broken
and already-written-of
tree alone
on its battered
hummock—

Above
among the shufflings
of the distant
cloud-rifts
vaporously
the unmoving
blue

THE RAPER FROM PASSENACK

was very kind. When she regained
her wits, he said, It's all right, Kid,
I took care of you.

What a mess she was in. Then he added,
You'll never forget me now.
And drove her home.

Only a man who is sick, she said
would do a thing like that.
It must be so.

No one who is not diseased could be
so insanely cruel. He wants to give it
to someone else—

to justify himself. But if I get a
venereal infection out of this
I won't be treated.

I refuse. You'll find me dead in bed
first. Why not? That's
the way she spoke,

I wish I could shoot him. How would
you like to know a murderer?
I may do it.

I'll know by the end of this week.
I wouldn't scream. I bit him
several times

but he was too strong for me.
I can't yet understand it. I don't
faint so easily.

When I came to myself and realized
what had happened all I could do
was to curse

and call him every vile name I could
think of. I was so glad
to be taken home.

I suppose it's my mind—the fear of
infection. I'd rather a million times
have been got pregnant.

But it's the foulness of it can't
be cured. And hatred, hatred of all men
—and disgust.

INVOCATION AND CONCLUSION

January!
The beginning of all things!
Sprung from the old burning nest
upward in the flame!

I was married at thirteen
My parents had nine kids
and we were on the street
That's why that old bugger—

He was twenty-six
and I hadn't even had
my changes yet. Now look at me!

GENESIS

Take some one in England with brains enough
or taste enough, what they call there,
possibly, an aristocrat—tho' seldom enough
And let him get a woman who's bitch enough
with child, then treat her characteristically
enough to make her, having guts enough,
quit the damned place and take a ship to New
York and with the son she got dare enough
to land herself another husband who has also
brains enough to marry her
and take her to St. Thomas where there's room
enough for the sprout to thrive and grow up.

SOLSTICE

The river is full
The time is ripe
Give murderous thoughts rest

No leaves on the trees
A mild sun darkens
the frosty earth

Quietness reigns
No birds, no wind
The shortest day of the year

is favorable

THE YACHTS

contend in a sea which the land partly encloses
shielding them from the too-heavy blows
of an ungoverned ocean which when it chooses

tortures the biggest hulls, the best man knows
to pit against its beatings, and sinks them pitilessly.
Mothlike in mists, scintillant in the minute

brilliance of cloudless days, with broad bellying sails
they glide to the wind tossing green water
from their sharp prows while over them the crew crawls

ant-like, solicitously grooming them, releasing,
making fast as they turn, lean far over and having
caught the wind again, side by side, head for the mark.

In a well guarded arena of open water surrounded by
lesser and greater craft which, sycophant, lumbering
and flittering follow them, they appear youthful, rare

as the light of a happy eye, live with the grace
of all that in the mind is fleckless, free and
naturally to be desired. Now the sea which holds them

is moody, lapping their glossy sides, as if feeling
for some slightest flaw but fails completely.
Today no race. Then the wind comes again. The yachts

move, jockeying for a start, the signal is set and they
are off. Now the waves strike at them but they are too
well made, they slip through, though they take in canvas.

Arms with hands grasping seek to clutch at the prows.
Bodies thrown recklessly in the way are cut aside.
It is a sea of faces about them in agony, in despair

until the horror of the race dawns staggering the mind,
the whole sea become an entanglement of watery bodies
lost to the world bearing what they cannot hold. Broken,

beaten, desolate, reaching from the dead to be taken up
they cry out, failing, failing! their cries rising
in waves still as the skillful yachts pass over.

YOUNG LOVE

What about all this writing?

O "Kiki"
O Miss Margaret Jarvis
The backhandspring
I: clean
    clean
    clean: yes . . New York

Wrigley's, appendicitis, John Marin:
skyscraper soup—

Either that or a bullet!

Once
anything might have happened
You lay relaxed on my knees—
the starry night
spread out warm and blind
above the hospital—

Pah!

It is unclean
which is not straight to the mark—

In my life the furniture eats me

the chairs, the floor
the walls
which heard your sobs
drank up my emotion—
they which alone know everything

and snitched on us in the morning—

What to want?

Drunk we go forward surely
Not I

beds, beds, beds
elevators, fruit, night-tables
breasts to see, white and blue—
to hold in the hand, to nozzle

It is not onion soup
Your sobs soaked through the walls
breaking the hospital to pieces
Everything
—windows, chairs
obscenely drunk, spinning—

white, blue, orange
—hot with our passion
wild tears, desperate rejoinders
my legs, turning slowly
end over end in the air!

But what would you have?

All I said was:
there, you see, it is broken
stockings, shoes, hairpins
your bed, I wrapped myself round you—

I watched.

You sobbed, you beat your pillow
you tore your hair
you dug your nails into your sides

I was your nightgown
                    I watched!

Clean is he alone
after whom stream
the broken pieces of the city—
flying apart at his approaches

but I merely
caressed you curiously
fifteen years ago and you still
go about the city, they say
patching up sick school children

HYMN TO LOVE ENDED
(*Imaginary translation from the Spanish*)

Through what extremes of passion
had you come, Sappho, to the peace
of deathless song?

As from an illness, as after drought
the streams released to flow
filling the fields with freshness
the birds drinking from every twig
and beasts from every hollow—
bellowing, singing of the unrestraint
to colors of a waking world.
                              So
after love a music streams above it.
For what is love? But music is
Villon beaten and cast off
Shakespeare from wisdom's grotto
looking doubtful at the world
Alighieri beginning all again
Goethe whom a rose ensnared
Li Po the drunkard, singers whom
love has overthrown—

To this company the birds themselves
and the sleek beasts belong and all
who will besides—when love is ended
to the waking of sweetest song.

AN ELEGY FOR D. H. LAWRENCE

Green points on the shrub
and poor Lawrence dead.
The night damp and misty
and Lawrence no more in the world
to answer April's promise
with a fury of labor
against waste, waste and life's
coldness.

Once he received a letter—
he never answered it—
praising him: so English

he had thereby raised himself
to an unenglish greatness.
Dead now and it grows clearer
what bitterness drove him.

This is the time.
The serpent in the grotto
water dripping from the stone
into a pool.
Mediterranean evenings. Ashes
of Cretan fires. And to the north
forsythia hung with
yellow bells in the cold.

Poor Lawrence
worn with a fury of sad labor
to create summer from
spring's decay. English
women. Men driven not to love
but to the ends of the earth.
The serpent turning his
stone-like head,
the fixed agate eyes turn also.

And unopened jonquils
hang their folded heads. No
summer. But for Lawrence
full praise in this
half cold half season—
before trees are in leaf and
tufted grass stars
unevenly the bare ground.

Slowly the serpent leans
to drink by the tinkling water
the forked tongue alert.
Then fold after fold,
glassy strength, passing
a given point,

as by desire drawn
forward bodily, he glides
smoothly in.

To stand by the sea or walk
again along a river's bank and talk
with a companion, to halt
watching where the edge of water
meets and lies upon
the unmoving shore—
Flood waters rise, and will rise,
rip the quiet valley
trap the gypsy and the girl.
She clings drowning to
a bush in flower.

Remember, now, Lawrence dead.
Blue squills in bloom—to
the scorched aridity of
the Mexican plateau. Or baked
public squares in the cities of
Mediterranean islands
where one waits for busses and
boats come slowly along the water
arriving.

But the sweep of spring over
temperate lands, meadows and woods
where the young walk and talk
incompletely,
straining to no summer,
hearing the frogs, speaking of
birds and insects—

Febrile spring moves not to heat
but always more slowly,
burdened by a weight of leaves.
Nothing now
to burst the bounds—
remains confined by them. Heat,

heat! Unknown. Poor Lawrence,
dead and only the drowned
fallen dancing from the deck
of a pleasure boat
unfading desire.

Rabbits, imaginings, the
drama, literature, satire.
The serpent cannot move
his stony eyes, scarcely sees
but touching the air
with his forked tongue surmises
and his body which dipped
into the cold water
is gone.

Violently the satiric sun
that leads April not to
the panting dance but to stillness
in, into the brain, dips
and is gone also.
And sisters return
through the dusk
to the measured rancor
of their unbending elders.

Greep, greep, greep the cricket
chants where the snake
with agate eyes leaned to the water.
Sorrow to the young
that Lawrence has passed
unwanted from England.
And in the gardens forsythia
and in the woods
now the crinkled spice-bush
in flower.

SUNDAY

Small barking sounds
Clatter of metal in a pan
A high fretting voice
and a low voice musical
as a string twanged—

The tempo is evenly drawn
give and take
A splash of water, the
ting a ring
of small pieces of metal
dropped, the clap of a door
A tune nameless as Time—

Then the voices—
Sound of feet barely moving
Slowly
And the bark, "What?"
"The same, the same, the—"
scrape of a chair
clickaty tee—

"Over Labor Day they'll
be gone"
"Jersey City, he's the
engineer—" "Ya"
"Being on the Erie R. R.
is quite convenient"

"No, I think they're—"
"I think she is. I think—"
"German-American"
"Of course the Govern—"

    . . . .

A distant door slammed.
Amen.

THE CATHOLIC BELLS

Tho' I'm no Catholic
I listen hard when the bells
in the yellow-brick tower
of their new church

ring down the leaves
ring in the frost upon them
and the death of the flowers
ring out the grackle

toward the south, the sky
darkened by them, ring in
the new baby of Mr. and Mrs.
Krantz which cannot

for the fat of its cheeks
open well its eyes, ring out
the parrot under its hood
jealous of the child

ring in Sunday morning
and old age which adds as it
takes away. Let them ring
only ring! over the oil

painting of a young priest
on the church wall advertising
last week's Novena to St.
Anthony, ring for the lame

young man in black with
gaunt cheeks and wearing a
Derby hat, who is hurrying
to 11 o'clock Mass (the

grapes still hanging to
the vines along the nearby

Concordia Halle like broken
teeth in the head of an

old man) Let them ring
for the eyes and ring for
the hands and ring for
the children of my friend

who no longer hears
them ring but with a smile
and in a low voice speaks
of the decisions of her

daughter and the proposals
and betrayals of her
husband's friends. O bells
ring for the ringing!

the beginning and the end
of the ringing! Ring ring
ring ring ring ring ring!
Catholic bells—!

THE RIGHT OF WAY (THE AUTO RIDE)

See Poem XI of *Spring and All*

SIMPLEX SIGILUM VERI

an american papermatch packet
closed, gilt with a panel insert,
the bank, a narrow building
black, in a blue sky, puffs of

white cloud, the small windows
in perspective, bright green grass—

a sixinch metal tray, polished
bronze, holding a blue pencil

hexagonal, its bright brassy
butt catching the window light,
the dullred eraser half worn
down and a cheap brownenameled

pen-holder rest on the brown
marbled field of the stained blotter
by an oystershell smudged
with cigarette ash, a primrose plant

in a gold-ringed saucer, flowerless—
surfaces of all sorts
bearing printed characters, bottles
words printed on the backs of

two telephone directories, titles
for poems, The Advertising Biographical
Calendar of Medicine, Wednesday 18
Thursday 19, Friday 20, papers

of various shades sticking out
from under others, throwing
the printing out of line: portrait
of all that which we have lost,

a truncated pyramid, bronzed
metal (probably the surface
only) to match the tray, to which
a square, hinged lid is fixed,

the inkstand, from whose
imagined top the Prince of Wales
having climbed up, once with all
his might drove a golf ball.

THE DEAD BABY

First published in 1927: See page 268.

THE BLACK WINDS (THE IMMEMORIAL WIND)

See Poem V of *Spring and All*

THE FARMER

See Poem III of *Spring and All*

THE WIND INCREASES

First printed in the *Della Primavera Trasportata al Morale* sequence:
See p. 339.

TO BE HUNGRY IS TO BE GREAT

The small, yellow grass-onion,
spring's first green, precursor
to Manhattan's pavements, when
plucked as it comes, in bunches,
washed, split and fried in
a pan, though inclined to be
a little slimy, if well cooked
and served hot on rye bread
is to beer a perfect appetizer—
and the best part
of it is they grow everywhere.

A POEM FOR NORMAN MACLEOD

The revolution
is accomplished
noble has been
changed to no bull

After that
has sickered down
slumming will
be done on Park Ave.

Or as Chief
One Horn said to
the constipated
prospector:

You big fool!
and with his knife
gashed a balsam
standing nearby

Gathering the
gum that oozed out
in a tin spoon
it did the trick

You can do lots
if you know
what's around you
No bull

YOU HAVE PISSED YOUR LIFE

Any way you walk
Any way you turn
Any way you stand
Any way you lie
You have pissed your life

From an ineffectual fool
butting his head blindly
against obstacles, become
brilliant—focusing,
performing accurately to
a given end—

Any way you walk
Any way you turn
Any way you stand
Any way you lie
You have pissed your life

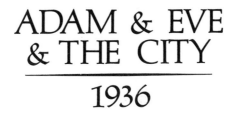

ADAM & EVE
& THE CITY
1936

ADAM
& EVE
& THE
CITY

WILLIAM)(ALCESTIS
CARLOS)(PRESS
WILLIAMS)(PERU, VT.
MCMXXXVI

TO A WOOD THRUSH

Singing across the orchard
before night, answered
from the depths
of the wood, inversely
and in a lower key—

First I tried to write
conventionally praising you
but found it no more
than my own thoughts
that I was giving. No.

What can I say?
                Vistas
of delight waking suddenly
before a cheated world.

FINE WORK WITH PITCH AND COPPER

Now they are resting
in the fleckless light
separately in unison

like the sacks
of sifted stone stacked
regularly by twos

about the flat roof
ready after lunch
to be opened and strewn

The copper in eight
foot strips has been
beaten lengthwise

down the center at right
angles and lies ready
to edge the coping

One still chewing
picks up a copper strip
and runs his eye along it

YOUNG WOMAN AT A WINDOW

See the second version of this poem on p. 373.

THE ROSE

First the warmth, variability
color and frailty

A grace of petals skirting
the tight-whorled cone

Come to generous abandon—
to the mind as to the eye

Wide! Wider!
Wide as if panting, until

the gold hawk's-eye speaks once
coldly its perfection

LA BELLE DAME DE TOUS LES JOURS

It speaks, it moves
there is a sound and alteration—

The hair
about the brow, the eyes
symmetrically turn—

This has no part
in what has been but smiles
in selfishness
unique—

            against the snow
new-fallen beyond
the tropic window-sill

A CHINESE TOY

Six whittled chickens
on a wooden bat

that peck within a
circle pulled

by strings fast to
a hanging weight

when shuttled by the
playful hand

ADAM

He grew up by the sea
on a hot island
inhabited by negroes—mostly.
There he built himself
a boat and a separate room
close to the water
for a piano on which he practiced—

by sheer doggedness
and strength of purpose
striving
like an Englishman
to emulate his Spanish friend
and idol—the weather!

And there he learned
to play the flute—not very well—

Thence he was driven—
out of Paradise—to taste
the death that duty brings
so daintily, so mincingly,
with such a noble air—
that enslaved him all his life
thereafter—

And he left behind
all the curious memories that come
with shells and hurricanes—
the smells
and sounds and glancing looks
that Latins know belong
to boredom and long torrid hours
and Englishmen
will never understand—whom
duty has marked
for special mention—with
a tropic of its own
and its own heavy-winged fowl
and flowers that vomit beauty
at midnight—

But the Latin has turned romance
to a purpose cold as ice.
He never sees
or seldom
what melted Adam's knees

to jelly and despair—and
held them up pontifically—

Underneath the whisperings
of tropic nights
there is a darker whispering
that death invents especially
for northern men
whom the tropics
have come to hold.

It would have been enough
to know that never,
never, never, never would
peace come as the sun comes
in the hot islands.
But there was
a special hell besides
where black women lie waiting
for a boy—

Naked on a raft
he could see the barracudas
waiting to castrate him
so the saying went—
Circumstances take longer—

But being an Englishman
though he had not lived in England
desde que tenia cinco años
he never turned back
but kept a cold eye always
on the inevitable end
never wincing—never to unbend—
God's handyman
going quietly into hell's mouth
for a paper of reference—
fetching water to posterity
a British passport

always in his pocket—
muleback over Costa Rica
eating pâtés of black ants

And the Latin ladies admired him
and under their smiles
dartled the dagger of despair—
in spite of
a most thorough trial—
found his English heart safe
in the roseate steel. Duty
the angel
which with whip in hand . . .
—along the low wall of paradise
where they sat and smiled
and flipped their fans
at him—

He never had but the one home
Staring Him in the eye
coldly
and with patience—
without a murmur, silently
a desperate, unvarying silence
to the unhurried last.

EVE

Pardon my injuries
now that you are old—
Forgive me my awkwardnesses
my impatience
and short replies—
I sometimes detect in your face
a puzzled pity for me
your son—
I have never been close to you
—mostly your own fault;

in *that* I am like you.
It is as though
you looked down from above
at me—not
with what they would describe
as pride but the same
that is in me: a sort
of shame that the world
should see you as I see you,
a somewhat infantile creature—
without subtlety—
defenseless.

And because you are defenseless
I too, horribly,
take advantage of you,
(as you of me)
my mother, keep you
imprisoned—in
the name of protection
when you want so wildly to escape
as I wish also
to escape and leap into chaos
(where Time has
not yet begun)

When Adam died
it came out clearly—
Not what commonly
might have been supposed but
a demon, fighting for the fire
it needed to breathe
to live again.
A last chance. You
kicked blindly before you
and nearly broke your leg
against the metal—then sank
exhausted.
And that is the horror
of my guilt—and the sweetness

even at this late date
in some kind of acknowledgment

I realize why you wish
to communicate with the dead—
And it is again I
who try to hush you
that you shall not
make a fool of yourself
and have them stare at you
with natural faces—
Trembling, sobbing
and grabbing at the futile hands
till a mind goes sour
watching you—and flies off
sick at the mumbling
from which nothing clearly
is ever spoken—

It not so much frightens
as shames me. I want to protect
you, to spare you the disgrace—
seeing you reach out that way
to self-inflicted emptiness—

As if you were not able
to protect yourself—
and me too—if we did not
have to be so guarded—

Therefore I make this last plea:

Forgive me
I have been a fool—
(and remain a fool)
If you are not already too blind
too deaf, too lost in the past
to know or to care—
I will write a book about you—
making you live (in a book!)

as you still desperately
want to live—
to live always—unforgiving

I'll give you brandy
or wine
whenever I think you need it
(need it!)
because it whips up
your mind and your senses
and brings color to your face
—to enkindle that life
too coarse for the usual,
that sly obscenity
that fertile darkness
in which passion mates—
reflecting
the lightnings of creation—
and the moon—
"*C'est la vieillesse
inexorable qu'arrive!*"

One would think
you would be reconciled with Time
instead of clawing at Him
that way, terrified
in the night—screaming out
unwilling, unappeased
and without shame—

Might He not take
that wasted carcass, crippled
and deformed, that ruined face
sightless, deafened—
the color gone—that seems
always listening, watching, waiting
ashamed only
of that single and last
degradation—

No. Never. Defenseless
still you would keep
every accoutrement
which He has loaned
till it shall be torn from
your grasp, a final grip
from those fingers
which cannot hold a knife
to cut the meat but which
in a hypnotic ecstasy
can so wrench a hand held out
to you that our bones
crack under the unwonted pressure—

ST. FRANCIS EINSTEIN OF THE DAFFODILS

*On the first visit of Professor Einstein to the United States
in the spring of 1921.*

"Sweet land"
at last!
out of the sea—
the Venusremembering wavelets
rippling with laughter—
freedom
for the daffodils!
—in a tearing wind
that shakes
the tufted orchards—
Einstein, tall as a violet
in the lattice-arbor corner
is tall as
a blossomy peartree

O Samos, Samos
dead and buried. Lesbia
a black cat in the freshturned
garden. All dead.

All flesh they sung
is rotten
Sing of it no longer—
Side by side young and old
take the sun together—
maples, green and red
yellowbells
and the vermilion quinceflower
together—

The peartree
with fœtid blossoms
sways its high topbranches
with contrary motions
and there are both pinkflowered
and coralflowered peachtrees
in the bare chickenyard
of the old negro
with white hair who hides
poisoned fish-heads
here and there
where stray cats find them—
find them

Spring days
swift and mutable
winds blowing four ways
hot and cold
shaking the flowers—
Now the northeast wind
moving in fogs leaves the grass
cold and dripping. The night
is dark. But in the night
the southeast wind approaches.
The owner of the orchard
lies in bed
with open windows
and throws off his covers
one by one

THE DEATH OF SEE

One morning
the wind scouring
the streets

I read: Poet
and woman
found shot dead

Pact seen in
murder—
Suicide in

artist's suite—
Their bodies
fully clothed

were found
half covered
by

a blanket—
See
was described as

a poet
but when or
where his

poems were
published M. could
not say. . . .

Which adds
a certain
gravity—

Suddenly
snow trees
flashing

upon the mind
from a clean
world

TO AN ELDER POET

To be able
and not to do it

Still as a flower

No flame,
a flower spent
with heat—

lovely flower
            hanging
in the rain

                Never!

Soberly

Whiter than day

Wait forever
shaken by the rain
            forever

UNNAMED
From "Paterson"

1

Your lovely hands
Your lovely tender hands!

Reflections of what grace
what heavenly joy

predicted for the world
in knowing you—
blest, as am I, and humbled
by such ecstasy.

2

When I saw
the flowers

I was
thunderstruck!

You should not
have been—

Tulips, she said
and smiled.

3

I bought a new
bathing suit

Just pants
and a brassiere—

I haven't shown
it

to my mother
yet.

4

Better than flowers
is a view of yourself
my darling—

I'm so glad you came
I thought I should never
see you again.

THE CRIMSON CYCLAMEN

(*To the Memory of Charles Demuth*)

White suffused with red
more rose than crimson
—all a color
the petals flare back
from the stooping craters
of those flowers
as from a wind rising—
And though the light
that enfolds and pierces
them discovers blues
and yellows there also—
and crimson's a dull word
beside such play—
yet the effect against
this winter where
they stand—is crimson—

It is miraculous
that flower should rise
by flower
alike in loveliness—
as though mirrors
of some perfection
could never be
too often shown—
silence holds them—
in that space. And
color has been construed
from emptiness
to waken there—

But the form came gradually.
The plant was there
before the flowers
as always—the leaves,
day by day changing. In
September when the first
pink pointed bud still
bowed below, all the leaves
heart-shaped
were already spread—
quirked and green
and stenciled with a paler
green
irregularly
across and round the edge—

Upon each leaf it is
a pattern more
of logic than a purpose
links each part to the rest,
an abstraction
playfully following
centripetal
devices, as of pure thought—
the edge tying by
convergent, crazy rays
with the center—
where that dips
cupping down to the
upright stem—the source
that has splayed out
fanwise and returns
upon itself in the design
thus decoratively—

Such are the leaves
freakish, of the air
as thought is, of roots
dark, complex from
subterranean revolutions

and rank odors
waiting for the moon—
The young leaves
coming among the rest
are more crisp
and deeply cupped
the edges rising first
impatient of the slower
stem—the older
level, the oldest
with the edge already
fallen a little backward—
the stem alone
holding the form
stiffly a while longer—

Under the leaf, the same
though the smooth green
is gone. Now the ribbed
design—if not
the purpose, is explained.
The stem's pink flanges,
strongly marked,
stand to the frail edge,
dividing, thinning
through the pink and downy
mesh—as the round stem
is pink also—cranking
to penciled lines
angularly deft
through all, to link together
the unnicked argument
to the last crinkled edge—
where the under and the over
meet and disappear
and the air alone begins
to go from them—
the conclusion left still
blunt, floating
if warped and quaintly flecked

whitened and streaked
resting
upon the tie of the stem—

But half hidden under them
such as they are
it begins that must
put thought to rest—

wakes in tinted beaks
still raising the head
and passion
is loosed—

its small lusts
addressed still to
the knees and to sleep—
abandoning argument

lifts
through the leaves
day by day
and one day opens!

The petals!
the petals undone
loosen all five and
swing up

The flower
flows to release—

Fast within a ring
where the compact
agencies
of conception

lie mathematically
ranged

round the
hair-like sting—

From such a pit
the color flows
over
a purple rim

upward to
the light! the light!
all around—
Five petals

as one
to flare, inverted
a full flower
each petal tortured

eccentrically
the while, warped edge
jostling
half-turned edge

side by side
until compact, tense
evenly stained
to the last fine edge

an ecstasy
from the empurpled ring
climbs up (though
firm there still)

each petal
by excess of tensions
in its own flesh
all rose—

rose red
standing until it

bends backward
upon the rest, above,

answering
ecstasy with excess
all together
acrobatically

not as if bound
(though still bound)
but upright
as if they hung

from above
to the streams
with which
they are veined and glow—
the frail fruit
by its frailty supreme
opening in the tense moment
to no bean
no completion
no root
no leaf and no stem
but color only and a form—

It is passion
earlier and later than thought
that rises above thought
at instant peril—peril
itself a flower
that lifts and draws it on—

Frailer than level thought
more convolute
rose red
highest
the soonest to wither
blacken

and fall upon itself
formless—

And the flowers
grow older and begin
to change, larger now
less tense, when at the full
relaxing, widening
the petals falling down
the color paling
through violaceous to
tinted white—

The structure of the petal
that was all red
beginning now to show
from a deep central vein
other finely scratched veins
dwindling to that edge
through which the light
more and more shows
fading through gradations
immeasurable to the eye—

The day rises and swifter
briefer
more frailly relaxed
than thought that still
holds good—the color
draws back while still
the flower grows
the rose of it nearly all lost
a darkness of dawning purple
paints a deeper afternoon—

The day passes
in a horizon of colors
all meeting
less severe in loveliness

the petals fallen now well back
till flower touches flower
all round
at the petal tips
merging into one flower—

TRANSLATIONS FROM THE SPANISH

1

CANCION
(Lupercio De Argensola)

Alivia sus fatigas
El labrador cansado
Quando su yerta barba escarcha cubre,
Pensando en las espigas
Del Agosto abrasado,
Y en los lagares ricos del Octubre.

The tired workman
Takes his ease
When his stiff beard's all frosted over
Thinking of blazing
August's corn
And the brimming wine-cribs of October.

2

Stir your fields to increase
Most happy Tórmes
For she will be soon here
Gathering flowers.

From fertile meadow
And unfruitful wood
The countryside round
Burgeon and bud

Lilies and wild pinks
In varied showers
For she will be soon here
Gathering flowers.

The dawn casts pearls
From her balconies,
Stirs the mild pastures
To burgeon and bud,
And the envious sun
His ruddy car empowers
For she will be soon here
Gathering flowers.

The gentle zephyr
Strokes his greenery
And in the fresh branches
Limpid nightingales
With their sweet singing
Greet day from those towers
For she will be soon here
Gathering flowers.

3

The dawn is upon us
And day begins to grow
Lest they come and find you here
Get up and go.

An end to endearing caresses
Though the master still be delaying
Ere sun to the earth comes heying
By whom all embraces are undone.
Without hardship there is no pleasure
And content without passion none.
Be assured to the wise fit occasion
Has not yet refused a full measure.
Get up and be gone.

If my love enkindle your bosom
With honest intent and true
That my soul may enjoy full pleasure
Give over now what in bed we do.
For who lames you lames me also
And my good name rests all with you.
Pray be gone for my dread
No longer consents to your staying.
Get up and go.

What though you are wrestling with sleep.
Good sense bids you end it
That the joys of a single encounter
May be pleasured many times o'er.
It is reasonable to remember
That that which today we abjure
Is a promise redoubled tomorrow.
Lest they come and find you here
Get up and go.

4

Tears that still lacked power
To lessen such cruelty
I will return them to the sea
Since from the sea they have come.

Of tears I've an overplus
With which love's sea has endowed me,
Till I must swim to be free
Since love, a sea, has o'erflowed me;
Tears that still mounting higher
To reach you still lacked the sum
I will return them to the sea
Since from the sea they have come.

In the face of harsh opposition
Tears bitterly wrung
Have sought this or that token

As much as torment could find tongue;
But since not all were availing
To lessen such cruelty,
I will return them to the sea
Since from the sea they have come.

5

Poplars of the meadow
Fountains of Madrid
That I am absent now
You murmur complaints of me.

All of you are saying
How sorry my chance is
The wind in the branches
The fountains playing
To all men conveying
I knew you once happy.
That I am absent now
You murmur complaints of me.

Justly may I wonder
Since at my leaving
The plants with sighs were heaving
And all tears the waters;
That you were such liars
I never thought could be.
That I am absent now
You murmur complaints of me

Being in your presence
Music you'd waken
Later I'm forsaken
When you discover my absence.
May God give me patience
Here in my misery,
That I am absent now
You murmur complaints of me.

PERPETUUM MOBILE: THE CITY

              —a dream
        we dreamed
              each
        separately
              we two

        of love
              and of
        desire—

        that fused
        in the night—

        in the distance
              over
        the meadows
              by day
        impossible—
              The city
        disappeared
              when
        we arrived—

              A dream
        a little false
        toward which
              now
        we stand
              and stare
        transfixed—

        All at once
              in the east
        rising!

              All white!

        small
as a flower—

a locust cluster
a shad bush
        blossoming

Over the swamps
        a wild
magnolia bud—
        greenish
white
a northern
        flower—

And so
        we live
        looking—

At night
        it wakes
On the black
        sky—

a dream
        toward which
we love—
at night
        more
than a little
        false—

We have bred
we have dug
we have figured up
our costs
we have bought
an old rug—

We batter at our
unsatisfactory
     brilliance—

There is no end
    to desire—

Let us break
    through
and go there—

in
    vain!

—delectable
    amusement:

Milling about—

Money! in
armored trucks—
Two men
    walking
at two paces from
    each other
their right hands
    at the hip—
on the butt of
an automatic—

till they themselves
hold up the bank
and themselves
    drive off
for themselves
    the money
in an armored car—

    For love!

Carefully
        carefully tying
carefully

        selected
wisps of long
dark hair
        wisp
by wisp
upon the stubs
of his kinky wool—
For two hours
three hours
        they worked—
        until
he coiled
        the thick
knot upon
that whorish
        head—

Dragged
        insensible
upon his face
by the lines—

—a running horse

        For love.

Their eyes
        blown out—

—for love, for love!

Neither the rain
Nor the storm—
can keep them

        for love!

from the daily
accomplishment
    of their
appointed rounds—

Guzzling
the creamy foods
    while
out of sight
    in
the sub-cellar—
the waste fat
the old vegetables
    chucked down
a chute
    the foulest
sink in the world—

And go
on the out-tide
ten thousand
    cots
floating to sea
    like weed
that held back
the pristine ships—
And fattened there
an eel
in the water pipe—

    No end—

There!

    There!

There!

    —a dream
of lights
    hiding

the iron reason
          and stone
a settled
          cloud—

City

          whose stars
of matchless
          splendor—
          and
in bright-edged
          clouds
the moon—

          bring

silence

          breathlessly—

Tearful city
          on a summer's day
the hard grey
          dwindling
in a wall of
          rain—

          farewell!

POEMS
1936–1939

THE YOUNG CAT AND THE CHRYSANTHEMUMS

You mince, you start
advancing indirectly—
your tail upright
knocking about among the
frail, heavily flowered
sprays.

Yes, you are lovely
with your ingratiating
manners, sleek sides and
small white paws but
I wish you had not come
here.

PATERSON: EPISODE 17

Beat hell out of it
Beautiful Thing
spotless cap
and crossed white straps
over the dark rippled cloth—
Lift the stick
above that easy head
where you sit by the ivied
church, one arm
buttressing you
long fingers spread out
among the clear grass prongs—
and drive it down
Beautiful Thing
that your caressing body kiss
and kiss again
that holy lawn—

And again: obliquely—
legs curled under you as a
   deer's leaping—
pose of supreme indifference
   sacrament
to a summer's day
   Beautiful Thing
in the unearned suburbs
   then pause
   the arm fallen—
what memories
of what forgotten face
brooding upon that lily stem?

   The incredible
nose straight from the brow
   the empurpled lips
and dazzled half-sleepy eyes
   Beautiful Thing
of some trusting animal
   makes a temple
of its place of savage slaughter
   revealing
the damaged will incites still
   to violence
consummately beautiful thing
and falls about your resting
   shoulders—

Gently! Gently!
as in all things an opposite
   that awakes
the fury, conceiving
   knowledge
by way of despair that has
   no place
to lay its glossy head—
Save only—Not alone!
   Never, if possible
alone! to escape the accepted

chopping block
and a square hat!—

And as reverie gains and
    your joints loosen
    the trick's done!
Day is covered and we see you—
    but not alone!
drunk and bedraggled to release
the strictness of beauty
under a sky full of stars
    Beautiful Thing
and a slow moon—
                                    The car
    had stopped long since
    when the others
came and dragged those out
    who had you there
    indifferent
to whatever the anesthetic
    Beautiful Thing
might slum away the bars—

Reek of it!
    What does it matter?
    could set free
only the one thing—
But you!
—in your white lace dress
    "the dying swan"
and high heeled slippers—tall
as you already were—
    till your head
through fruitful exaggeration
was reaching the sky and the
prickles of its ecstasy
    Beautiful Thing!

And the guys from Paterson
    beat up

the guys from Newark and told
them to stay the hell out
of their territory and then
socked you one
   across the nose
   Beautiful Thing
for good luck and emphasis
   cracking it
till I must believe that all
desired women have had each
   in the end
   a busted nose
and live afterward marked up
   Beautiful Thing
   for memory's sake
to be credible in their deeds

Then back to the party!
   and they maled
and femaled you jealously
   Beautiful Thing
as if to discover when and
   by what miracle
there should escape what?
still to be possessed
out of what part
   Beautiful Thing
should it look?
   or be extinguished—
Three days in the same dress
   up and down—
   It would take
a Dominie to be patient
   Beautiful Thing
with you—

The stroke begins again—
   regularly
automatic
   contrapuntal to

the flogging
like the beat of famous lines
in the few excellent poems
   woven to make you
   gracious
and on frequent occasions
   foul drunk
   Beautiful Thing
pulse of release
   to the attentive
and obedient mind.

ADVENT OF TODAY

South wind
striking in—torn
spume—trees

inverted over trees
scudding low
a sea become winged

bringing today
out of yesterday
in bursts of rain—

a darkened presence
above
detail of October grasses

veiled at once
in a downpour—
conflicting rattle of

the rain against
the storm's slow majesty—
leaves

rising
instead of falling
the sun

coming and going
toward the
middle parts of the sky

THE GIRL

with big breasts
under a blue sweater

bareheaded—
crossing the street

reading a newspaper
stops, turns

and looks down
as though

she had seen a dime
on the pavement

CLASSIC SCENE

A power-house
in the shape of
a red brick chair
90 feet high

on the seat of which
sit the figures
of two metal
stacks—aluminum—

commanding an area
of squalid shacks
side by side—
from one of which

buff smoke
streams while under
a grey sky
the other remains

passive today—

THE SUN

lifts heavily
and cloud and sea
weigh upon the
unwaiting air—

Hasteless
the silence is
divided
by small waves

that wash away
night whose wave
is without
sound and gone—

Old categories
slacken
memoryless—
weed and shells where

in the night
a high tide left
its mark
and block of half

burned wood washed
clean—
The slovenly bearded
rocks hiss—

Obscene refuse
charms
this modern shore—
Listen!

it is a sea-snail
singing—
Relax, relent—
the sun has climbed

the sand is
drying—Lie
by the broken boat—
the eel-grass

bends
and is released
again—Go down, go
down past knowledge

shelly lace—
among the rot
of children
screaming

their delight—
logged
in the penetrable
nothingness

whose heavy body
opens
to their leaps
without a wound—

WIND OF THE VILLAGE

Seated above the dead
who are silent these two months
I kiss empty shoes
and grasp furiously
the heart's hand
and of the soul that supports it.
Let my voice lift to the mountains
and crash to the earth again in thunder
is my throat's supplication
from this day and forever.
Draw near to my clamor
village of the same milk as I,
tree that with its roots
holds me imprisoned,
for I am here myself to show my love
and here to defend you
with my blood as with word of mouth
that are as two faithful rifles.
If I was born of this earth,
if I have issued from a womb
wretched and impoverished,
it was only that I might be
the nightingale of misfortunes,
echo of evil luck,
to sing over and over
for those who must hear,
all that to poverty, all that to anguish,
all that to country is referred.
Yesterday the people wakened
naked and with nothing to wear,
hungry with nothing to eat,
and today has dawned
heavily tormented
bleeding in fact.
With guns in their hands
they wish themselves lions
to put an end to the savage beasts

who would ruin them as before.
Although you lack arms
village of ten times ten thousand powers
concede no rest to your bones,
punish those who dastardly wound you,
while you are possessed of fists,
nails, spit, and there lives in you
heart, guts,
a man's parts, and your teeth.
Brave as the wind is brave,
and light as the lightest airs,
kill those who would kill you,
hate him who hates
the peace of your hearts,
and the wombs of your women.
Don't let them wound you from behind
live face to face with them and die
with chests to the bullets
as broad as a wall.
I sing with the voice of a lute,
for your heroes, my own village,
your anguish one with my own,
your misfortunes that are made
of the same metal and weeping,
the same fiber
your thoughts and my own,
your heart and my blood,
your grief and the laurels which I bring
An outer buttress to nothingness
seems this life to me.
I am here to live but
while the soul lies sleeping,
and here to die
when my hour shall come,
in the bosom of my people,
from now on and forever.
Life is drunk over and over
and death is one swallow only.

AUTUMN

A stand of people
by an open

grave underneath
the heavy leaves

celebrates
the cut and fill

for the new road
where

an old man
on his knees

reaps a basket-
ful of

matted grasses for
his goats

AFRICA

Quit writing
and in Morocco
raise a beard

Go without a hat
like poor Clew
who braved

the desert heat.
Or if you will
like Herb

sit on a hotel
balcony and
watch your ship

while the girls
bring wines
and food

to you privately.
The language?
Make money.

Organize
The language.
Right.

WEASEL SNOUT

Staring she
kindles
the street windows

to daintiness—
Under
her driving looks

gems plainly
colored blue and
red and

green grow
fabulous again—She
is the modern marvel

the ray from
whose bulbous eyes
starts

through glass walls
to animate
dead things—

SHE WHO TURNS HER HEAD

She turns her head
to breathe the morning air
bright April on her
        pale face
and yellow hair

Hey look! they turn
from their horseplay
Look! reminiscent of the
        night
striking by day

As one who has come
from dancing
half naked under lights
        she plucks
her clothes about her
and fights to seem
indifferent before the
overpowering mastery
        of this
garish dream

THE TERM

A rumpled sheet
of brown paper
about the length

and apparent bulk
of a man was
rolling with the

wind slowly over
and over in
the street as

a car drove down
upon it and
crushed it to

the ground. Unlike
a man it rose
again rolling

with the wind over
and over to be as
it was before.

MAN AND NATURE

The roar and clatter
behind a cataclysmic beacon
crash by trailing
the shaken body.

The cat remains,
green eyes and dragging
tail under
the frozen street light.

THE POOR

It's the anarchy of poverty
delights me, the old

yellow wooden house indented
among the new brick tenements

Or a cast-iron balcony
with panels showing oak branches
in full leaf. It fits
the dress of the children

reflecting every stage and
custom of necessity—
Chimneys, roofs, fences of
wood and metal in an unfenced

age and enclosing next to
nothing at all: the old man
in a sweater and soft black
hat who sweeps the sidewalk—

his own ten feet of it—
in a wind that fitfully
turning his corner has
overwhelmed the entire city

BETWEEN WALLS

the back wings
of the

hospital where
nothing

will grow lie
cinders

in which shine
the broken

pieces of a green
bottle

A BASTARD PEACE

—where a heavy
woven-wire fence
topped with jagged ends, encloses
a long cinder-field by the river—

A concrete disposal tank at
one end, small wooden
pit-covers scattered about—above
sewer intakes, most probably—

Down the center's a service path
graced on one side by
a dandelion in bloom—and a white
butterfly—

The sun parches still
the parched grass. Along
the fence, blocked from the water
leans the washed-out street—

Three cracked houses—
a willow, two chickens, a
small boy, with a home-made push cart,
walking by, waving a whip—

Gid ap! No other traffic or
like to be.
There to rest, to improvise and
unbend! Through the fence

beyond the field and shining
water, 12 o'clock blows
but nobody goes
other than the kids from school—

LOVELY AD

All her charms
are bubbles
from a tilted
cigarette—

And look!
she sees
to light them
his face!

Whereas for us
his sleek
black hair
is hint enough.

THE DEFECTIVE RECORD

Cut the bank for the fill.
Dump sand
pumped out of the river
into the old swale

killing whatever was
there before—including
even the muskrats. Who did it?
There's the guy.

Him in the blue shirt and
turquoise skullcap.
Level it down
for him to build a house

on to build a
house on to build a house on
to build a house
on to build a house on to . . .

MIDDLE

of this profusion
a robin flies carrying
food on its tongue
and a flag

red white and
blue hangs
motionless. Return
from the sick

wean the mind
again from among
the foliage also of
infection. There

is a brass band at
the monument
and the children
that paraded

the blistering streets
are giving lustily
to the memory
of our war dead.

Remain and listen or
use up the time
perhaps
among the side streets

watching the elms
and rhododendrons the
peonies and
changeless laurels.

AT THE BAR

Hi, open up a dozen.

Wha'cha tryin' ta do—
charge ya batteries?

Make it two.

Easy girl!
You'll blow a fuse if
ya keep that up.

GRAPH FOR ACTION

Don't say, "humbly."
"Respectfully," yes
but not "humbly."

And the Committee
both farted
and that settled it.

BREAKFAST

Twenty sparrows
on

a scattered
turd:

Share and share
alike.

TO GREET A LETTER-CARRIER

Why'n't you bring me
a good letter? One with
lots of money in it.
I could make use of that.
Atta boy! Atta boy!

THESE

are the desolate, dark weeks
when nature in its barrenness
equals the stupidity of man.

The year plunges into night
and the heart plunges
lower than night

to an empty, windswept place
without sun, stars or moon
but a peculiar light as of thought

that spins a dark fire—
whirling upon itself until,
in the cold, it kindles

to make a man aware of nothing
that he knows, not loneliness
itself—Not a ghost but

would be embraced—emptiness,
despair—(They
whine and whistle) among

the flashes and booms of war;
houses of whose rooms
the cold is greater than can be thought,

the people gone that we loved,
the beds lying empty, the couches
damp, the chairs unused—

Hide it away somewhere
out of the mind, let it get roots
and grow, unrelated to jealous

ears and eyes—for itself.
In this mine they come to dig—all.
Is this the counterfoil to sweetest

music? The source of poetry that
seeing the clock stopped, says,
The clock has stopped

that ticked yesterday so well?
and hears the sound of lakewater
splashing—that is now stone.

MORNING

on the hill is cool! Even the dead
grass stems that start with the wind along
the crude board fence are less than harsh.

—a broken fringe of wooden and brick fronts
above the city, fading out,
beyond the watertank on stilts,
an isolated house or two here and there,
into the bare fields.

                    The sky is immensely
wide! No one about. The houses badly
numbered.

              Sun benches at the curb bespeak
another season, truncated poplars

that having served for shade
served also later for the fire. Rough
cobbles and abandoned car rails interrupted
by precipitous cross streets.

                              Down-hill
in the small, separate gardens (Keep out
you) bare fruit trees and among tangled
cords of unpruned grapevines low houses
showered by unobstructed light.

                              Pulley lines
to poles, on one a blue
and white tablecloth bellying easily.
Feather beds from windows and swathed in
old linoleum and burlap, fig trees. Barrels
over shrubs.

                              Level of
the hill, two old men walking and talking
come on together.

                              —Firewood, all lengths
and qualities stacked behind patched
out-houses. Uses for ashes.
And a church spire sketched on the sky,
of sheet-metal and open beams, to resemble
a church spire—

                              —These Wops are wise

                              —and walk about
absorbed among stray dogs and sparrows,
pigeons wheeling overhead, their
feces falling—

                        or shawled and jug in hand
beside a concrete wall down which,
from a loose water-pipe, a stain descends,
the wall descending also, holding up

a garden—On its side the pattern of
the boards that made the forms is still
discernible. —to the oil-streaked
highway—

   Whence, turn and look where,
at the crest, the shoulders of a man
are disappearing gradually below the worn
fox-fur of tattered grasses—

     And round again, the
two old men in caps crossing at
a gutter now, *Pago, Pago!* still absorbed.

—a young man's face staring
from a dirty window—Women's Hats—and
at the door a cat, with one fore-foot on
the top step, looks back—

      Scatubitch!

     Sacks of flour
piled inside the bakery window, their
paley trade-marks flattened to
the glass—

   And with a stick,
scratching within the littered field—
old plaster, bits of brick—to find what
coming? In God's name! Washed out, worn
out, scavengered and rescavengered—

Spirit of place rise from these ashes
repeating secretly an obscure refrain:

This is my house and here I live.
Here I was born and this is my office—

—passionately leans examining, stirring
with the stick, a child following.

Roots, salads? Medicinal, stomachic?
Of what sort? Abortifacient? To be dug,
split, submitted to the sun, brewed
cooled in a teacup and applied?

                     Kid Hot
Jock, in red paint, smeared along
the fence.—and still remains, of—
if and if, as the sun rises, rolls and
comes again.

          But every day, every day
she goes and kneels—

              died of tuberculosis
when he came back from the war, nobody
else in our family ever had it except a
baby once after that—

                   alone on the cold
floor beside the candled altar, stifled
weeping—and moans for his lost
departed soul the tears falling
and wiped away, turbid with her grime.

Covered, swaddled, pinched and saved
shrivelled, broken—to be rewetted and
used again.

POROUS

    Cattail fluff
    blows in
    at the bank door,

    and on wings
    of chance
    the money floats out,

lighter than a dream,
through the heavy walls
and vanishes.

THE HALFWORLD

Desperate young man
with haggard face
and flapping pants—

As best they can
under the street lights
the shadows are

wrapping you about—
in your fatigue
and isolation, in all

the beauty of your
commonplace against
the incestuous

and leaning stars—

THE HARD LISTENER

The powerless emperor
makes himself dull
writing poems in a garden
while his armies
kill and burn. But we,
in poverty lacking love,
keep some relation
to the truth of man's
infelicity: say
the late flowers, unspoiled

by insects and waiting
only for the cold.

THE RETURN TO WORK

Promenading their
skirted galleons of sex,
the two office assistants

rock unevenly
together
down the broad stairs,

one
(as I follow slowly
in the trade wind

of my admiration)
gently
slapping her thighs.

THE LAST WORDS OF MY ENGLISH GRANDMOTHER

There were some dirty plates
and a glass of milk
beside her on a small table
near the rank, disheveled bed—

Wrinkled and nearly blind
she lay and snored
rousing with anger in her tones
to cry for food,

Gimme something to eat—
They're starving me—

I'm all right I won't go
to the hospital. No, no, no

Give me something to eat
Let me take you
to the hospital, I said
and after you are well

you can do as you please.
She smiled, Yes
you do what you please first
then I can do what I please—

Oh, oh, oh! she cried
as the ambulance men lifted
her to the stretcher—
Is this what you call

making me comfortable?
By now her mind was clear—
Oh you think you're smart
you young people,

she said, but I'll tell you
you don't know anything.
Then we started.
On the way

we passed a long row
of elms. She looked at them
awhile out of
the ambulance window and said,

What are all those
fuzzy-looking things out there?
Trees? Well, I'm tired
of them and rolled her head away.

Appendix A: A Note on the Text

In ordering the poems for this edition we have retained the integrity of Williams' individual volumes with the exception of the collected volumes of 1934, 1938, 1950, and 1951. Poems that appear only in these collections, and all uncollected poems, are arranged by date of first publication. The only exceptions to this chronological arrangement (apart from posthumously published works) are seven poems first published many years after they were written: "Martin and Katherine," "Misericordia," "Min Schleppner," "For Viola: De Gustibus," "The Drunkard," "Impromptu: The Suckers," and "The Young Cat and the Chrysanthemums." They are printed under their dates of composition. The sequence "Della Primavera Trasportata al Morale" presents a special problem. These poems were part of a prose/poetry composition, a sequel to *The Descent of Winter*, that Williams drafted in 1928. A truncated version of the sequence was published in 1930, but all the poems were not gathered together until 1938. We have preserved the integrity of the final sequence and printed it under 1930.

We have used the text of the 1951 *Collected Earlier Poems* for the poems included in that volume, since this was the last printing of these poems that Williams supervised; but we have eliminated the numerous errors in the 1951 text caused by the circumstances of its preparation. Williams prepared the 1951 text for the printer in two stages. The first was a combination of retyped poems and pasted-up poems from earlier printings that followed the sequence of the 1938 *Complete Collected Poems* (catalogued in Yale University's Beinecke Library as Williams Za49). In all, 60% of the poems were pasted in. Most of the pasted-up versions came from the *Complete Collected Poems*, but Williams occasionally used an alternative printed text. His correspondence makes clear that these alternatives were not chosen for textual reasons, but because they were more easily available or prevented the cutting-up of rare editions. In the case of some of the *Spring and All* poems, for example, Williams preferred to cut up the 1923 *Go Go* text rather than the more valuable *Spring and All* volume.

Williams did not do the typing himself. This task was undertaken by Kathleen Hoagland, a friend and fellow writer who lived at 131 Ridge Road—about half a mile from the Williams home at No. 9. Because of this close proximity, no correspondence (short of a brief hand-written note) appears to have taken place between author and typist concerning the preparation of typescripts for *Collected Earlier Poems* or the other two volumes being readied almost simultaneously, *Collected Later Poems* and the *Autobiography*.

The Za49 arrangement contains many corrections in Williams' hand on the typescript, and a small number of changes on the pasted-up poems. Kitty Hoagland then incorporated most of these changes into her retyping of the complete text. The carbons of this retyped version are catalogued at the Beinecke Library as Za50, and contain no corrections.

If Williams read over this retyped script (Za50) he did so in cursory fashion, not noticing that the typist had missed a small number of corrections marked in Za49 and had introduced a large number of new errors. The originals of the Za50 carbons have disappeared, but it is certain that they formed the copy-text for the printing of *Collected Earlier Poems*, since many of the errors introduced in Za50 found their way into the 1951 volume. Only obvious spelling errors were corrected, probably by the New Directions copy editor. For example: Za50's "Mezo" for "Mezzo" in the title of "Mezzo Forte" was caught, but not "offsprings" for "offspring" in the third line of "Mujer," or the erroneous "the" between "for" and "rest" in the next line of the poem.

A number of factors prevented Williams (never a scrupulous proofreader) from giving close attention to the final typescript of *Collected Earlier Poems*. At this time (1950 and early 1951) he was negotiating with a new publisher, Random House, and working not only on *Collected Earlier Poems* but on *Collected Later Poems*, the *Autobiography*, *Paterson IV*, and *Make Light of It*. He also undertook in the fall of 1950 a pressurized teaching and lecturing tour of the West Coast. This heavy work load undoubtedly contributed to the stroke in March 1951 that incapacitated Williams during the last months before the publication of *Collected Earlier Poems* (December 1951).

In addition to the distractions of work and illness, another factor that may have kept Williams from a close reading of the final typescript was his concern for the new "arrangement" of the volume (see the Preface to this edition for further details). The Za49 and Za50 scripts both follow the organization of the 1938 *Complete Collected Poems*. Williams' "hell of a good idea" for the new arrangement probably occurred after he returned the corrected Za49 to the typist for retyping. While leaving the Za50 carbons in their original order, he almost certainly experimented with reordering the originals, giving more attention to organization than to a close reading of the typescript.

Williams' experience with the *Collected Later Poems* a few months earlier should have alerted him to the need for carefully checking the work of his typist. That volume first appeared missing ten poems that the typist had failed to return with the final typescript. In the *Collected Earlier Poems* no poems disappeared between the Za49 and Za50 versions, but a page containing the last two stanzas of "Middle" was evidently lost and the poem was printed in truncated form.

Whenever our collation for this edition revealed differences between the 1951 text and the 1938 *Complete Collected Poems*, we examined Za49 and Za50 to discover whether the changes had Williams' sanction (i.e. were present in Za49) or whether they were introduced by the Za50 retyping. The changes introduced into the 1951 text by Za49 and Za50 form two distinct kinds: while Williams' own changes on Za49 are in the direction of concreteness, concision, and increased reading speed, the Za50 errors weaken his intent through such changes as the omission of deliberately repeated pronouns and the substitution of the indefinite for the definite article. We have accepted all changes introduced into the 1951 text by Za49 except for a small number of obvious errors that Williams failed to note, but we have not accepted changes introduced by Za50. In a handful of poems we have corrected obvious errors that derive from the 1938 or earlier printings.

Most of the poems in *Collected Earlier Poems* that did not appear in *Complete Collected Poems* were set up from typescripts now catalogued at the Beinecke Library as Za196 and Za197. As with Za49 and Za50, these poems were retyped from typescripts corrected by Williams, and some of the final scripts contain errors that subsequently appeared in print. In using these typescripts we have followed the same principles as those described for Za49 and Za50. For poems not found in *Collected Earlier Poems* or *Complete Collected Poems*, we have turned to sources such as the *Poetry* and *Little Review* files for confirmation of the text.

In his corrections of the Za49 typescript Williams gave his typist only sporadic help in the matter of stanza breaks within poems. Our collation revealed that in the printing of *Complete Collected Poems* stanza breaks were sometimes erroneously introduced after lines that had appeared at the bottom of the page in earlier printings. However, typescripts and previous printings, and the patterning of the poem itself, often showed that in such cases the end of a page should not have been treated as the end of a stanza. In a few poems, an end-of-page stanza break in an earlier printing is ignored in *Complete Collected Poems*.

Errors of this kind are not common in *Complete Collected Poems*, but the peculiar circumstances surrounding the production of *Collected Earlier Poems* led to many more instances in the 1951 text. In preparing the Za49 script the typist received little guidance as to whether a stanza ended at the bottom of a page or continued on to the next; and in retyping from the corrected typescript she had to make more such decisions, as did the New Directions copy editor and the compositor. Not surprisingly, many poems opened up or closed in random fashion, making Williams' stanzaic patterns seem arbitrary— whereas his usual practice from early on in his career was to be highly inventive in his use of stanzaic forms from poem to poem, but to be consistent in the stanzaic patterning within each poem. We have restored the intended spacing on the evidence of early typescripts, previous printings, and the typescripts at the Beinecke Library.

Neither Williams nor his publishers gave much attention to line runovers. *Complete Collected Poems* usually reproduces the lineation of earlier book printings, the Za49 and Za50 typescripts follow this, and consequently so does *Collected Earlier Poems*. The result in the 1951 volume is an inconsistent treatment of line lengths. Lines in *The Tempers, Al Que Quiere!*, and *Sour Grapes* were frequently run over, these books being small in format, while the larger page sizes of subsequent volumes permitted longer line lengths. As with the issue of erroneous spacing within stanzas, an examination of the various printings, earlier typescripts, and Williams' developing poetic practice has helped us to determine when he intended a new line and when an early runover has been reproduced throughout successive printings. In this edition we have avoided runovers as much as possible, but where a line is a runover it is indented a standard paragraph indent from the left. All other indentations are part of Williams' design for his poems.

Where a poem differs substantially between an early and a final version, and where the printings are separated by a number of years, we have printed each version in its chronological place. Where two very different versions appeared in print closer in time, we have usually reprinted the earlier version in the notes. Five poems in *An Early Martyr* and one in *Adam & Eve & The City* differ very little from their first publication years before, and we have printed them only once under the dates of their first appearances.

In 1957 John C. Thirlwall published sixty-three "Lost Poems of William Carlos Williams" in *New Directions 16*. Most of these poems had been previously published, although not collected; but twelve had never before been published. We have not given this collection the authority of a later printing because of the numerous errors in transcription and Williams' minimal involvement with the project. Williams' correspondence with James Laughlin makes it clear that the work of selecting, arranging, and transcribing the texts was entirely Thirlwall's—although Williams was delighted to see so many poems "inadvertently omitted from my past volumes" in print (WCW to James Laughlin, 4 Dec. 1956; Yale Za 295). In making this edition we have returned to the earlier periodical publications of these poems, and have noted the very few substantial variants between periodical appearance and *New Directions 16* that are not the result of mistranscription. None of the poems first published in *New Directions 16* appears in this volume, although Thirlwall assigned dates in the 1930s to several of them. Manuscript and stylistic evidence clearly shows that these dates are too early, and the poems will be included in Volume II.

In preparing this edition we collated every known printing of each poem, and examined typescript and manuscript materials wherever possible. In general, Williams revised most heavily between first periodical and book publication. As he wrote to Louis Zukofsky on 29 April 1931: "My only excuse is that most modern work is written to be printed and cannot be considered to exist until it is so" (Humanities Research Center, University of Texas). The textual notes in Appendix B record all verbal variants between printings—with the exception of the categories listed below—and lineation changes of major interest. However, limitations of space and the complexity of recording multiple variants in lineation and format have made it impossible to record all changes between printings or all corrections to the text. We have not noted the following kinds of variants and corrections unless they seem to have important critical significance:

1) changes in punctuation.
2) changes in lineation or in runovers.
3) changes of spacing within stanzas.
4) changes in the positioning of a line (see the note on "Rain").
5) verbal variants in anthology printings with which Williams had no connection.
6) spelling variants.
7) changes in hyphenation between printings (We have retained the hyphenations of the 1951 text).
8) obvious typographical, printing, and transcription errors.

Because of the irregular line structures in many of WCW's poems, it is often difficult to tell whether the end of a page marks the close of a stanza or verse paragraph. In this edition the following pages end with a break:

16   25   36   41   48   53   63   64   72   74   75   76   87   90

94   95   96   107   111   115   123   138   141   146   160   171   190   191

195   196   200   204   205   212   215   217   218   221   222   226   227   228

233   239   242   243   248   251   255   256   257   260   266   269   271   273

279   286   287   291   292   299   304   305   308   322   323   324   325   326

327   328   330   332   333   335   336   337   340   343   344   345   347   348

349   353   355   357   358   359   360   361   362   363   364   365   366   367

369   370   379   380   382   384   385   386   388   389   391   401   405   406

416   418   419   426   427   430   431   432   433   434   439   443   444   445

449   450   451   458   462

Appendix B: Annotations

In addition to a record of significant verbal changes in the published versions of the poems, we have provided a number of explanatory notes drawn from both published and unpublished sources. We have not aimed at a "complete" annotation, and have excluded matters of general cultural knowledge that can be found in standard dictionaries or the *Encyclopedia Britannica.*

We have not repeated most of the bibliographical information concerning first and subsequent printings that can be found in Emily Wallace's *A Bibliography of William Carlos Williams,* and have tried to make the necessary citations as concise as possible. We have, however, given full bibliographical information for publications not listed in Wallace, and have indicated the sources for all poems not included in *The Collected Earlier Poems* and *The Collected Later Poems* (these are marked by an asterisk).

Since it is sometimes difficult to identify a poetic "line" in Williams' work, we have counted each printed line in giving references by line numbers.

The following abbreviations are used in the annotations:

A   *The Autobiography of William Carlos Williams* (1951)

AQQ   *Al Que Quiere!* (1917)

BUFFALO   Neil Baldwin and Steven L. Meyers, *The Manuscripts and Letters of William Carlos Williams in the Poetry Collection of the Lockwood Memorial Library, State University of New York at Buffalo: A Descriptive Catalogue* (1978)

CCP   *The Complete Collected Poems* (1938)

CEP   *The Collected Earlier Poems* (1951)

CLP   *The Collected Later Poems* (1950)

CP1934   *Collected Poems, 1921-1931* (1934)

IWWP   *I Wanted to Write a Poem: The Autobiography of the Works of a Poet,* ed. Edith Heal (1958)

MARIANI   Paul Mariani, *William Carlos Williams: A New World Naked* (1981)

ND16   John C. Thirlwall, "The Lost Poems of William Carlos Williams," *New Directions 16* (1957)

SE   *Selected Essays of William Carlos Williams* (1954)

SG   *Sour Grapes* (1921)

SL   *Selected Letters of William Carlos Williams,* ed. John C. Thirlwall (1957)

SP   *Selected Poems* (1949)

T   John C. Thirlwall's annotated copy of *The Collected Earlier Poems.* In the late 1950s Thirlwall went through most of CEP with Williams and transcribed in the margins, often in a form of personal shorthand, WCW's comments on individual poems and on his poetic principles. We have drawn heavily from this new source (only a few of the entries have been previously published, in *Interviews with William Carlos Williams*, ed. Linda Welshimer Wagner [New Directions, 1976]). The reader should keep in mind that in these comments—as in the *Autobiography*—Williams is not always accurate in his factual recollections, and that he is viewing his earlier work from the perspective of the late poems, especially *Paterson V*.

WALLACE   Emily Mitchell Wallace, *A Bibliography of William Carlos Williams* (1968)

WCWR   *William Carlos Williams Review* (before 1980 the *William Carlos Williams Newsletter*)

YALE   The Williams archive at the Beinecke Rare Book and Manuscript Library, Yale University

THE TEMPERS (1913)

Dedication: "To Carlos Hoheb." WCW's mother, born Elena Hoheb, cherished the memory of her brother Carlos, who had practiced medicine in Puerto Rico and Haiti. She wished her older son William to carry on the tradition.

PEACE ON EARTH   When this poem was submitted to *Poetry* (Chicago), where it appeared in June 1913, the editor Harriet Monroe insisted that the names of the constellations be capitalized, and WCW consented. "Why doubt that the reader will see the stars in 'Peace on Earth,' when you saw them? Yet to capitalize as you suggest is good: please do so" (WCW to HM, 5 March 1913; SL 24). For WCW's subsequent problems with the house style of *Poetry* see the note on "Spirit of '76," p. 491.

"Just making a berceuse that would hold together, using material that I knew" (T).

POSTLUDE   "One of the first poems that ever impressed me with my ability. Rarefied atmosphere of the Pre-Raphaelite Brotherhood. This was my idea of what the classics were" (T). "Influence of Keats and Yeats, Dowson" (T).

15   you there / you're there (*New Freewoman*, Sept. 1913; *The Glebe*, Feb. 1914; *Des Imagistes* [1914]).

18   "breasts" underscored in T with the marginal comment: "attracted and repelled by sex."

24-26   Omitted in *Poetry* (June 1913), *The Tempers*, and *Profile* (1932); restored in CCP. "Omitted in *Poetry* at Harriet Monroe's suggestion" (T).

FIRST PRAISE   "I was always building it up and conscious of this falseness. I should have written about things around me, but I didn't know how. I was unhappy because I wasn't doing what I wanted. I was just on the verge of saying right, but I couldn't get it out. I knew nothing of language except what I'd heard in Keats or the Pre-Raphaelite Brotherhood" (T).

2   my Lady   WCW's fiancée Florence (Floss) Herman. In the first stanza he

is recalling a stay with Floss and her family in the summer of 1910 at Cooks Falls on the Beaver Kill in southern New York (T). See A129.

5   brown / grey   (*The Tempers*, CCP)

HOMAGE   "Elvira" was Elvira Stolt, "a friend of the Hermans, a romantic woman, a Hedda Gabler. I fell for her to the extent of writing a poem. This is Pound, pure Pound. Floss and Mrs. Herman hated her" (T).

5   Candles / As candles   (*The Poetry Review*, Oct. 1912)
15-16   Which leadeth from love
          Has no passers.   (*Poetry Review*)

THE FOOL'S SONG   "This came from my fumbling reading of Philosophy—Herbert Spencer in particular. A little touch of Kant" (T).

FROM "THE BIRTH OF VENUS," SONG   "The shore at West Haven [Connecticut]. I was patting the little girls and getting hot as hell" (T).

IMMORTAL   "Addressed to Viola Baxter" (T). In 1907 Ezra Pound introduced WCW to Viola Baxter, an attractive young woman interested in the arts whom he had met while at Hamilton College. To WCW she represented New York sophistication, and WCW maintained a flirtatious relationship with her during the years of his engagement and even after his marriage in 1912. She was married to Virgil Jordan in 1914.

Title: "Proof of Immortality"   (*Poetry*, June 1913)
1   Yes, there / For there   (*Poetry*)

MEZZO FORTE   "Imagination of Grace Smith, a tough baby, who married Dickinson" (T). Grace Smith went to school with Florence Herman (later Mrs. W. C. Williams) and married Fairleigh Dickinson, Sr., one of the founders of the Becton-Dickinson surgical products company.

CRUDE LAMENT   "Mother" is glossed "R. H. R." (T). WCW's mother was christened Raquel Hélène Rose Hoheb.

THE ORDEAL   "Band of poets more or less isolated—fraternity led by E. P. [Ezra Pound]" (T).

THE DEATH OF FRANCO OF COLOGNE: HIS PROPHECY OF BEETHOVEN   Franco was the "inventor of musical notation." "From my German reading. We were bound to invent new poetry as he the scale. I was searching for something beyond rime. And I found free verse in Whitman in *Leaves of Grass*, given to me by Floss in March 1913. I've always had the feeling that good things happen to me in March" (T).

PORTENT   "I was predicting my own wonderful future. I was the dusky child who was going to show 'em" (T).

CON BRIO "This I always liked because I was just beginning to find my way around, to say what I wanted—written without changing a word" (T).

AD INFINITUM "For Viola [Baxter]" (T).

*TRANSLATIONS FROM THE SPANISH, "EL ROMANCERO" "Romancero" is Spanish for a ballad, usually anonymous. WCW translated from the second volume of a four-volume collection, *Poesías Selectas Castellanas*, Recogidas y Ordenadas por D. Manuel Josef Quintana, Nueva Edición, Madrid 1817. This volume was given to WCW by Ezra Pound (IWWP 16-17 and Wallace 38-39); volumes III and IV remained with Pound and are now in the Ezra Pound Library at the University of Texas.
The first lines in Spanish are:
I. Although you do your best to regard me ("Aunque con semblante ayrado")
II. Ah, little green eyes ("Ay ojuelos verdes")
III. Poplars of the meadow ("Álamos del prado"). Compare the later translation of this poem in *Adam & Eve & The City*, p. 429.
IV. The day draweth nearer ("El alba nos mira"). Compare the later translation in *Adam & Eve*, p. 427.

HIC JACET "E. P. [who arranged for publication of *The Tempers*] thought this the best of all" (T). Pound included the poem in *Profile* (1932).

CONTEMPORANIA Probably a response to Pound's "Contemporania" series (*Poetry*, April 1913), especially "Salutation the Second," where Pound speaks of having "just come from the country."

POEMS 1909-1917

*THE USES OF POETRY First published in *Poems* (1909). Reprinted as "The Uses of Poetry (for H. D.)" in ND16.

*LOVE *Poems* (1909). Reprinted in Reed Whittemore, *William Carlos Williams: Poet from Jersey* (1975), p. 50.

*ON A PROPOSED TRIP SOUTH *Poems* (1909). Reprinted in Whittemore, p. 51.

*AND THUS WITH ALL PRAISE First published in Linda Wagner, *The Poems of William Carlos Williams* (1964), p. 76. In the Buffalo archive this poem and the following one are grouped with three unpublished poems under the heading "Poems—1910-1912" (Buffalo A254).

*MARTIN AND KATHERINE First printed in *The Little Review* (Spring-Summer 1926) with "Misericordia" as "Two Fugitive Poems (1910)" in the "Interests of 1926" sequence. In ND16 it is titled "The Wartburg," and on a Library of Congress recording "Sonnet: 1909" (Wallace F2). At Buffalo it is also dated 1909 (A254, A379) and listed as "1909/The Wartburg" in some arrangements for WCW's 1944 collection *The Wedge* (D6).

At this time WCW was fascinated by the life of Martin Luther, and especially by Luther's decision to marry a former nun, Katherina von Bora, "to spite the devil." At one time he even thought of writing a play called *Luther at Wittenberg—1526.* In Dec. 1909 he visited the ruins of the convent at Grimma where Katherina had lived before her marriage to Luther in 1525, and in March 1910 he stayed at Wartburg and visited the castle where in 1521 Luther began his German translation of the New Testament (A 110; Mariani 84-85, 99-100).

*MISERICORDIA First published with "Martin and Katherine" in *The Little Review* (Spring-Summer 1926) as "Two Fugitive Poems (1910)" in the "Interests of 1926" sequence. In *The Little Review* the poem "The gayest of bright flowers" (see p. 259) was erroneously printed as part of this sonnet.

In "Misericordia" Katherina von Bora may be addressing her new "Master," Luther.

*MIN SCHLEPPNER First published in *The Massachusetts Review* (Winter 1962) with the note: "This poem was recently called to WCW's attention by his brother, the architect Edgar I. Williams, to whom he sent it in 1910. Written in Leipzig, it shows Williams still using conventional rhyme."

*I WILL SING A JOYOUS SONG First published without a title as a Lockwood Memorial Library Christmas Broadside (1974) and reprinted in WCWR, 1 (Fall 1975) with a background note by Emily Wallace. The "occasion" for the poem was a reconciliation between WCW and his fiancée, Florence Herman.

*FOR VIOLA: DE GUSTIBUS First printed in *Selected Letters* as part of a May 1912 letter from WCW to Viola Baxter (see note on Viola Baxter, p. 474). The title is taken from a typescript at Yale (Za197), where the poem is slightly different:

> Viola you are
> Caviar of caviar!
> Of all I love you best,
> Oh my Japanese bird's nest!
> No herring from Norway
> Can touch you for savor! nay
> Pimiento itself
> Is flat as an empty shelf
> Compared to your piquantsy
> Oh quince of my despondency!

*A MAN TO A WOMAN *The Poetry Review* (Oct. 1912).

*IN SAN MARCO, VENEZIA *The Poetry Review* (Oct. 1912).

SICILIAN EMIGRANT'S SONG Subtitled: "In New York Harbor" (*Poetry,* June 1913).
3 "I passed through Palermo in 1910" (T).

*ON FIRST OPENING *The Lyric Year* First published in *Poetry* (June 1913) in the "Correspondence" section. In July 1912 WCW met Ferdinand Earle, who would later marry Florence Herman's sister Charlotte (to whom WCW was greatly attracted). Earle was editor of an annual collection *The Lyric Year,* which he described in the preface as "a selection from one year's work of a hundred American poets. . . . Ten thousand poems by nearly two thousand writers of verse have been personally examined by the Editor for this competition." Earle solicited some of WCW's poems for the 1912 volume, but a month later told him that the "other editors" had rejected them (Mariani 100-101).

*THE WANDERER: A ROCOCO STUDY First version published in *The Egoist* (March 1914). For the later version included in CEP see pp. 108-117. WCW's comments on the poem are given in the annotations to the later version.

*AT DAWN The first poem of a nine-poem sequence called "Invocations" (*The Egoist,* March 1914) which includes "At Dawn," "Rendezvous," "Gulls," "To the Outer World," "La Flor," "Offering," "A La Lune," "In Harbor," "The Revelation." "Gulls," "In Harbor," and "The Revelation" appear in CEP.

*RENDEZVOUS *The Egoist* (March 1914).

*TO THE OUTER WORLD *The Egoist* (March 1914).

*LA FLOR *The Egoist* (March 1914). Dedication "for E. P." added in ND16. The poem alludes to Ezra Pound's "An Immorality" (1912) which begins: "Sing we for love and idleness, / Naught else is worth the having."

*OFFERING *The Egoist* (March 1914).

*A LA LUNE *The Egoist* (March 1914).

THE REVELATION The following version published in *The Egoist* (March 1914) contains five additional lines and differs in other ways from the version in CP1934, CCP, and CEP.

> I awoke happy, the house
> Was strange, voices
> Were across a gap
> Through which a girl
> Came and paused,

Reaching out to me
With never a word.

Then I remembered
What I had dreamed:
A beautiful girl
Whom I know well
Leaned on the door of my car
And stroked my hand
While her soul
Streamed up to me
From her quiet eyes.

I shall pass her on the street,
We will say trivial things
To each other,
But I shall never cease
To search her eyes
For that quiet look
Henceforth.

WCW's retrospective comment in the 1950s: "I saw an old woman on the street the other day and something emanated from her to me. I am still looking in every face for that rare combination. 'That's for me.' It's always a woman. It may be a man, since there's no sex. The essence of art—Demuth, Sheeler" (T).

TRANSITIONAL First published in *The Egoist* (Dec. 1914). "My definition of what the poet's attitude to the world should be. Not philosophical, not practical, but poetic—a view of life" (T).
  9   of the / O' the   (*Egoist*)
  11   befits / fits   (*Egoist*)

*INVITATION   *The Egoist* (Dec. 1914).

*AUX IMAGISTES   *The Egoist* (Dec. 1914). Ezra Pound published his "A Few Don'ts by an Imagiste" in *Poetry* (March 1913), and the anthology *Des Imagistes* (which included WCW's "Postlude") appeared in March 1914.

*PEACE   *The Egoist* (Dec. 1914).

*PASTORALS AND SELF-PORTRAITS   From a typescript filed with a letter from WCW to Viola Baxter Jordan of 24 Dec. 1914 (Yale ZaJordan). This sequence was first published in Rod Townley, *The Early Poetry of William Carlos Williams* (1975), pp. 177-185. "Grotesque" was previously published by Mike Weaver in *William Carlos Williams: The American Background* (1971).
  For a later version of PASTORAL 1. see p. 70.

*slow movement   *Poetry* (May 1915). Dedication "(for E. P.)" in ND16. Before they were regularized by *Poetry* the last two lines read:

> merely faint and sleepy
> as they are now.

*a confidence   *Poetry* (May 1915).

*metric figure (veils of clarity)   *Others* (Feb. 1916).

*epigramme   *Others* (Feb. 1916).

*stillness   *Others: An Anthology of the New Verse* (1916).

a love song: first version, 1915   First titled "Love Song" (*Poetry*, Nov. 1916), then "A Love Song, First Version: 1915" (*The Broken Span* [1941]), and later "First Version: 1915" (CEP). In CEP this poem is placed immediately before the later version from *Al Que Quiere!* (see p. 107).

"I thought it verbose and wanted to cut it down to its essentials. It was as good a love poem as I could write to Flossie—But I was always repulsed by her. She was never passionately loving. I was completely devoted to her" (T).

*naked (what fool would feel)   *Poetry* (Nov. 1916).

*marriage   *Poetry* (Nov. 1916).

*the old worshipper   *Poetry* (Nov. 1916). Dedication "(for Jim Hyslop)" in ND16. James A. Hyslop, WCW's close boyhood friend (A 19-24), later became a distinguished entomologist.

the young housewife   "Whenever a man sees a beautiful woman it's an occasion for poetry—compensating beauty with beauty" (T).

spring song (having died)   "One of my despairing moods, which I inherited from my mother, who was always depressed and disillusioned with life. I wanted to be sentimental and sorry for myself—literary despair. I was impressed by myself in my despairs" (T). Of "The Shadow" (p. 50), which follows this poem in CEP, WCW commented: "The same mood. I was romantically sorry for myself. I wanted to be poetic: the structure is very regular, perhaps in the mood of Algernon Charles Swinburne or Christina Rossetti. But I was unhappy with it" (T).

9   there is something / there is
                   something   (*Others*, Dec. 1916)

In its early printings the poem is divided between lines 4-5 only. The division into four stanzas in CCP and CEP is an example of WCW's tendency toward regularity in his post-1920s poetry.

*NIGHT   *The Poetry Journal* (Dec. 1916).

*SICK AFRICAN   *The Masses* (Jan. 1917).

*CHINESE NIGHTINGALE   *The Masses* (Jan. 1917). Sam Wu is the Wu Kee of
"The Young Laundryman" (p. 122).

AL QUE QUIERE! (1917)

WCW first translated the title as "To him who wants it" in a letter to Mari-
anne Moore of 21 Feb. 1917 (SL 40):
"I want to call my book:

A Book of Poems:

AL QUE QUIERE!

—which means: To him who wants
it—but I like the Spanish just as I like a Chinese image cut out of stone: it
is decorative and has a certain integral charm. But such a title is not demo-
cratic—does not truly represent the contents of the book, so I have added:

A Book of Poems:

AL QUE QUIERE!

or

THE PLEASURES OF DEMOCRACY.

Now I like this conglomerate title! It is nearly a perfect image of my
own grinning mug (seen from the inside), but my publisher objects—and
I shake and wobble."

The book was published as simply *Al Que Quiere!*
The dustjacket of the 1917 edition has this statement: "To Whom It May
Concern! This book is a collection of poems by William Carlos Williams. You,
gentle reader, will probably not like it, because it is brutally powerful and
scornfully crude. Fortunately, neither the author nor the publisher care much
whether you like it or not. The author has done his work, and if you *do* read
the book you will agree that he doesn't give a damn for your opinion. . . .
And we, the publishers, don't much care whether you buy the book or not.
It only costs a dollar, so that we can't make much profit out of it. But we
have the satisfaction of offering that which will outweigh, in spite of its eighty
small pages, a dozen volumes of pretty lyrics. We have the profound satis-
faction of publishing a book in which, we venture to predict, the poets of
the future will dig for material as the poets of today dig in Whitman's *Leaves
of Grass*."
Al Que Quiere! has an epigraph taken from *El hombre que parecia un
caballo* (1915), a story by the well-known Guatemalan writer Rafael Arévalo

Martínez. WCW's translation of the story, made with the help of his father, was published in *The Little Review* (Dec. 1918) under the title "The Man Who Resembled a Horse." Following are the corrected text of the epigraph and WCW's translation.

"Había sido un arbusto desmedrado que prolonga sus filamentos hasta encontrar el humus necesario en una tierra nueva. Y cómo me nutría! Me nutría con la beatitud con que las hojas trémulas de clorofila se extienden al sol; con la beatitud con que una raíz encuentra un cadáver en descomposición; con la beatitud con que los convalecientes dan sus pasos vacilantes en las mañanas de primavera, bañadas de luz; . . ."

"I had been an adventurous shrub which prolongs its filaments until it finds the necessary humus in new earth. And how I fed! I fed with the joy of tremulous leaves of chlorafile that spread themselves to the sun; with the joy with which a root encounters a decomposing corpse; with the joy with which convalescents take their vacillating steps in the light-flooded mornings of spring; . . ."

SUB TERRA   "I saw a bunch of kids from the Union School leaping around a dead dog. The children were cheered by the spectacle and like a bunch of Indian kids jumping around a bear the hunters had brought in" (T).
    18   *that* will / *that* shall (AQQ, CCP). Italicization and change to "will" indicated on corrected typescript (Yale Za49). CEP omits the italicization.

    21-22   Oh, I have you!
          Yes, you are about me in a sense   (*Poetry*, May 1915)

    31-32   You I want, my companions!
          God! if I could only fathom   (*Poetry*)

PASTORAL (WHEN I WAS YOUNGER)   "Unconsciously I was playing with the form of the line, and getting into the American idiom" (T).

CHICORY AND DAISIES   "I liked this because of the elimination of the inessential in the composition. I cut it down and down and down. To use immediate images, the visual image which moved me—and then to cut down. This is squeezed up to make it vivid" (T).
In *Rogue* (June 1915) the poem is titled "Lyric," is not divided into sections, and has the following variants:

    14-20   Cool,
          Luxuriant,
          Sky blue!
          The earth cracks and shrivels up
          The wind moans piteously
          The sky goes out
          If you should fail.
            Reflect.

METRIC FIGURE (THERE IS A BIRD)   "If I had written conventionally I might have got it in the *Atlantic*. I couldn't write conventionally, but I was not a good enough critic to analyze the difference. I was not accepted in the magazines because of my revolt against the English tradition" (T).

7 Phoebus! / Phoenix!   (*Poetry*, May 1915)

*WOMAN WALKING   First version in *The Egoist* (Dec. 1914) has no stanza breaks, and other variants.

4 [omitted in *The Egoist*]

8-11 To the left, a single tree;
      To the right, jutting in,
      A dark crimson corner of roof.
      God knows I'm tired of it all.
      And God knows what a blessing it is   (*Egoist*)

20 a different / different   (*Egoist*)
24 brows / eye sockets   (*Egoist*)

GULLS   In 1958 WCW recalled that the poem was written in 1912, before the move to 9 Ridge Road (T). "I was always very conscious of my townspeople—having no official philosophy of my own I had to invent one. Living across from the Episcopal Church I was very conscious of the old connection. On Sunday I used to hear the responses and my blood boiled when I heard the general confession. I didn't feel like a sinner and they didn't mean it" (T).

18 Easter, it was / It was Easter   (*The Egoist*, Aug. 1914, where the poem is untitled).

"It was a beautiful day and I was conscious that I was looked on askance for not conforming. It is a religious poem" (T).

APPEAL   In Thirlwall's copy of CEP line 13 is glossed "E. P." [Ezra Pound].

IN HARBOR   "H. D. [Hilda Doolittle] liked this—a triple rhythm anapaestic. I was still a kid" (T).

3-4 Go out timid child and snuggle in
     Among the great ships, talking so quietly.
         (*Catholic Anthology* [1915])

6 lifted / Raised   (*The Egoist*, Aug. 1914)
11-18 It is a quiet sound—
       Rest! That's all I care for now.
       The smell of them will put us presently to sleep.
       Smell them! It is the sea water mingling here
           into the river—
       Perhaps it is something else—but what matter?

       The sea water! It is smooth and quiet here!
       And they move slowly, little by little trying

> The hawsers that drip and groan with their agony.
> And it is certainly of the high seas that they
>   are talking.   (*The Egoist*)

17   drop / drip   (*Catholic Anthology*)

WINTER SUNSET   "The hopeless feeling that comes over me on a winter day. That is why I'm a poet setting poetry against a hopeless nature. I'm a pessimist and I must hike myself up by my bootstraps. My mother was a moody person and her moods affected me" (T).

PASTORAL (THE LITTLE SPARROWS)   See the earlier version on p. 42.
14   Meanwhile, / Then again,   (*Others*, Aug. 1915; *Others: An Anthology* [1916]).

M. B.   The poem is about Maxwell Bodenheim, a fellow contributor to *Others*, who stayed for a while in a "borrowed room" at WCW's home, 9 Ridge Road, Rutherford (T; IWWP 19).
11   a sparkling lady / a lady in white   (*The Poetry Journal*, Dec. 1916).

TRACT   "I'm tired of everything I wrote in these formative years. I was always searching for a regular format of the line, just as I wanted to be regular in my life—to conform. But I thought my friends were damn fools, because they didn't know any better way of conducting their lives. Still they conformed better than I to a code. I wanted to conform but I couldn't so I wrote my poetry" (T).
The 135 lines of this poem's earliest versions (*Others*, Feb. 1916, and *Others: An Anthology* [1916]) are consolidated to 70 lines in AQQ, CCP and CEP (eleven lines were omitted altogether). In the *Al Que Quiere!* version breaks within lines reflect the earlier lineation. Thus the first eleven lines in *Others* (Feb. 1916):

> I will teach you
> my townspeople
> how to perform
> a funeral—
> for you have it
> over a troop
> of artists—
> unless one should
> scour the world—
> you have the ground sense
> necessary.

become in AQQ:

> I will teach you   my townspeople
> how to perform   a funeral—
> for you have it   over a troop

> of artists—
> unless one should   scour the world—
> you have the ground sense   necessary.

This spacing disappears in CCP.

44   had come / had to come   (*Others; Others: An Anthology*)
46   though / tho'   (*Others; Others: An Anthology*)
68   pockets. / pocket—   (*Others; Others: An Anthology*)

Between lines 68 and 69 the *Others* texts have:

> remember that, and
> this:
> there is one land—
> and your two feet
> are sucked down
> so hard on it that
> you cannot raise them—
> where men are
> truly equal
> for they all have
> nothing.

PROMENADE   This poem "is about Billy, my son, when he was first born" (IWWP 23).

EL HOMBRE   See Wallace Stevens' "interpretation" of this poem, "Nuances of a Theme by Williams."

3   Shine / shining   (*Others*, Dec. 1916).
4   toward which you lend
     no part.   (*Others; Others: An Anthology* [1917]).

HERO   "I could face whatever was necessary, but I didn't go looking for it—like Odysseus" (T).

3-4   "Anything that drives men to face the perils of nature. Argonauts. All men want to leave the confinement of the home—to *War*" (T).

CANTHARA   The poem concerns "Spanish fly and the legend about it" (IWWP 24). *Cantharides:* a preparation of powdered Spanish fly, thought to be an aphrodisiac.

MUJER   " 'Mujer'—our wonderful Mother Kitty. . . . The last line in the poem will tell you our constant Mother Kitty predicament" (IWWP 24-25).

3   offspring / offsprings   (CEP)
4   for rest / for the rest   (CEP) We have restored these two readings which occur in all earlier printings and in the corrected typescript for CEP (Yale Za49).

SUMMER SONG (WANDERER MOON)   The following early version was published in *Poetry*, Nov. 1916; note the *Poetry* house-style of initial indentation and capitalization at the start of each line. Thirlwall inserted the last three lines from *Poetry* into his copy of CEP and WCW commented: "Trite omit."

> Wanderer moon,
> Smiling
> A faintly ironical smile
> At this brilliant,
> Dew-moistened
> Summer morning—
> A detached,
> Sleepily indifferent
> Smile,
> A wanderer's smile—
> If I should
> Buy a shirt
> Your color, and
> Put on a necktie
> Sky-blue,
> Where would they carry me?
> Over the hills and
> Far away?
> Where would they carry me?

LOVE SONG (SWEEP THE HOUSE CLEAN)   "Conscious of the presence of Floss, my girl" (T).

*FOREIGN   This poem appears only in AQQ. It must have been their shared interest in sexual theorizing, together with their mixed racial origins, that led WCW to compare himself with the Russian writer Mikhail Artsybashev: see Christopher MacGowan, *William Carlos Williams's Early Poetry: The Visual Arts Background* (1984), p. 50.

A PRELUDE   The setting is the "shore of Savin Rock [at West Haven, Conn.], the environment I loved" (T).
   Title: "New Prelude" (*Others*, Dec. 1916; *Others: An Anthology* [1917]).

HISTORY   WCW called this poem a "continuation of the mood of 'March'" (T); "March" is printed immediately before "History" in CEP. The setting is the Metropolitan Museum of Art in New York City. In 1913 the Museum acquired the late Egyptian sarcophagus of Uresh-nofer, who was a priest of the goddess Mut. On the cover of the sarcophagus is the figure of the sky-goddess Nut. See "A Late Egyptian Sarcophagus," *Bulletin of the Metropolitan Museum of Art*, Vol. IX (1914).
   When "History" was published in *Poetry* (July 1917) the editor Harriet Monroe insisted upon omitting sections 1, 2 and 5—exempting only lines 23-25. Williams agreed under protest: "It offends my sense of completeness to have you wish to remove parts of poems for reasons that are to me so trivial that they are positively ridiculous yet beggars must not be choosers: I have few opportunities to print my work—the truth is out!" (WCW to Harriet

Monroe, 25 May 1917; *Poetry* Magazine Papers, 1912-1935, Box 40 Folder 26-28, Department of Special Collections, University of Chicago Library; hereafter referred to as *Poetry* Archive, University of Chicago). In the *Poetry* version lines 23-25 become section I, section 3 becomes II, and section 4 becomes III.

14   wind belched / belched wind   (AQQ)

15   delicately / deliberately   (CEP) "Delicately" is the reading of AQQ and the corrected typescript (Yale Za196); correction also found in T.

24   priest / priestess   (*Poetry*, AQQ)

41   priest / priestess   (AQQ)

48   shall / will   (AQQ)

54   priest / priestess
        his / her   (*Poetry*, AQQ)

55   his / her   (*Poetry*, AQQ)

56   over flesh / over the flesh   (CEP) We have restored the reading of all previous printings and the corrected typescript (Yale Za196).

70   Omitted in *Poetry*, AQQ.

78   face / country   (*Poetry*)

85-86   Lay / the finger upon this granite   Not in *Poetry* (not included in the typescript sent to *Poetry*).

102-103   We have restored the lineation of all printings before CEP and the corrected typescript (Yale Za196).

GOOD NIGHT   "Trying to describe what was going on as accurately and rhythmically as possible. Yet not in the Tennysonian poetic form. Not the girls of Provence but those of my own time and place" (T).

25   sound / sounds   (CEP) We have restored the reading of all previous printings and the corrected typescript (Yale Za49).

32   my / a   (CEP) We have restored the reading of all previous printings and the corrected typescript (Yale Za49).

DANSE RUSSE   Diaghilev, Nijinsky, and the Ballets Russes were in New York in 1916.

1   If I when / If when   (CEP) Error in retyping of the corrected typescript (Yale Za49).

2   "Kathleen" was the nursemaid of the Williams children for nearly five years. See the note on "K. McB." (p. 489).

8   dance / danced   *Others: An Anthology* [1917])
        danse   (AQQ)

10   round / around   (*Others*, Dec. 1916; *Others: An Anthology*).

PORTRAIT OF A WOMAN IN BED   Although late in life WCW sometimes claimed to have read this poem at the 1913 Armory Show (e.g. T, A 136), he actually read it and "Overture to a Dance of Locomotives" (p. 146) at the 1917 Independents exhibition. The poem's speaker, Mrs. Robitza, is also the main character in WCW's play "The Comic Life of Elia Brobitza," published in *Others* (April-May 1919).

In his comments to Thirlwall WCW says that the poem is his "idea of what happened" when Mrs. Robitza, "a Polish woman, cook of the Castle," confronted the "overseer of the poor, Mr. Dunne," who was trying to evict her from her house. "I wanted to throw her in the face of the town. The whores are better than my townspeople" (T).

4 shirt / skirt (*Others*, Dec. 1916; *Profile* [1932]).

10-11 For these two lines *Profile* substitutes "ha!" Ezra Pound, who edited *Profile*, may have censored the lines.

13 got Omitted in *Others, Profile.*

21 it's high! "forehead" (T).

22 brains and blood / blood and brains (*Others*)

37 is / was (*Others*)

38 isn't / wasn't (*Others*)

48 county / country (CEP) We have restored the reading of all previous printings and the corrected typescript (Yale Za49).

VIRTUE "*Virtue* is personified in *Paterson* V, in the virgin and to have a baby" (T). For WCW's sexual theories see his reply to Dora Marsden, "The Great Sex Spiral," *The Egoist* (April and Aug. 1917); and Mike Weaver, *William Carlos Williams: The American Background* (1971), pp. 23-29.

*PORTRAIT OF A YOUNG MAN WITH A BAD HEART Appears only in AQQ.

KELLER GEGEN DOM "Consciousness of loss of religion after the example of Matthew Arnold" (T). WCW may possibly have had in mind Auerbach's Keller in Leipzig, the setting for Scene V of the First Part of Goethe's *Faust.*

8 opens / opening (*Others*, Dec. 1916)

SMELL! "The alertness of senses is one of my themes from the beginning. I was keen for any sensation—sensuous, of all the senses. I didn't want to drink because it might dull my senses" (T).

1 Oh / O (*Poetry*, July 1917)

7 deep / deep a (*Poetry*)

8 We quicken our desires, O nose of mine, (*Poetry*)

BALLET "I was too much influenced by Imagistic technique. When I look at what the boys and girls of our day are doing, I don't know whether I like it or not. The reader must infer from the vividness of the image the meaning" (T).

SYMPATHETIC PORTRAIT OF A CHILD

Title: *Touché* (*Others*, Feb. 1916; *Others: An Anthology* [1916]).

17 best as she / best she (*Others, Others: An Anthology*, CEP) We have restored the AQQ and CCP reading because the source of CEP's change is the uncorrected typescript (Yale Za50).

THE OGRE "I was sympathetic with her but had to be careful. Compare this with 'The Use of Force' [WCW's short story] with its rape suggestion" (T).

8   This / But this   (*Others*, Aug. 1915; *Others: An Anthology* [1916]).

RIPOSTE   "For E. P. I was a fencer" (T). WCW, like Ezra Pound, had been a fencer at the U. of Pennsylvania. Pound's 1912 collection of poetry is titled *Ripostes*.

"The lines fell entirely by my ear. Whether it came out 4 or 5 lines made no difference to me. I was learning, but I knew I wouldn't be regular" (T).

THE OLD MEN   "I had the idea that old age would quiet sexual passion, and beauty take its place. Art is more important than sex" (T).

12-15   over young men and even
over dark-faced husbands
whose minds are a street
with arc-lights,   (*Others*, Dec. 1916)

SPRING STRAINS   WCW said the poem was based on his 1909 experiences in Germany: "I used to climb the Torn all by myself jumping from crag to crag" (T).

2-3   We have preferred the form as in *Others*, Dec. 1916; *Others: An Anthology* [1917]; and AQQ. In CCP these lines are printed as one, apparently interpreting "the sky" in AQQ as a run-on, and this form is repeated in SP and CEP.

TREES   "Oak tree in back yard" (T).

In the Poetry Collection of the U. of Buffalo there is a parody of Joyce Kilmer's "Trees" (1913) which may date from around this time; it was first published by Emily Wallace in *William Carlos Williams: Papers by Kenneth Burke, Emily Mitchell Wallace, Norman Holmes Pearson, A. M. Sullivan*, ed. Charles Angoff (1974), p. 28.

Trees

Of all the things that I could be
I had to be a lousy tree,

A tree that stands out in the street
With little dogs around my feet.

I'm nothing else but this, alas,
A comfort station in the grass.

I lift my leafy arms to pray,
Get away, little doggie, get away!

A nest of robins I must wear
And what they do gets in my hair.

Of all the things I had to be
I had to be a goddam tree.

A PORTRAIT IN GREYS   WCW indicated that the poem was about his wife: "longer lines to give the contemplative effect of quiet. Regret that we were not excited by the same things" (T). In the poetry of this period "grey" seems to be associated with Florence Williams.

3   backward / backwards   (CEP) Error in retyping the corrected typescript (Yale Za49).

*INVITATION (YOU WHO HAD THE SENSE)   First published in AQQ.

*DIVERTIMIENTO   Appears only in AQQ.

JANUARY MORNING   By section XV, line 2 ("old woman") WCW noted "Mother" (T).
"Park Avenue" (section XV) is a street in Rutherford near WCW's home.

TO A SOLITARY DISCIPLE   Apparently WCW had no one in mind: "I was sure there'd be only *one*, if that many" (T).
34   of morning / of the morning   (*Others*, Feb. 1916; *Others: An Anthology* [1916]).

DEDICATION FOR A PLOT OF GROUND   For information on WCW's grandmother, Emily Dickinson [or Dickenson] Wellcome, see Mariani and "The Last Words of My English Grandmother" (pp. 253 and 464). The "plot of ground" is evidently her house and land at West Haven in Connecticut (T).
4   Dickinson / Richardson   (AQQ)

K. MCB.   Titled "K. McD." in *Others*, Dec. 1916. Kathleen McBride or Kathleen McDonnell (WCW uses both names) was the young girl from the state orphanage who was the nursemaid for the Williams boys during World War I. Later WCW got her a job at the Babies' Hospital.
4   in April! / April!   (CEP) We have restored the reading of all previous printings and the corrected typescript (Za49).

LOVE SONG (I LIE HERE THINKING OF YOU)   See earlier version, p. 53. On 1 March 1916 WCW wrote to Harriet Monroe of *Poetry* magazine: "It would be a long story to tell you how I came to change the version of the rotten 'Love Song' to what it was in my last. For the present suffice it to say that whichever version you like best will satisfy me also. The point is that technically I am only interested in the two main stanzas but of course, left by themselves, they make a bare looking whole. The 'rugged beginning' though it is more than half rhetoric makes a better impression" [*Poetry* Archive, University of Chicago]. Harriet Monroe printed the earlier version, itself a condensation of a version previously forwarded to *Poetry* by Ezra Pound.
16-17   "I was thinking of [Charles] Demuth's picture of the sky over the horizon" (T).

THE WANDERER   See first version from *The Egoist* (March 1914), pp. 27-36. "*The Wanderer*, featuring my grandmother [Emily Dickinson Wellcome], the river, the Passaic River . . . my first 'long' poem, which in turn led to *Pater-son*" (A 60-61). For a more extended comment by WCW on "The Wanderer" see *Interviews with William Carlos Williams*, ed. Linda Welshimer Wagner (1976), p. 76.

49   is   Omitted in *Catholic Anthology* (1915), AQQ.

83   *live* / live   (CEP) We have restored the reading of all previous print-ings and the corrected typescript (Yale Za49).

Section title: THE STRIKE / PATERSON—THE STRIKE (*Catholic Anthol-ogy*, AQQ, CCP, SP). In 1913 Paterson, N. J., was torn apart by a strike of the silk workers, whose jobs were threatened by new machines. The "ruling classes" relied on force to suppress the strike, which figures in Book III of *Paterson*.

145   where / were   (*Catholic Anthology*, AQQ)

Section Title: ST. JAMES' GROVE   Santiago Grove in Rutherford, N. J., near the Passaic River.

309   spoke / She spoke   (*Catholic Anthology*)

320   to you remembering / to rememb'ring   (*Catholic Anthology*)

POEMS 1918-1921

*LOVE SONG (HE: YOU HAVE COME BETWEEN ME)   *The Little Review* (June 1918).

8   The single printing in *The Little Review* has: "I have spread my arms out with wide feeling you about me." We have omitted "with" to make sense of the line.

LE MÉDECIN MALGRÉ LUI   Title of a Molière comedy based on a fable about a woodcutter who, to avoid a beating, pretends he is a doctor.

6   Build shelves in
    The little laboratory;   (*Poetry*, July 1918)

23-24   And the cleaner's
        And grew a decent beard   (*Poetry*)

THE YOUNG LAUNDRYMAN   This poem is part of an eighteen-poem sequence, "Broken Windows," published in *Poetry* (March 1919). Fourteen of the poems appear in *Sour Grapes*, thirteen of them together, but not in the "Broken Win-dows" order. In a letter to Harriet Monroe of 23 Nov. 1918 WCW says that the order of the sequence is "immaterial," but that it should start with "Berket and the Stars" and end with "Man in a Room" (*Poetry* Archive, U. of Chi-cago).

5   heels / heel   (*Poetry*, March 1919)

*STROLLER   *Poetry* (March 1919).

MAN IN A ROOM   "Always stuck in my crop as a compressed way of writ-ing—intended to be a sonnet, but I was revolting against the discipline of a sonnet" (T).

A CORONAL

2   New books and / New and   (*The Little Review*, Jan. 1920)
5   bow / blow   (CEP) "Bow" is in all earlier printings and in the corrected typescript for CEP (Yale Za49).
10   her / our   (*Little Review*)
14   her mouth rounded and cresses   (*Little Review*)

TO MARK ANTHONY IN HEAVEN

19-21   above the battle's fury
         reflecting—
         clouds and trees and grass
         for then
         you are listening in heaven.   (*The Little Review*, Jan. 1920).

*IT IS A SMALL PLANT   Untitled as part of a seven-poem sequence "Flowers of August" published in *Others for 1919* (1920) which includes: I. Daisy, II. Queenannslace, III. It is a small plant, IV. Healall, V. Great Mullen, VI. Butterandeggs, VII. Thistle. Poems I, II, and V appear in *Sour Grapes*.

*HEALALL   *Others for 1919* (1920).

*BUTTERANDEGGS   *Others for 1919* (1920).

*THISTLE   *Others for 1919* (1920).

*SPIRIT OF '76   This letter to Harriet Monroe appeared in *Poetry* (June 1920). Williams' first published poem in which the lines do not begin with capital letters (unless they are the beginnings of sentences) is "Metric Figure (Veils of clarity)" in *Others* (Feb. 1916). From then onward this strategy is an integral part of his poetics. But from "A Love Song: First Version, 1915," sent to *Poetry* in Feb. 1916, through the "Broken Windows" sequence (*Poetry*, Feb. 1919), Harriet Monroe insisted upon printing WCW's poems with capitalization at the beginning of each line. WCW's letters to her from 1916 to 1919 frequently attack this practice, although he accepted "the silly custom" on sufferance in order to get his work in print. On 9 Sept. 1918 he lodged a typical protest: "As to capitals, do as you please but by putting a capital at the beginning of each line against the plain rules of grammar you will always mar the effect of the poem" (*Poetry* Archive, University of Chicago).

WCW's next poem in *Poetry* after "Spirit of '76" was "A Goodnight" (Jan. 1921), which appeared with the lower-case line openings unaltered.

When in these early years WCW reprinted poems that had appeared in *Poetry* he restored the original punctuation—as with the fourteen poems of the "Broken Windows" sequence in *Sour Grapes*. However, when "Man in a Room" was reprinted for the first time in CP1934 WCW allowed the capital letters to stand, as he did with "To Be Closely Written . . . ," "The Young Laundryman," and "A Love Song: First Version, 1915" when they were reprinted in CEP. We have accepted the *Poetry* format for these poems because WCW did. We have also retained the initial capital letters in three other poems that were printed in *Poetry* after Feb. 1916 but were not included in CEP—"Naked," "Marriage," and "The Old Worshipper"—because no type-script is extant in the *Poetry* files. In these poems we have, however, ignored the *Poetry* house-style of indenting the first lines of stanzas, as we have in two of the pre-1916 *Poetry* texts, "Slow Movement" and "A Confidence."

PORTRAIT OF A LADY   The painting WCW has in mind is Fragonard's "The Swing." Although they differ greatly in style and motive, Fragonard and Watteau were often linked together in popular writing on art in the early twentieth century.

In the first printing in *The Dial* (Aug. 1920) these two lines appear after line 21:

> —the petals from some hidden
> appletree—Which shore?

*MARIANNE MOORE   *Contact* (Dec. 1920).

*ST. FRANCIS EINSTEIN OF THE DAFFODILS   See the later version on p. 414. This version appeared in *Contact* (Summer 1921) as a "sample poem" beneath the following statement:

ANNOUNCEMENT AND SAMPLE POEM.

Henceforth the writings of William Carlos Williams will be offered for sale at prices fixed by the author. Prospective purchasers will apply through CON-TACT which at present is the sole agent. A minimum price of fifty dollars will be charged for all poems, those of most excellence, as in all commercial ex-change, being rated higher in price. Critical essays, imaginative prose and plays will be offered at prices varying according to the length and success of the work. The artist will however continue to contribute his work gratis to what-ever publication, in his own opinion, furthers the interests of good writing in the United States.

In this issue WCW also offered a "Sample Prose Piece" and a "Sample Criti-cal Statement" as part of his attack on commercialism in literature.

*TO THE SHADE OF PO CHÜ-I, THE CATS' MONTH, DAYBREAK   These three poems were sent to *The Little Review* ca. 1920 as part of a sequence of six poems that also included "Winter Trees" (*The Dial*, Jan. 1921) and "Complaint" and "The Cold Night" (*Sour Grapes*). They were discovered by Dennis M. Read in the *Little Review* files at the Golda Meir Library, University of Wisconsin-Milwau-kee, and published in *American Literature*, 58 (1986). We have reproduced the spacing and punctuation of WCW's typescript as an example of what his early poems looked like before they were subjected to the house-styles of various magazines.

SOUR GRAPES (1921)

Dedication: To Alfred Kreymborg. The dedication is partly ironic, since WCW's close friendship with Kreymborg formed during the heyday of the magazine *Others* had begun to sour by 1921 (see IWWP 31-32).

"Sour Grapes are to a painter as attractive as any other grape, whereas the world would think I wasn't getting what I wanted. So I turned it round in my mind and said, 'To hell with you!' " (T).

THE LATE SINGER
4   with the black / with black   (*The Egoist,* July 1919)
11   hangs / floats   (*The Egoist*)

MARCH   WCW submitted a much longer version of this poem to *The Egoist,* where it appeared in Oct. 1916 after extensive pruning by Hilda Doolittle (who had taken over the post of assistant editor from her husband Richard Aldington after he joined the army). WCW included the letter from H. D. justifying these cuts in his "Prologue" to *Kora in Hell* (dated 1 Sept. 1918). It reads in part:

14 Aug. 1916
Dear Bill:—
  I trust you will not hate me for wanting to delete from your poem all the flippancies. The reason I want to do this is that the beautiful lines are so very beautiful—so in the tone and spirit of your *Postlude*—(which to me stands, a Nike, supreme among your poems). I think there is *real* beauty—and real beauty is a rare and sacred thing in this generation—in all the pyramid, Ashurban-i-pal bits and in the Fiesole and in the wind at the very last. . . . I feel in the hey-ding-ding touch running through your poem a derivative tendency which, to me, is not *you*—not your very self. . . .   [*Imaginations,* pp. 12-13]

H.D.'s deletions, to judge from a typescript at Buffalo (A195), were more extensive than the cuts in the final printed version. Many of the excised lines make explicit the implicit theme of the poem: that in previous springtimes artists created new works permanently expressive of their "March," and that the modern poet must break conventions to do the same. The longer version contains an "Interlude" between sections III and IV that details some of the constraints under which the modern poet writes.

Interlude

Now my cheeks are on fire—
    now my mind is whirling!
Here's my feet to kiss, you
        cold winds!
Take them if you want to.

> Yes, blow—sneak in, you common
>   dirt-winds!
> Blow, you miserable senators!
> Blow, you pot-bellied congressmen!
> Blow, you deadly preachers
>   of the gospel!
> You can chill my feet
> but my cheeks are aflame
>   above you.

And elsewhere the longer version refers to "flowers / thronging / thicker than the Germans through Brussels!"

The original version also enlists Herrick and Synge as members of the pantheon celebrated in the poem, whereas the published version links the poet's task explicitly to that of visual artists. The "hey-ding-ding touch" that H. D. found derivative, and that WCW defends in his "Prologue," is most evident in this passage which follows the present line 8 and closes the first section of the uncut version.

> Precarious pretty flowers of
>   spring
> then hey-ding-a-ding!
> God damn winter the more heartily.
> I'm your companion! Then since
> neither of us need shine alone
> —now that we have me—why,
>
>   Hey-ding-a-ling!
> Winter has lost his sting
>   his sting!
> (one might equally well say
>   his stink!
> but we've spoilt that first
> fine stanza sufficiently)
>
> And so—my song
> let's gather rose-buds while
>   we may
> (Herrick, what an exquisite old
> preacher-pagan you were, I salute you
> in passing)
> let's gather rose-buds while
>   we may
> and this song—this rose-bud
> is for the month of March.

In the "Prologue" to *Kora in Hell* WCW used this editorial interference as an occasion for proclaiming "I'll write whatever I damn please, whenever I damn please and as I damn please," but he eventually accepted the validity of H. D.'s criticisms. In Thirlwall's copy of CEP this excised passage is copied in with the gloss: "Influenced by Palgrave's *Golden Treasury* cf. T. Nashe" (Thomas Nashe's "Spring," with its refrain "Cuckoo, jug-jug, pu-we, to-witta-woo!," is the first poem in Francis Palgrave's famous anthology). Although WCW marked "Stet" by many of the excised passages in the Buffalo typescript, "March" in *Sour Grapes* and subsequent printings follows *The Egoist* with the exception of minor changes in spacing and punctuation.

18-19   band of young poets   The *Others* poets of the artists' colony at Grantwood, N. J. (T).

Section III   Although WCW annotates this "Metropolitan Museum" (T), he probably has in mind the Assyrian relief in the British Museum showing Ashurbanipal slaying a lion.

45ff. "I was conscious of a renascence of learning in the U. S. A." (T).

Section IV "Visit with Ed" (T). WCW and his brother Edgar visited Florence and Fiesole in March 1910. The Fra Angelico Annunciation is not in Fiesole but in the convent of San Marco, Florence.

84   But! now for / But now! now for   (*Egoist*)

86   springtime   "Dawn of new renascence—publication of poetry—*Des Imagistes*" (T).

108   cold fellows!   "Villon's ink freezing in the pot . . . I was reading Villon in French" (T).

BERKET AND THE STARS   "Story told me by my mother. When her Carlos [WCW's uncle] was a medical student in Paris" (T).

4   the vender /a vendor   (CEP) We have restored the reading of all previous printings and the corrected typescript (Yale Za49).

A CELEBRATION   "Same gal as in 'Romance Moderne'—extension" (T).

12   the Palace   Grand Central Palace on Lexington Avenue, where the Society of Independents exhibition took place in 1917 (see "Overture to a Dance of Locomotives").

35   odd / old   (CEP)

36   of a violet / of violet   (CEP)

44   Rafael Arévalo Martínez   See the epigraph to *Al Que Quiere!* (p. 480).

47   my side so / my side for so   (CEP) In lines 35, 36, and 47 we have restored the reading of all previous printings and the corrected typescript (Yale Za49).

52   branch / spray   (*The Egoist*, May 1918)

APRIL (IF YOU HAD COME AWAY WITH ME)
First published in *The Egoist* (Dec. 1919) as:

CHICAGO

If you will come away with me
into another state
we can be quiet together.
But here the sun coming up

> out of the nothing beyond the lake is
> too low in the sky,
> there is too great a pushing
> against him,
> too much of sumac buds, pink
> in the head
> with the clear gum upon them,
> too many opening hearts of
> lilac leaves,
> too many, too many swollen,
> limp poplar tassels on the
> bare branches!
> It is too strong in the air.
> I have no rest against this
> springtime!
> The pounding of the hoofs on the
> raw sods
> stays with me half through the night.
> I awake smiling but tired.

The "here" (l. 4) of this version shifts to "there" in later printings, and the tense from present and future to past. This first version seems to have been written during or shortly after WCW's visit to Chicago in spring 1919, where he lectured on poetry (see "Notes from a Talk on Poetry," *Poetry* [July 1919]) and had a brief affair with Marion Strobel, the associate editor of *Poetry* (Mariani 159). In his comments to Thirlwall WCW linked this poem with "A Goodnight" and "The Late Singer" as "Chicago" poems.

A GOODNIGHT   Written for Marion Strobel, the associate editor of *Poetry* magazine (A 161).
   Title: "A Good Night" (CEP)
   44   At table / At the table   (CEP) We have restored this reading and the title, which are in all printings prior to CEP and in the corrected typescript (Yale Za49).

OVERTURE TO A DANCE OF LOCOMOTIVES   "Pennsylvania Station" (T). WCW read this "futurist" poem and "Portrait of a Woman in Bed" at the Independents exhibition of avant-garde art that opened at the Grand Central Palace in April 1917.
   In *Sour Grapes* the poem is divided into two sections, I (lines 1-20) and II (lines 21-44). In CCP the sections are combined and the II eliminated. The I remained in all printings through CEP; we have removed it.
   18   disaccordant / discordant   (CEP) We have restored the reading of all previous printings and the Yale typescripts.

ROMANCE MODERNE   The poet is flirting with a young woman in the back seat of an automobile, while her husband and the poet's wife are seated in front. The poem ends with a quarrel between the poet and his wife. "I wanted to be free and attached at the same time" (T).

17   This line is preceded in *Others* (Feb. 1919) by: "Huge sliding surfaces clatter by."

71   woman? / woman.   (CEP) We have restored the reading of all previous printings and the corrected typescript (Yale Za49).

THE DESOLATE FIELD   "Tribute to Floss Williams" (T).
10   —and my heart stops amazed (*The Dial*, Aug. 1920)

APPROACH OF WINTER
8-9   and fall where the hard
        carmine of the salvias—   (*The Dial*, Jan. 1921)
11   edge / edges   (*The Dial*)

BLIZZARD
1   Snow: / Snow falls: (*The Dial*, Aug. 1920)
14   track / tracks   (CEP) We have restored the reading of all earlier printings and the corrected typescript (Yale Za49).

TO WAKEN AN OLD LADY
17   by a / with a   (*The Dial*, Aug. 1920)

SPRING STORM
9   But water, water is seething   (*The Dial*, Aug. 1920)

*THE DELICACIES   First published in *The Egoist* (Oct. 1917). "For some reason I included a short prose piece called 'The Delicacies'—an impression of beautiful food at a party, image after image piled up, an impression in rhythmic prose" (IWWP 35).

TIME THE HANGMAN
1   Abner, poor old / Abner, old   (SG) Abner was a black man who drove for Doc Hollister, a local family doctor.
5   kill / choke   (*Poetry*, March 1919)

TO A FRIEND   "Lizzie Anderson" was a local black girl whose illegitimate baby was delivered by WCW. She may be the subject of *Kora in Hell* XVI. 2 [*Imaginations*, p. 61].
Title: "A Friend of Mine" (*Poetry*, March 1919)
5-6   Does one with a little two-pointed smile
        Change the law—pouff!—into a mouthful of
            phrases? (*Poetry*)

THE SOUGHING WIND
1   some fall / and some fall   (*Poetry*, March 1919; *Anthology of Magazine Verse for 1919* [1919])

2   frost—so goes / frost goes   (*Anthology*)

PLAY   "Imitating E. P. [Ezra Pound]" (T).

LINES
1   greygreen / grey green   (CEP) We have restored the reading in SG, CCP, and the corrected typescript (Yale Za49).

COMPLETE DESTRUCTION
4   match / fire   (SG)

DAISY   The printing in *Others for 1919* [1920] concludes with two additional lines:

> The sun has shortened his desire
> to a petal's span!

PRIMROSE   "Close observation—trying to sum up what I saw. A true imagistic poem. Written at the shore in Connecticut" (T).

QUEEN-ANNE'S-LACE   "Flossie again" (T).
Title: "Queenannslace" and "Queen-Ann's-Lace" in other printings.
6   raise / rise   (*Others for 1919* [1920])

GREAT MULLEN   In Thirlwall's copy of CEP "grey" in the last line is underscored and annotated: "Fight with Floss." See the note on "A Portrait in Greys," p. 489.
8   Ha! / Ha, ha   (*Others for 1919* [1920])
         Ha, ha!   (SG, CCP, SP) Change made on the corrected typescript for CEP (Yale Za49).

WAITING
13   children as dear / children dear   (*The Little Review*, Jan. 1920)

ARRIVAL
8   The tawdry / That tawdry   (SP)

TO A FRIEND CONCERNING SEVERAL LADIES   "I was always experimenting with the line. I had reached no final method. Everything had a validity for me" (T).
39   behind. / behind?   (CEP) We have restored the reading of the earlier printings and the corrected typescript (Yale Za49).

THE DISPUTANTS
1   bowl / bowl!   (CEP) We have restored the reading of the earlier printings and the corrected typescript (Yale Za49).

THE TULIP BED   "I was very conscious of the Impressionists' use of color— Monet, Manet were very alive to me" (T).

THE NIGHTINGALES   In *Sour Grapes* the poem is printed without a stanza break and with an additional line, so that 4-5 read:

> flat worsted flowers
> under my feet.

In IWWP (66) WCW recalled "writing several poems as quatrains at first, then in the normal process of concentrating the poem, getting rid of redundancies in the line—and in the attempt to make it go faster—the quatrain changed into a three line stanza, or a five line stanza became a quatrain, as in [the revised version of "The Nightingales"]. "See how much better it conforms to the page, how much better it looks?"

BLUEFLAGS   "Bill and Paul [WCW's sons]" (T).

THE WIDOW'S LAMENT IN SPRINGTIME   "My imagination of what mother would be thinking" (T).
   12   load / loaded   (SP)
   19   turn / turned   (CEP, *Perspectives USA* [Fall 1952])
In these two instances we have restored the original readings in all printings through CCP, which fit the syntax of the poem.

LIGHT HEARTED WILLIAM
   Title: "Lighthearted William" (CEP)
   1   Light hearted / Lighthearted   (CEP) In both these cases we have restored the reading of earlier printings and the corrected typescript (Yale Za49).

PORTRAIT OF THE AUTHOR   "I didn't like this, crumpled it up and threw it in the waste basket. Bob McAlmon fished it out and told me it was one of my best. But I thought it artificial" (T).
   16   O my brother   "Everyman" (T).
   31   is the madness / is madness   (*Contact,* Spring 1921)
   40-41   that splits comfort, crushes my house   (*Contact*)

THE LONELY STREET   First published in the magazine of the Rutherford High School, *The Rutherfordian* (March 1921), along with a half-facetious letter claiming that the poem will be an antidote to the poetic styles and subjects usually found in the magazine.

THE GREAT FIGURE   "Once on a hot July day coming back exhausted from the Post Graduate Clinic, I dropped in as I sometimes did at Marsden [Hartley's] studio on Fifteenth Street for a talk, a little drink maybe and to see what he was doing. As I approached his number I heard a great clatter of bells and the roar of a fire engine passing the end of the street down Ninth Avenue. I turned just in time to see a golden figure 5 on a red background flash by. The impression was so sudden and forceful that I took a piece of paper out of my pocket and wrote a short poem about it" (A 172). Later Charles Demuth interpreted the poem in his famous 1928 poster "I Saw the Figure 5 in Gold," which WCW called "the most distinguished American painting that I have seen in years" (SL 97).

In 1955 WCW told Henry Wells: ". . . in the case of *The Great Figure* I think you missed the irony of the word *great*, the contemptuous feeling I had at that time for all 'great' figures in public life compared with that figure 5 riding in state with full panoply down the streets of the city ignored by everyone but the artist" (from notes in a folder with WCW's letter to Henry W. Wells of 27 July 1955 [General Manuscript Collection, Rare Book and Manuscript Library, Columbia University]).

7 In SG this line is followed by an additional line: "with weight and urgency."

SPRING AND ALL (1923)

Dedication: "To Charles Demuth"

During his second year at the University of Pennsylvania's Medical School (1903-4) WCW met the young painter Charles Demuth, who was studying art in Philadelphia. "I met Charles Demuth over a dish of prunes at Mrs. Chain's boarding house on Locust Street and formed a lifelong friendship on the spot with dear Charlie, now long since dead" (A 52). Demuth, who studied in Paris before World War One, played a leading role in the American assimilation of European avant-garde movements, and was one of WCW's major contacts with the New York art world. His 1928 poster-painting "I Saw the Figure 5 in Gold" was inspired by WCW's "The Great Figure" (1921).

"The Crimson Cyclamen" in *Adam & Eve & The City* is WCW's elegy for Demuth, who died in 1935.

The titles given to the poems of *Spring and All* in other printings, and the rearrangements of the sequence, are best shown in tabular form. Poems marked with a dagger were included in CP1934. All the poems were reprinted without titles in CCP (1938).

    I.   Spring and All
    II.   †The Pot of Flowers (The Hothouse Plant in *Secession*, Jan. 1923; The Pot of Primroses in CP1934)
    III.   The Farmer
    IV.   †Flight to the City (Cornucopia in *The Chapbook*, April 1923)
    V.   The Black Winds (The Immemorial Wind in *An Early Martyr* [1935])
    VI.   To Have Done Nothing
    VII.   The Rose
    VIII.   †At the Faucet of June
    IX.   Young Love (Young Romance in *An Early Martyr*)
    X.   †The Eyeglasses
    XI.   The Right of Way (The Auto Ride in *An Early Martyr*)
    XII.   †Composition

XIII. The Agonized Spires
XIV. Death the Barber
XV. †Light Becomes Darkness
XVI. To an Old Jaundiced Woman (The Attempt in *Secession,* Aug. 1922)
XVII. Shoot it Jimmy!
XVIII. †To Elsie
XIX. Horned Purple
XX. The Sea
XXI. Quietness
XXII. †The Red Wheelbarrow
[Quietness and The Red Wheelbarrow were reversed in CCP and CEP, so that they became XXII and XXI. This occurred in the preparation of CCP when WCW decided to transpose the poems so that the "better poem" (The Red Wheelbarrow) would "have the better presentation and not be cut in half by the page" (WCW to James Laughlin, 1 Aug. 1938)].
XXIII. †Rigamarole (Rigmarole in *Go Go* [1923]; The Veritable Night in *Der Querschnitt,* Fall 1924)
XXIV. †The Avenue of Poplars
XXV. †Rapid Transit
XXVI. †At the Ball Game
XXVII. The Wildflower [numbered XXVIII in CCP and CEP where The Hermaphroditic Telephones, first published in *Go Go,* is inserted into the sequence as XXVII].

Sanscrit or even Latin (p. 179) Probably a reference to the esoteric notes in T. S. Eliot's *The Waste Land,* published in Dec. 1922.

POEM I "One of the best images I have ever perpetrated, which even Yvor Winters liked. But just at this point he parted company from me for the classic forms" (T). Yvor Winters, poet and critic, began his career as an admirer and imitator of the Imagist poets and especially of Williams; but by the end of the 1920s he had formulated a neo-classic poetic that excluded most of Williams' verse (although he continued to praise the technique of this particular poem). WCW felt that he had lost another "disciple."
3   driven / driving   (*Broom,* Nov. 1923)
4   northeast / northwest   (*Broom*)
12   dead, brown / brown   (*Broom*)
21   stiff curl / curl   (*Broom*)
26   come upon / overtaken   (*Broom*)

POEM II In *The Hieroglyphics of a New Speech* (1969) Bram Dijkstra argues that this poem "is a literal rendering into poetry of Demuth's watercolor 'Tuberoses,' which was painted in 1922, and soon after became a part of Williams' own collection" (p. 172; the painting is reproduced as Plate XX).

Dora Marsden's philosophic algebra (p. 184) Dora Marsden was founder and editor of *The Freewoman* and the *New Freewoman* (after 1913 *The Egoist*), to which she frequently contributed essays on philosophy and psychology. In "The Great Sex Spiral, A Criticism of Miss Marsden's 'Lingual Psychology' " (*The Egoist*, April and August 1917), WCW criticized her confusion of "male and female psychology." See Mike Weaver, *William Carlos Williams: The American Background* (1971), pp. 23-29.

POEM III   "Merely an image, not strictly a poem" (T).

POEM IV   "For the 13-year-old girl next door in Rutherford. Fresh, and rough and tough" (T).

The final period in this poem and others in the CEP *Spring and All* text (VII, VIII, XV, XXI, XXIII, XXVII, XXVIII) resulted from the use of the *Go Go* version as paste-ups in Za49. When some of the poems from the 1923 *Spring and All* were collected in *Go Go* (1923) without the surrounding prose, WCW felt that they looked unfinished and supplied final periods (Mariani 206). In the original *Spring and All* Poem II ends with a period and Poem XXV with the abbreviation "Co."

Alfred Kreymborg (p. 188) See note on the dedication to *Sour Grapes* (p. 493).

Hartley. . . his "Adventures" (p. 189) The painter Marsden Hartley played an important role in WCW's New York life after World War One. WCW recognized Hartley's talent as an expressionistic artist, but was often uncomfortable with both the man and his work. "A tragic figure. I really loved the man, but we didn't always get along together, except at a distance" (A 171).

In his collection of essays *Adventures in the Arts* (1921) Hartley argues that the artist should concentrate on his native environment and the simple relations that exist in the natural world. His typical heroes are the American Indian and the "primitive" painter Henri Rousseau.

POEM V   [comment on last stanza] "To hell with poetry and anything in life—a pessimistic poem. All these poems are emotional complexes, but they didn't get me anywhere" (T).

23   Hartley praises Miss Wirt   In the chapter "A Charming Equestrienne" of his *Adventures in the Arts* (1921) Marsden Hartley praises the circus rider May Wirth whose art "gives the body a chance to show its exquisite rhythmic beauty . . . the beautiful plastic of the body, harmonically arranged for personal delight" (p. 178).

34   bowmen of Shu   See "Song of the Bowmen of Shu" in Ezra Pound's *Cathay* (1915).

POEM VI   "I was trying to think aloud" (T).

[POEM VII]   Not numbered in the original text. "I was experimenting in the mode of the French painters—the fragmentation of Picasso" (T).

[comment at end of poem] "I was tremendously impressed by the images of Rimbaud" (T).

POEM VIII

15 J. P. M. WCW thought the older J. Pierpont Morgan (1837-1913) collected "dead" European art at the expense of vital American artists. J. Pierpont Morgan, Jr. (1867-1943) was also a powerful financier who dealt in "motor cars."

Here is a shutter, a bunch of grapes, a sheet of music, a picture of sea and mountains . . . (p. 197) WCW is describing a painting by one of his favorite artists, Juan Gris: "The Open Window." It was reproduced in black-and-white in *Broom*, 1 (Jan. 1922), 264.

*POEM IX Whereas all the other poems in *Spring and All* follow our amended CEP text, we have printed this poem in its 1923 form since it differs substantially from CEP in spacing and format. We print the CEP text in *An Early Martyr* (p. 389).

2-3 The name "Purvis" appears in the margin of Thirlwall's annotated copy of CEP. Miss Margaret Blake Purvis was a member of the first class to graduate from the nursing program of the French Hospital in New York (1907); at that time WCW was an intern at the Hospital (Rapport du Président, *Société Française de Bienfaisance de New York*, Octobre 1907). For general background to this poem see Chapter 15, "French Hospital," in the *Autobiography*.

"Kiki" may have been Margaret Purvis's nickname. WCW could also have had in mind "Kiki of Montparnasse," the Parisian model of the 1920s who was celebrated by Man Ray and Hemingway; or the *gamine* of the play *Kiki*, which had a long run on the New York stage in 1921-23.

8-9 Wrigley's Chewing Gum had launched a large advertising campaign for "Spearmint" in 1907.

John Marin The American painter who, like WCW, was born in Rutherford, N.J. He produced a number of expressionistic views of the New York skyline that might well be called "skyscraper soup." In the late 1950s Williams told Emily Farnham, the biographer of Charles Demuth: "I could never see Marin as an artist. Surely drawing is a basic thing in painting?" ("Charles Demuth: His Life, Psychology, and Works," Dissertation, Ohio State 1959, p. 990.)

The Improvisations (p. 203) WCW's *Kora in Hell: Improvisations* (1920).

France's "lie" (pp. 204, 199) A translation of Anatole France's *La vie en fleur* appeared in *The Dial* (Oct.-Dec. 1921). The last paragraph reads: "All I can say is that what I have done I have done in good faith. I repeat: I love truth. I believe that humanity has need of it; but surely it has a much greater need of falsehood which flatters and consoles and gives infinite hopes. Without falsehood humanity would perish of despair and ennui" (*Dial*, 71 [Dec. 1921], 692).

POEM X   [comment dated 6/11/60] "I got the variable foot here, but I didn't realize it. The line was important to me but the continuity of sense was fragmentary" (T).

In Thirlwall's copy of CEP the last line of Poem X is emended to "tranquilly like a lake Titicaca—," with the comment: "to get the exact force of tranquillity."

POEM XI   "Importance of an unrelated event to me—the really important people, whom I can salute" (T).

POEM XV   Gloss by line 20, "rotating the object" underscored: "as the movies do" (T).

POEM XVI   In all printings prior to CEP lines 9-10 read:

> elysian slobber
> from her mouth
> upon

The line "from her mouth" was eliminated in the cut-and-paste of the typescript for CEP (Yale Za49): this may be a deliberate excision.

POEM XVII   "Constructed to retain the rhythmic character" (T).
2   nuts / meow   (*The Dial*, Aug. 1923)

POEM XVIII   "Elsie" was the retarded nursemaid from the State Orphanage who worked for the Williams family after Kathleen McBride left (see note on "K. McB.," p. 489; and A 251). WCW may be referring to the same person when he tells the story of "Sadie" and the stolen silverware (A 244-46). Beside the title "To Elsie" in Thirlwall's copy of CEP is the note: "Pyromaniac. Subject of story of robbers—gagged and silver hidden. Succeeded Kate McDonnell."

Pío Baroja (p. 220) WCW identified with the Basque author who studied medicine, then took over a bakery, and finally turned to writing about the poor and contemporary social problems.

POEM XIX   "Very important to me—I was moved by a boy that I saw. I was carried away by the actual thing and forgot about the construction. I was usually torn between the scene and the rhythmic identity. Here I forgot the rhythmic identity, because the scene was forced on me as a fact" (T).

POEM XX   "An awkward thing. I never tried it again" (T).
8   O la la O   Change on typescript for CEP (Yale Za49) that was not printed. CEP and 1923 text read "O la la."
16   Oom barroom   Change on typescript for CEP (Yale Za49) that was not printed. CEP reads "coom barroom" and 1923 text "coom barrooom."

POEM XXIV   "I was writing in my own language, and whatever the language suggested I wrote. I was following the beat in my own mind, of the American idiom" (T).

32   *Les Trois Frères* A cave in the south of France, discovered in 1914, that contains monumental Upper Paleolithic paintings.

POEM XXV   "I was studying a presentation of the language as it actually is used. Compare 'April' [p. 329]" (T).

9   Don't / Do not   In all printings prior to CEP. Change occurs in corrected typescript (Yale Za49).

14-15   The following lines were omitted, probably deliberately, between lines 14 and 15 in the corrected typescript (Yale Za49):

> What's the use of sweating over
> this sort of thing, Carl: here
> it is all set up—

"Carl" may be Carl Van Doren, who had recently published in *The New Republic* (21 March 1922) an academic essay on "American Realism."

POEM XXVII   Lines 5 and 6 were combined in CEP as the result of an error in Za50. We have restored the reading of all previous printings and the corrected typescript (Yale Za49).

POEMS 1922-1928

*PICTURE SHOWING   Untitled in *Manuscripts* (Feb. 1922). The British-built dirigible ZR-2, largest in the world at that time, exploded over England on 24 Aug. 1921. Although the dirigible had not yet been taken over by the U.S. Navy, sixteen American officers and men were aboard. Their bodies were returned to the U.S. on the British warship *Dauntless,* and funeral services were held at the Brooklyn Naval Yard. A photograph in the *New York Tribune,* 17 Sept. 1921, shows the caskets on the deck of the British ship.

*MY LUV   Untitled in the only printing, *Manuscripts* (Feb. 1922).

THE BULL
17   round / great   (*The Dial,* Feb. 1922; *An "Objectivists" Anthology* [1932]).
18   smooths / smooth   (CEP)
25   Milkless / milkless   (CEP) In lines 18 and 25 we have restored the reading of all printings before CEP and of the corrected typescript (Yale Za49).

THE JUNGLE
2   the trees / the great trees   (*The Dial,* Feb. 1922; *An "Objectivists" Anthology* [1932])
5   reptiles / the reptiles   (*The Dial*)
9   but / It is   (*The Dial*)

10   a girl, waiting, all at once—   (*The Dial*)

FISH   "A story told by Carolina Benson, an old friend of the family, in Vermont in the summer of 1921" (T).

13-14   In *Broom* (April 1922) there is an additional stanza between these lines:

> Men call from the cliffs
> or blow horns
> that the fishermen
> shall go down to the shore
> to their boats and nets
> to make the catch.

27   in / into   (*Broom*)
55   as the / as to the   (*Broom*)
71   then / and   (*Broom*)
93   *huldra* / the *huldra*   (*Broom*)

93-96   In Norwegian legend, a *hulder* is a wicked, alluring siren that inhabits hills and mountains (beautiful in appearance, but with a long tail). A *nøkk* is a water sprite (in the shape of a man, horse, etc.).

*HULA-HULA   *Broom* (Aug. 1922). *Tangerine* was a hit musical comedy of 1921-22 with a tropical setting and grass-skirted chorus girls. Brighton Beach is on Coney Island in Brooklyn.

*VIEW   *Forum* (Sept. 1922).

*WHEN FRESH, IT WAS SWEET   First published in *The Dial*, 73 (Dec. 1922), 617-619. The poem was discovered by Christopher MacGowan and published with a commentary in the WCWR, 6 (Fall 1980). It records WCW's response to a performance of *Katinka* by Nikita Balieff's Chauve-Souris, or Bat, Company. The Moscow troupe appeared in New York through much of 1922. Al Jolson (see line 31) attended both the Feb. 4th opening and the April 9th charity performance.

Katinka, "a ballet set to an old Russian polka, was distinguished for its novel stage setting in imitation of a wooden toy music box, with the dancers as automatic figures" (*New York Evening Post*, 6 Feb. 1922).

*FROM A BOOK   *Rhythmus* (April-May 1923).

NEW ENGLAND
Title: "Down-town" (*An "Objectivists" Anthology* [1932]; CP1934; ND16).

1-6   New England is the condition
of bedrooms whose

electricity is brickish or
made into T beams—They

dangle them on wire cables
to the tops of Woolworth buildings   (*Contact,* June 1923)

3   brickish / brackish   (*An "Objectivists" Anthology;* CP1934; ND16)

11-13   the lintel of his cap standing
to have his picture taken

on the butt of a girder   (*Contact*)

15   lonely cock atop / lonely atop   (*An "Objectivists" Anthology;* CP1934; CCP; ND16). This return to the 1923 *Contact* reading is the only instance in CEP of a verbal change that restores an earlier form not found in the corrected typescript (Yale Za49) or the uncorrected retyped text (Za50).

17   —a thought / reminiscient   (*Contact*)

THE DRUNKARD   In the fall of 1923, at the beginning of his 1923-24 "sabbatical" from his medical practice, WCW and his wife took an apartment in New York City. There he wrote a letter to his mother which begins: "Here I am settled in a room in New York in order to work out my destiny." Later in the letter he says: "There is a poem inclosed which I hope you will like better than some of my incomprehensible latter work. I think you will like the one I am sending. It seems that this is the sort of thing I am going to do. Art is a curious command. We must do what we are bidden to do and we can only go so far as the light permits. I am always earnest, as you if any one knows must know, but no doubt I puzzle even you—as I do myself."

The enclosed poem was "The Drunkard," which was not published at that time. Years later WCW "recovered" the poem and it appeared in *The Beloit Poetry Journal* (Spring 1951) with a headnote (beginning "Dear Mother" and ending "Plenty of love, from your son. Willie") which almost exactly reproduces the passage from WCW's 1923 letter quoted above. This headnote was somewhat revised when the poem was reprinted in CEP.

*THE NEW CATHEDRAL OVERLOOKING THE PARK   First published (untitled) as a poem in *Broom* (Nov. 1923); it appears as prose in *Spring and All* (p. 180). The cathedral is the Church of St. John the Divine in New York City, begun in 1892.

AT NIGHT   Untitled in *Broom* (Nov. 1923).
1-2   The stars, that are small lights,
are my nightly companions, my friends
now that I know them foreign.
The security I feel in them
cannot be broken. Separate, inscrutable
(*Broom*)
4   by / with   (*Broom*)

*HOW HAS THE WAY BEEN FOUND?   Untitled in the only printing, *Broom* (Nov. 1923).

THE HERMAPHRODITIC TELEPHONES   Added to *Spring and All* as the penultimate poem (XXVII) in CCP and CEP.

*FULL MOON   *The Dial* (Jan. 1924). With one change in punctuation this poem later became part of the "Della Primavera Trasportata al Morale" sequence (see p. 336).

*LAST WORDS OF MY GRANDMOTHER   *the transatlantic review* (March 1924). See the later version on p. 464. Emily Dickinson Wellcome died in 1920: see A 167.

IT IS A LIVING CORAL   "Employing ordinary images musically, and keeping them bouncing" (T). In this, one of the most allusive of WCW's poems, the author of *In the American Grain* (1925) takes a stroll through his nation's Capitol. For a description of the art in the Capitol at that time see Charles E. Fairman, *Art and Artists of the Capitol of the United States of America* (1927).

Title: Printed as the first line of the poem in An *"Objectivists"* Anthology (1932).

4   *E Pluribus Unum*   In the fresco allegory in the canopy of the dome, "The Apotheosis of George Washington," Washington is surrounded by thirteen maidens with a banner emblazoned "E Pluribus Unum."

8   Armed Liberty   The statue of Freedom atop the dome of the Capitol.

14   iron / of iron   (*The Arts,* Aug. 1924)

18   of / of the   (*The Arts*)

19   the / like the   (*The Arts*)

21-23   Congress . . . Commission   In 1859 an Art Commission was established to examine all designs for sculpture or painting. It was discontinued the next year.

26-31   sculptured group . . . Washington   There is no group exactly like this. WCW may have in mind "Fame and Peace Crowning George Washington," above the Rotunda Bronze Door, East Central Portico; more likely, he has misread the allegory of "The Apotheosis of George Washington" in the dome.

32   Commerce Minerva   Allegorical figures in the fresco on the canopy of the dome.

35   at / at the   (*The Arts*)

36-42   John Blake White's painting "Miss Mott Directing Generals Marion and Lee to Burn Her Mansion to Dislodge the British," in the Senate Wing. *Appleton's* says of Rebecca Brewton Motte (1739-1815): "Her husband died during the Revolution, leaving his large estate . . . During the occupation of South Carolina by the British, her mansion in Orangeburg county, on Congaree river, was seized by the invaders . . . Francis Marion and Henry Lee laid siege to Fort Motte, as the post was called, and, when informed of the approach of British reinforcements, deliberated over the plan of setting fire to the house, but were reluctant to destroy Mrs. Motte's property. She dispelled their scruples, and brought out an African bow and arrows specially adapted for the purpose, with which the roof was ignited, causing the garrison to surrender speedily. Mrs. Motte then provided a banquet for the officers on both sides."

49-50   Baptism of Pocahontas   John G. Chapman's painting in the Rotunda.

57-58   George L. Shoup, former Senator from Idaho, whose statue was placed by his home state in Statuary Hall.

61-63   it fetches naked / Indian / women from a river   This scene, and the one with Columbus below (lines 69-71), correspond to nothing in the Capitol and seem to have seeped in from WCW's reading for *In the American Grain*.

64-73   Trumbull Varnum Henderson . . . Banks White . . . Kerr   Portraits of former speakers of the House, in Speaker's Lobby: Jonathan Trumbull, Joseph B. Varnum, David B. Henderson, Nathaniel Banks, John White, Michael C. Kerr.

66-67   Frances Willard's corset   Frances E. Willard, reformer, founder of the Woman's Christian Temperance Union. Her statue was the first of a woman in Statuary Hall.

77-83   Perry . . . Lake Erie   William H. Powell's painting of "The Battle of Lake Erie," in the Senate Wing.

83   The version in *The Arts* adds these lines at the close:

> The trivial rhythm of
> great events
>
> But who's Fantin
> Latour
>
> Venus and Cupid this
> escape
>
> into an etching for
> Heaven
>
> is disorder but art
> is kind

INTERESTS OF 1926   This poem was originally titled "Insanity or Genius," and was the first item in a miscellany of poetry and prose published in *The Little Review* (Spring-Summer 1926) under the general heading "Interests of 1926." Following "Insanity or Genius" were "Two Fugitive Poems (1910)" ["Martin and Katherine" and "Misericordia," see p. 23]; "Poem: Daniel Boone"; and a prose improvisation "Stolen Letter" (Dear Aunt N.). We have not reprinted the prose improvisation. A separate poem, "The gayest of bright flowers," was printed by mistake as a part of "Misericordia" (see below).

7   wading . . . over / wading—on   (*The Little Review*)

9   smile of / reflecting smile   (*The Little Review*)

10   the / of the   (*The Little Review*)

11   compassion / sweet compassion   (*The Little Review*)

*POEM (DANIEL BOONE)   *The Little Review* (Spring-Summer 1926).

*THE GAYEST OF BRIGHT FLOWERS   *The Little Review* (Spring-Summer 1926).
On the typescript that WCW submitted to the *Little Review* the items in the
"Interests of 1926" sequence (see above) are numbered, as are the pages of the
typescript. This poem is at the top of a page, and the editors erroneously de-
leted the sequence number as if it were a page number.

STRUGGLE OF WINGS   First printed in *The Dial* (July 1926) as an "incomplete"
poem. "Direct transmission—a purely literary thing built out of surrealist ma-
terials" (T). In the CP1934 and CEP printings WCW retained most of the ap-
paratus that signals the poem's provisional state, although this later version
contains many changes from *The Dial* and is no longer designated "incom-
plete."
   47   Inness   George Inness, the New Jersey landscape artist who frequently
painted the Hackensack Meadows.
   The following is *The Dial* version in full:

> Roundclouds occluding patches of the blue
> sky rival steam bluntly towering,
> slowspinning billows which rival
> the resting snow, which rivals the sun
>
> beaten out upon it, flashing
> (laughing) to a (struggle of wings) which
> fills the still air—still but not cold—
> or, cold yet burning . . .
>
> It is the snow risen above itself, it is
> winter pressed breast to breast
> with its own whiteness, transparent
> yet visible against the sky:
>
> Together, with their pigeons' heads whose
> stupid eyes deceive no one—as their wings meet
> contending—they hold something up between them
> which wants to fall to the ground . . .
>
> and there's the River with thin ice upon it
> fanning out from the (marble) shores half over the
> black water, the free middlewater racing under its
> ripples that move crosswise on the stream.
>
> But the wings and bodies of the pigeonlike creatures
> keep fluttering above me, turning together
> hiding that which is between them. It seems
> to rest not in their claws but upon their breasts—
>
> It is a baby!
> Now it is very clear (*) They are keeping the child
> (naked in the air) warm and safe between them.
> The eyes of the birds are fixed in

a bestial ecstasy. They strive together panting.
It is an antithesis of logic, very
theoretical. To his face the baby claps
the bearded face of Socrates . . .

Ho, ho! He's dropped it. It was a mask.
Now indeed the encounter throws aside all dissim-
ulation. The false birdheads drop back, arms
spring from the wingedges, all the parts

of two women become distinct, the anatomy
familiar and complete to the smallest detail:
A meaning plainly antipoetical . . . and
. . . all there is is won

      [.   .   .   .   .   .   .

It is Poesy, born of a man and two women
Exit No. 4, the string from the windowshade
has a noose at the bottom, a noose? or
a ring—bound with white cord, knotted
around the circumference designedly in a design—
      And all there is is won

And it is Inness on the meadows and fruit is
yellow ripening in windows every minute
growing brighter in the bulblight by the
cabbages and spuds—
      And all there is is won

What are black 4A Ms after all but black
4A Ms like anything else: a tree,
a fork, a leaf, a pane of glass—?
      And all there is is won

A relic of old decency, a very personal friend
      And all there is is won

          [*Envoi*

Pic, your crows feed at your windowsill
asso, try and get near mine . . .
      And all there is is won

      [.   .   .   .   .   .

.   .   .   .   .   .   All
up and down the Rio Grande the sand is sand
on every hand (Grand chorus and finale)

      [.   .   .   .   .   .

Out of such drab trash as this
by a metamorphosis
bright as wallpaper or crayon
or where the sun casts ray on ray on
flowers in a dish, weave, weave
for Poesy a gaudy sleeve
a scarf, a cap and find him gloves
white as the backs of turtledoves.
Make him magnificently bright
like the Little Man that's hight
Jesus Christ upon the altars
and oleochromes and sundry psalters
of his people. Cloath him
richly, those who loath him
will besmirch him fast enough.
A surcease to sombre stuff
black's black, black's one thing
but he's not a blackbird, bring
something else for him to wear.
See! he is young, he has black hair
all right then, a red vest . . .

So I say he shall be dressed

[*Incomplete*]

*TREE Published in *The Dial* (Jan. 1927). Although some critics have argued that this is one of WCW's earliest poems, it seems to date from the 1920s. See Mariani, p. 778.

PATERSON Parts of this poem were reworked into Book One of *Paterson* (1946). See *Paterson* (New Directions, 1963), pp. 9, 27-28.
39 Alex Shorn Son of a local bootblack whose shop was visible from the living room of 9 Ridge Road.

*MARCH IS A LIGHT *The Dial* (March 1927).

YOUNG SYCAMORE
Title: Followed by a colon in *The Dial* (March 1927).
1 I must / I feel that I must (*The Dial*).

LINES ON RECEIVING THE DIAL'S AWARD: 1927 "The *Dial*'s award, though it was given for general excellence in writing during the year (1926) was specifically pointed up by their publication of . . . *Paterson*, on which I based the later and more extended poem" (A 243).
Title: date omitted in *The Dial* (March 1927), CP1934, CCP.
9 upon one side / upon the side We have restored the reading of all pre-CEP printings and the corrected typescript (Yale Za49).

12   Captain Bragg   During the Mexican War Capt. Braxton Bragg served as artillery captain under Gen. Zachary Taylor. There was a widely-publicized but apocryphal story that during the final Mexican attack at the Battle of Buena Vista Gen. Taylor said: "A little more grape, Captain Bragg."

ALL THE FANCY THINGS   A poem about WCW's mother.
9   Green / The green car   (*The Dial*, June 1927)
15   or what there is, a thin   (*The Dial*)

BRILLIANT SAD SUN
1-2   We have restored the large initial L found in the first two printings and the corrected typescript for CEP (Yale Za49).
10   that / this   (*The Dial*, June 1927)
15-18   beside that purity?

> With empty pitcher dangling in the sun
> her coarse voice croaks   (*The Dial*)

20   Patti   Adelina Patti, the Spanish-born opera singer, was one of the most celebrated sopranos of her time; her sister, Carlotta, was also a professional soprano.
21   Mayaguez   The town in Puerto Rico where WCW's mother grew up.

IMPROMPTU: THE SUCKERS   "I believed that they [Sacco and Vanzetti] had been double-crossed, that New England was ganging up on these men" (T). In its first publication in *The Broken Span* (1941) and later in *Selected Poems* (1949) the poem is dated 1927; internal evidence shows that it was written around Aug. 7-10, 1927, when the execution of Sacco and Vanzetti was still scheduled for Aug. 11 ("on the eleventh to get the current," line 34). At the last moment the execution was stayed until Aug. 23.
4   pleas / plea   (*The Broken Span*)
10-18   The investigative committee that advised against clemency for Sacco and Vanzetti was composed of Abbott Lawrence Lowell, President of Harvard; Samuel W. Stratton, President of MIT; and Robert A. Grant, a former judge.
26   school / schools   (*The Broken Span*)

FROM: A FOLDED SKYSCRAPER   This prose-poetry sequence was published in *The American Caravan* (1927). "Hemmed-in Males" and "The Winds" were not printed together when the prose was dropped in CP1934 and subsequent printings.
   The first prose piece is about WCW's grandmother, Emily Dickinson Wellcome; the second is a meditation on Ezra Pound and the American idiom.
   In 1959 WCW told John Thirlwall that there "were two or three or four abortive beginnings [for *Paterson*] associated wth 'The Folded Skyscraper' " (*New Directions* 17 [1961], p. 269).

HEMMED-IN MALES   In *The American Caravan* the title appears as "*Hemmed in males—hemmedin males—hemmedin males.*"

2   black sand   "A woman's pubic hair" (T).

8   George   "A janitor in the Lincoln School [Rutherford]" (T).

17-18   John L. Sullivan and Jake Kilrain, prize fighters; Adrian Constantine ("Pop") Anson, professional baseball player.

29   black sand's got me   "I was making fun of anyone who objected to the dirty images. I'll make a poem out of anything. I was trying to defy woman" (T).

THE WINDS

1-3   many winds, flowing edge to edge
      their clear edges meeting—
      as thought meets thought
      in pity and contention
      —the winds of this northern March
            (*American Caravan*)

5   field / fields   (*American Caravan*)

10   clouds / the clouds (*American Caravan*; CP1934; CCP). Change made on corrected typescript (Yale Za49).

WINTER

11   leather-green / leathery green   (*transition*, Dec. 1927)

14-19   marking
      the sky
      over them

      This is winter
      winter winter
      green
      spearshaped leaves

      leathery
      in the falling snow   (*transition*)

THE MEN

6   bridges are / bridge is   (*The Dial*, June 1928)

10   run the waters / runs the water   (*The Dial*)

12   bulbous towers / russian towers, bulbous   (*The Dial*)

14   so dreamily / dreamily, futilely   (*The Dial*)

17   mill chimneys / factory chimneys   (*The Dial*)

THE ATLANTIC CITY CONVENTION, A COMPOSITION IN TWO PARTS: POEM AND SPEECH
Published in *The Second American Caravan* (1928). "The Waitress" was reprinted subsequently without the prose.

THE WAITRESS

23   what / the   (*Second American Caravan*)

43   cold / long cold   (*Second American Caravan*)
44   the / a   (*Second American Caravan*)
47   reflections / reflection   (*Second American Caravan*)

ON GAY WALLPAPER   In the first printing in *The Dial* (Nov. 1928) lines 18-19 are telescoped so that the poem ends:

> where the day blows in
>
> The scalloped curtains to
> the sound of rain

The later change in lineation made in *An "Objectivists" Anthology* (1932) allows the stanza pattern to reflect the "threes" of the wallpaper.

THE LILY
4   And in the air a humming-bird   (*The Dial*, Nov. 1928)

THE SOURCE   The version printed in *The Dial* (Nov. 1928) and CP1934 divides the poem into three sections rather than two, with the third section beginning at line 42.

THE DESCENT OF WINTER (1928)

Although this sequence appeared in a little magazine, Ezra Pound's *The Exile* (Autumn 1928), we have followed WCW's practice in CCP and CEP and treated it as a separate volume.

*9/27   Omitted in subsequent printings.

9/29   WCW began *The Descent of Winter* in late Sept.-early Oct. 1927, while returning from France on the S.S. *Pennland*. His wife had stayed in Europe to be with their two sons, who were enrolled for the year in a school near Geneva.

9/30   A compressed version of the second half of this poem was published in *An Early Martyr* as "The Sadness of the Sea" (p. 383).
We have printed the revised version of this poem in the main text. In *The Exile* it read:

> There are no perfect waves—
> Your writings are a sea
> full of misspellings and
> faulty sentences. Level. Troubled.
> A center distant from the land
> touched by the wings of nearly
> silent birds that never seem
> to rest, yet it bears me

seriously—to land, but without
you.

This is the sadness of the sea—
waves like words all broken—
a sameness of lifting and falling mood.

I lean watching the detail
of brittle crest, the delicate
imperfect foam, the yellow weed
one piece like another—
There is no hope, or maybe
a coral island slowly
slowly forming and waiting
for birds to drop the seeds
will make it habitable

10/21   In CP1934 the poem begins in the middle of the second line with
"the orange flames."
2   aflame / in flames   (The Exile)
10   steadily continues / continues steadily   (CP1934)

10/28   In WCW's journal of 1927, from which The Descent of Winter
was adapted (Buffalo D2), he writes: "Today to invent a character is what I
am at. A girl. Dolores Marie Pischak." But on 22 Nov. 1927 WCW wrote to
his wife Florence, who was abroad with the children: "That [woman's name
inked out] Dolores Marie Veronica Magdalena actually or at any rate did
come into my office today and ask me to screw her. She couldn't be got out.
Imagine. How I didn't do it I don't know, except by thinking like hell of you.
The wild thoughts that go through the head at such times are like mad eagles:
Do it. To hell with everything. You're a fool. What of it. It doesn't mean a
thing, do it anyway. Jesus! And all the time the body is trembling like a leaf,
like sick meat with desire. She begged for it [and] couldn't be got out. A
young woman—dripping with desire unsatisfied. . . ." (Mariani 265-66).

10/28   When the prose from The Descent of Winter was reprinted in
Selected Essays (1954) as "Notes in Diary Form," several cuts were made; we
have recorded the significant changes. In this entry the following lines (p. 299)
were eliminated after "Or let us take a run up to the White Mountains or
Lake Mohonk":
Not Bethlehem (New Hampshire) any more, the Jews have ruined that like
lice all over the lawns. Horrible to see. The dirty things. Eating everywhere.
Parasites.

10/28   WCW gave this poem the title "Summer" in a notebook in the
James G. Leippert collection at the Library of Congress.

10/29   Line 5: "its organ its tarpaulin" (CEP). An unnoticed error in Yale
typescripts Za49 and Za50.

11/1   Variant in line 14:
And in runningpants and / And in runningpants (CP1934)

11/2   Variant in line 14:
track / tracks (CEP) We have restored the reading in all printings prior to CEP and in the corrected typescript (Yale Za49).

11/2   A MORNING IMAGINATION OF RUSSIA   "A sympathetic human feeling—non-political—roused by thoughts of Russia" (T).
In An "Objectivists" Anthology (1932) lines 8-11 read:

> on the intense green grass where in patches
> oak leaves were pressed hard down
> by the night rain. There were no cities

34   Tan dar a dei!   The refrain of the nightingale in Walther von der Vogelweide's song "Unter der linden." WCW may well have known the original medieval German poem, but he could have found the phrase in Thomas Lovell Beddoes's translation.
43   was / had been   (An "Objectivists" Anthology [1932]; CP1934)

11/6   This prose passage (pp. 306-308) does not appear in SE.

Henry Ford . . . Chas. Sheeler (p. 307). WCW met the painter and photographer Charles Sheeler in 1923, and became a great admirer of his work (see A 320-22). In 1939 he wrote an introduction to a Museum of Modern Art catalogue of Sheeler's works, and in 1954 he contributed a foreword to the catalogue of a Sheeler Retrospective Exhibition. In 1927 Sheeler made a famous series of photographs of the Ford Motor Company plant at River Rouge, Michigan.

"Nevada" (p. 308)   The rodeo star "Nevada" Jack Rose. He was on board the S.S. Pennland in Sept.-Oct. 1927 when WCW returned to the U.S. and began The Descent of Winter (see SL 77).

11/8   Around 1890 the Williams family lived in the "Bagellon House" in then-rural East Rutherford, near Charlie Wadsworth's printing shop (see A 6-8).

11/10   Line 4: We have restored "hall," present in all printings prior to CEP and in the corrected typescript (Yale Za49).

11/13   SHAKESPEARE
E pur si muove (p. 311) According to legend, Galileo—after being forced by the Inquisition to recant the Copernican theory—rose to his feet, stamped the ground, and exclaimed "Eppur si muove!" ("Yet it does move!").

11/13   TRAVELLING IN FAST COMPANY   Omitted in SE.

11/22   Titled "10/22" and printed in that chronological position in CP1934. The CP1934 version ends:

> but aloof
> as if from another world

11/28   CP1934 omits "really" in line 1.

12/15   In a notebook in the James G. Leippert collection at the Library of Congress WCW titled this poem: "The Girl of the Golden West."

12/18   The passage beginning ". . . who was away much of the time studying" and ending ". . . fine shirts and a few things like that" (pp. 316-317) was omitted in SE.

Krug (p. 316)   A business associate of WCW's grandfather Solomon Hoheb (see Mariani 15-16).

POEMS 1929-1935

*QUESTION AND ANSWER   *New Masses* (Jan. 1929).

*SIMPLEX SIGILUM VERI   *Blues* (Fall 1929). See the later version on p. 398.

THE FLOWER (A PETAL, COLORLESS)
3-4   The George Washington Bridge over the Hudson, under construction 1927-1931, as seen from a ferry. WCW may have been contrasting his "incomplete" bridge with Hart Crane's *The Bridge,* parts of which were being published to great acclaim in *The Dial, The Little Review,* and even T. S. Eliot's *The Criterion* (see Mariani 279-80).
9-10   of it is mine, but visibly it is
          petal of a flower for all that—my own.   (*Imagist Anthology* [1930])
18   131 West Passaic Avenue in Rutherford, where WCW was born.
19-20   in which I happen to have been born:
          A heap of dirt, if you care   (*Imagist Anthology*)
21   sunstreaked / snow-streaked   (*Imagist Anthology*)
26   can find to throw / can throw   (*Imagist Anthology*)
27   Madame Lenine   The French spelling of the name of Lenin's widow, who was an educational leader in Russia.
32   San Diego   WCW may have in mind the little magazine *Troubadour* (1928-32), published in San Diego, which placed a special emphasis on regional literature. Or he may have been thinking of Kenneth Rexroth in San Francisco, whose rambunctious letter to *Blues* (Fall 1929) criticizing the current literary scene (including WCW) was published beneath an equally tendentious letter from "Augustus Tiberius" in San Diego.
35   the stamens / stamens   (*Imagist Anthology; U.S.A.* [Spring 1930])
41   ill / sick   (*Imagist Anthology*)

54   strings of lights / stringsoflights   (*Imagist Anthology*)

55-56   not my own, in which I have not
         the least part. Another petal reaches   (*U.S.A.*)

58   when / where   (*U.S.A.*)
       a child bathing in a small / child bathing in a   (*Imagist Anthology*)

60   them / it   (*Imagist Anthology*)

63   could / may   (*U.S.A.*)

THE ATTIC WHICH IS DESIRE: We have restored the colon to the title, as in all printings before CEP and in the corrected typescript (Yale Za49). This poem describes the view from the west window of WCW's attic study at 9 Ridge Road, which was constructed in 1929-30.

8-10   where storms

> sobbing and
> whispering
>
> confess—
> Here from the
> street by   (*Blues*, Spring 1930)

*THE MOON—   *Blues* (Spring 1930).

BIRDS AND FLOWERS   Originally printed in two sections in *The Miscellany* (March 1930), with section I combining the first two sections of the final version. Section III was published separately in its final form and numbered "3" in *An "Objectivists" Anthology* (1932).

The version in *The Miscellany* begins with an additional three-line stanza:

> The cold
> has been struck aside as by
> the flash of an eye—

Other variants in *The Miscellany* are listed below:

2   time— / time; it is

10   globed / globed as a balloon

15   And / Come now. And

17   ankles / straight and slender ankles

18   way, as / way; the

19   grown / of growing

20   in / that is in

23-24   birds so briefly resting
           they seem still in flight . . .

28-29   this day is fine, this day I
           love you. This day

31-33   more than a mottled bird in
           under my ribs where
           anatomists say the heart is—

41-42   ourselves we make a desert
         for everyone. If we blossom—

         If we blossom!

         winter shall wear a new
         blossom—
                      a snowdrop.

43   Nothing is lost (I cannot
     wait for a title) the white

56-62   It is, that the eye
         has grown inward and the mind
         spread its embrace until
         whole acres of thought are coming
         into bud, hard in the wind that
         brushed the stiff petals.

*CHILD AND VEGETABLES   *This Quarter* (April-June 1930).

DELLA PRIMAVERA TRASPORTATA AL MORALE   WCW drafted this sequence in
April 1928, shortly after finishing *The Descent of Winter*. The title page of
the first typescript of the sequence (Buffalo D2) reads: "Della PRIMAVERA
Transportata AL MORALE, by William Carlos Williams M. D., Preceeded
By an introduction: THE DESCENT OF WINTER." It appears that WCW
first intended to continue the prose/poetry form of *The Descent of Winter*,
but the work soon evolved into a suite of poems which preoccupied WCW
for the next two years.
On 2 March 1930 WCW wrote to Ezra Pound that "an incomplete, early
version" of the sequence would appear in the *Imagist Anthology* (1930) but
that he was sending Pound the "complete" and "final" version. The group of
poems in the *Imagist Anthology*, which is headed "(*incomplete*)," includes
"April," "The Trees," "The Wind Increases" (in a form that incorporates
"The Bird's Companion"), "Love in a Truck *or* The Sea-Elephant," "Rain,"
and "The Flower." In CP1934 the sequence contains "April," "The Trees,"
"The Birds' Companion," "The Sea-Elephant," "Rain," "The House," "Death,"
and "The Botticellian Trees." In CCP and CEP the sequence takes the final
form we have reprinted. We have followed WCW's intention in treating the
poems as an integral unit, and have placed them in 1930 when the sequence
had been fully drafted and a first truncated version published.
The title of the sequence has an interesting history. (*Trasportata* is incor-
rectly spelled *Transportata* in WCW's typescript and through all the editions:
the Italian might best be rendered as "A Moral Interpretation of Springtime").
It derives from a book of Italian poetry that Ezra Pound had left behind in
Rutherford years before, *Varie Poesie* Dell'Abate Pietro Metastasio (Venezia,
1795). At the end of his "Prologue" to *Kora in Hell* WCW claims it was this
volume that gave him the format for *Kora in Hell*, where the notes and im-
provisations are separated by ruled lines. Many years later, when recalling

this in a conversation with Edith Heal (the editor of *I Wanted to Write a Poem*), WCW said: "I came upon a book Pound had left in the house written by an Abbot who had to make excuses for himself for dealing with poetry so he called his book: *Varie Poesie Dell'* (Springtime transported to the Moral)."

Edith Heal recorded this comment in her Columbia M.A. thesis, but when the thesis was converted into a book she must have checked with WCW and discovered that he had been mistaken, since in IWWP (p. 27) the correct title is given. The phrase "Della Primavera Trasportata al Morale" occurs nowhere in *Varie Poesie*, although "primavera" is one of Metastasio's favorite subjects and "Sonetto III" (which contains the words "trasportata" and "primavera") contains the gist of WCW's title. It seems most likely that WCW created the title out of his memories of Metastasio to fit his mood of the late 1920s. In the annotations to Thirlwall's copy of CEP "Metastasio" is written by the title.

APRIL (THE BEGINNING—OR)   We have restored the title that this poem has in all printings before CEP and in the corrected typescript (Yale Za49). In CEP the sequence title is printed as the title of the poem, and "April" becomes a section title.

Unless otherwise noted all the following variants are in the *Imagist Anthology* (1930). Some of them may be questionable, since the printing for this volume was unusually careless. WCW is listed as the author of *Tempera, Four Grapes,* and *In the American Grave*!

6   Loose it (again)
11   shoot / shoots
15   trunk / trunks   (*Imagist Anthology*, CP1934, CCP). Changed on the typescript for CEP (Yale Za49).

15-17   strain
          the violent
          trunks and limbs of
          the supporting trees—
                    —yellow
          the arched stick

29   iris blades unsheathed
       stabbing—

40-42   in that its desire

               though it was like
          this in part it was deformed

48   and April
       for all that—

50-56   the rest is all reserved
       With this proviso
          virgin (?) negress

at the glass in
blueglass venetian
     beads—

63-64 [omitted]
97/98 we / I
99   *The* Academy (St.)
112 and I also believe in the right
      of the people to make and unmake
      their own laws—
119 negro— / negro and—

121-26   I believe
              in your love
              the first dandelion
              a heavenly blossom
              at the edge of
              the concrete—
     the fishman's bugle announces
     the warm wind—
                  taraaaaaaa
                  taraaaaaaa

131-37   Stop : Stop
     you would kiss "me" with "kindness":

140-43 Thus, in that light and only in
      that light can I say—

      Winter : Spring (a copy)
      abandoned (?) to you. The world lost—

160-61 [omitted]
167-68 No trucking on this street
169-75 [omitted]
177   —a tree / as a tree

FULL MOON   Lines 7-16, present in the first version (*The Dial*, Jan. 1924; see p. 252), were cut in *An "Objectivists" Anthology* (1932) and CP1934 but restored in CCP and CEP when the poem became part of the "Della Primavera" sequence.

THE TREES   "I was trying to get speed in verse. There is not time enough in the modern world to be prolix. I was feeling for an impetuous rhythm—a Declaration of Independence from every restraint" (T). The different versions found in the *Imagist Anthology* (May 1930) and *The Miscellany* (Nov. 1930) are printed in full below.

          The trees—being trees
          thrash and scream

guffaw and curse—
wholly abandoned
new with buds—
damning the race of men—

Christ, the bastards
haven't even sense enough
to stay out in the rain—

Wha ha ha ha

wheeeeeee
clacka tacka tacka
tacka tacka
wha ha ha ha ha
ha ha ha

knocking knees buds
bursting from each pore
even the trunk's self
putting out leafheads—

The cold wind
has had us his own
winter long, his kiss
did not leave
a part of us untouched—

Wailing at the gate
heartbreak at the bridgehead—

What gone
and whence returning?
Seedless, spent

Science
—wheeeee!

              ghosts
sapped of strength—
desire dead
in the heart—

Philosophy!
—haw haw haw haw
and memory broken.

Loose desire.
"Do what you please"
We naked cry to you

Listen!
there were never satyrs

never mænads
never eagle-headed gods—

these were men
from whose hands sprung
love
bursting the wood—
Trees were their
companions—
    (*Imagist Anthology*)

The trees—being trees
thrash and scream
wholly abandoned
new with buds—

Christ (man) God in
Heaven Almighty
why have you created me
for lice to crawl on?

              they lash
resisting the wind—

God (man) Almighty King
in Heaven since men
have no thought
other—

        than to kill,
the only hole left—
we, the undersigned,
the trees, rooted
make a vocabulary
of our green pricks
to resemble
the sharp stars—
while we are hot,
hot and the wind whips
us till the triple
crotch wrenches and
groans—

Christ, the bastards
haven't sense enough
to stay out in the rain—

Wha ha ha ha

There stands "Shakespeare"

on his branch of
glass not even his
name certain—

and here he stands for
this is he—
in money
unable to pull his foot
out—

wheeeee
who aw ah eeeee
clacka tacka tacka
tacka tacka
wha ha ha ha ha
ha ha ha

knocking knees buds
bursting from each pore
even the trunk's self
putting out leafheads—

The cold wind
has had us his own
winter long, his kiss
did not leave
a part of us untouched—

Blight the
race of men. Chop
them down.

Wailing at the gate
heartbreak at the bridgehead—

Seedless, spent

Science
—wheeeee!
ghosts
sapped of strength—
desire dead
in the heart—

Philosophy!
—haw haw haw haw

Where is the memory
unpocked with
the disease of school—

Loose desire,

we, naked, cry to you
"Do what you please."

You cannot,
no wind winterlong
in the hollows of
your flesh—
icy with pleasure—

There were never satyrs
never maenads
never eagle-headed gods—
This is
the language of desire—

these were men—
Trees their
companions—

nothing
on the earth then
not now to be had here—
but for a decaying
memory; nothing
to be learned now
not long since forgotten.
                    (*The Miscellany*)

THE WIND INCREASES
24 body / bodies (*Imagist Anthology* [1930])
The *Imagist Anthology* version contains 10 additional lines, the last 8 of
which—slightly revised—became a separate poem, "The Bird's Companion,"
in CP1934.

                    enameled, fluted
                              and shellsharp—

               as love

                         newborn
               each day upon the twig
                    which may die

                    springs your love
               fresh up
                    lusty for the sun
               the bird's companion—

THE BIRD'S COMPANION   The form "birds' " is used in the title and line 8 of
the printings in CP1934, CCP, and SP. The CEP form is supported by the
typescript at Buffalo and the first printing in the *Imagist Anthology*.

THE HOUSE
23   in it at / in at   (*Front*, Feb. 1931)

THE SEA-ELEPHANT   The setting is a Barnum & Bailey Circus at Madison Square Garden. "Blouaugh!" is the cry of the sea-elephant (T).
Title: "Love in a Truck *or* The Sea-Elephant" (*Imagist Anthology* [1930], *The Miscellany* [Nov. 1930]).
34   torn / ripped   (*Imagist Anthology, Miscellany*)
80   icummen / ycomen   (*Imagist Anthology, Miscellany*). The reference is to the medieval lyric "Sumer is icumen in, / Lhude sing cuccu!" WCW may have in mind Ezra Pound's "Ancient Music" (1916), which begins: "Winter is icummen in, / Lhude sing Goddamm." Writing on 8 Dec. 1929 to Lincoln Kirstein, who had accepted the poem for *Hound & Horn*, WCW said:

> As to the last four lines: I believe you have spotted a weakness in my middle English! . . . What I should have said was simply 'ycomen', mocking the old songs by using an old English form of speech.
> Weeeel, let's make a change in the last line, let's say—

> > the bounty
> > of . . and spring
> > they say—
> > spring is here (SL 111)

But the poem never appeared in *Hound & Horn*, and the change was not made.

RAIN   "In some ways this is the best poem I have ever done" (T).

1-2   As the rain moistens
        everything
        as does   (*Imagist Anthology* [1930])

"Rain" exists in seven printed versions, and it would take many pages of notes to record all the differences in spacing, lineation, punctuation, and spelling. Such a description is beyond the scope of this edition. However, we have reproduced below the first printing of the poem in *Hound & Horn* (Oct.-Dec. 1929) to give the interested reader a sense of the variations in spacing and format between two printings of a Williams poem. Here, as elsewhere, it is often difficult to determine which variations were intended by WCW and which were the products of house-styling and printers' whims.

> As the rain falls
> so does
> your love
>
> bathe every
>   open
> object of the world—

In houses
the priceless dry
        rooms
of illicit love
where we live
hear the wash of the
        rain—

There
    paintings
and fine
        metalware
woven stuffs—
all the whorishness
of our

    delight

sees
from its window
the spring wash
of your love
        the falling
rain—

The trees
are become
beasts fresh risen
from
    the sea—
water

trickles
from the crevices of
their hides—

So my life is spent
    to keep out love
with which
she rains upon

    the world

of spring

    drips

so spreads

the words

far apart to let in

her love—

And running in between
the drops

the rain

is a kind physician

the rain
of her thoughts over
the ocean
every

where

walking with
invisible swift feet
over

the helpless
waves—

Unworldly love
that has no hope
of the world

and that
cannot change the world
to its delight—

The rain
falls upon the earth
and grass and flowers

come
    perfectly

into form from its
        liquid

clearness

    But love is
unworldly

        and nothing
comes of it but love

following
and falling endlessly
from
        her thoughts.

DEATH (HE'S DEAD)   The first version in *Blues* (Fall 1930) prints the follow-
ing additional lines:
after 25   You could
        jump up and down on him
        and he wouldn't bend.
after 28   he's dead
        he makes love a hopeless
        howl—
after 37   He's let him go
        but he hasn't gone yet
Lines 41-46 in *Blues* read:
                the light—
                    calabashes—

        such as he used to bring
        home from South
        America when he would
        go there on business trips—
        in the years gone by

        dead, carved out of
        flesh, a mockery
                    which
        love cannot touch—

        Love can only bury it
        and hide its face—for shame.

The reference here is to WCW's own father.

THE BOTTICELLIAN TREES

28   quick with desire / with hot ardor   (*Poetry,* Feb. 1931; *Profile* [1932];
CP1934; CCP; SP). The change was made on the corrected typescript (Za49).

A MARRIAGE RITUAL

Title: "Wedded are the River and the Sky" (*Scribner's Magazine,* July
1930; *Modern Things* [1934]). In *The Broken Span* and *Selected Poems* the
date 1928 is added to the title.

The versions in *Scribner's Magazine* and *Modern Things* are so different
from each other, and from the final version, that we give them in full.

> Winter's icy sky
> marks the silhouette of the city
> and under it the icy
> waters of the river. This
> is my own! a fruit, a flower,
> an animal by itself—
>
> It does not recognize me
> and never will. Still
> it is my own and my heart
> goes out to it—
>
> dumbly—
> but eloquently in my own breast
> for you whom I love and to whom
> I cannot explain what
> my love is, nor
> how it varies, though I waste it—
>
> It is the light
> from a river
> flowing through refuse and
> the sticks of weeds, the banks
> rimmed with falling shell-ice
> lilac from above—
> as if with thought of you—
>
> Mine this face and its moods
> my moods, a
> riffled whiteness, shaken by the
> flow, that's constant in
> its swiftness as a pool—
>
> A Polack in the stinging
> wind, her arms wrapped to her
> breast, comes near to look
> at—what? downstream.
>
> It is
> an old-world flavor: the poor

the unthrifty, passionately
biassed by what errors
of conviction.

Now a boy
is rolling a great metal drum
up from below the river bank.
The woman and the boy—
two thievish figures—struggle
with the object . . . in
this light!

And still there is
a leafless bush—or tree, just
at the water's edge and—

my face

constant to you. . . .
(*Scribner's Magazine*)

Wintry sky, silhouette
of a city and under that
the waters—

You whom I love!

a riffled
whiteness shaken by the
flow, that's constant in
its swiftness as a pool.

But now a woman in the
stinging wind, her arms
wrapped to her breasts
comes near. An old-world
flavor. A boy is rolling
a metal drum up
from below the near bank.
The woman and the boy
two thievish figures
struggle with the object
—in this light!

—and falling
shell-ice lilac from above
rims the far shore—
(*Modern Things*)

THE UNFROCKED PRIEST   This is the first of several pre-1939 poems that
WCW included in *Collected Later Poems*.

23 What / Nothing (*Poetry*, July 1930)
28 standing? / standing (*Poetry*)

POEM (AS THE CAT)
10-11 into the round
        of the empty (*Poetry*, July 1930)

*FLOWERS BY THE SEA *Pagany* (Fall 1930). See the later version on p. 378.

SEA-TROUT AND BUTTERFISH The first version in *Pagany* (Fall 1930) is patterned into 3-line stanzas.

> The contours and the shine
> hold the eye powerless against the stillness
> of dead things, caught and lying
>
> orange-finned and the two
> half its size, pout-mouthed beside it
> on the white dish, untouched.
>
> Silver scales, the weight
> and swift lines wake thought to flight
> in the water, through it
>
> sharp turns, quick tails
> whipping the streams aside. Then the eye
> comes down once more, eagerly
>
> appraises the unravelled
> secret of the sea, separates this from
> that and the fine fins sharp spines

8 aslant / aside (*Poetry*, Oct. 1933; *Active Anthology* [1933])

*SUNDAY *American Caravan IV* (1931). See the later version on p. 396. Rutherford was on the Erie Railroad.

A CRYSTAL MAZE The two sections originally appeared separately as two different versions of the poem in *American Caravan IV* (1931) and *The Westminster Magazine* (1934). WCW gathered the texts together for CLP and numbered them as sections.
5   of a cigarette—or some, (*American Caravan IV*)
20 emerge / emerging (*American Caravan IV*)
46 twelve / twelve men (*Westminster Magazine*)
53 uncalled for / unnecessary (*Westminster Magazine*)

*READIE POME Published in *Readies for Bob Brown's Machine* (1931). Robert Carlton Brown, who had been a patron of the *Others* artists at Grantwood, N.J., later settled in France. He was convinced that "speed reading" by means of a reading machine would create a new way of writing, as different from traditional literature as the cinema is from the stage; and he decided to publish an anthology of pieces suitable for his machine. WCW was one of some forty writers (including Ezra Pound and Gertrude Stein) who contributed to the collection.

*TWO ASPECTS OF APRIL   First published in *The Rutherfordian* (Spring 1932) and reprinted in the WCWR, 9 (Fall 1983).

THE COD HEAD   In a letter to Kenneth Burke (transcribed by Thirlwall) WCW insisted that the cod head was a cod head and not just any fish-head, since cod was the only thing being caught. He also identified the "red cross" (l. 14) as the mark on the back of a large jellyfish or "stingever" (T).

3-4   oscillate—
       firmament to fishes   (*The Cod Head* [1932])
9-10   at night agitate
       wildly phosphores-   (*The Cod Head*)
12   flaccid / gellatinous   (*The Cod Head*)
15-16   lives—darkly
       the bottom skids   (*Contempo*, April 1932; *Contact*, May 1932)

19-30   Clearer—three fathom
         amorphous
         wavering rocks darkly

         two fathom—the
         vitreous body
         through which the oar tips—

         Small scudding fish
         deep down—and now a
         lulling

         lift and fall
         red stars—
         a severed cod-head

         between two
         green stones—lifting
         falling
           (*The Cod Head*)

20-22   ing rocks—a vitreous
         body through

         which the oartips—
         (*Contempo, Contact*)

THE RED LILY   Titled "The Canada Lily" in *Contact* (May 1932).
11   crossroads / cross road   (*An "Objectivists" Anthology* [1932])

THIS FLORIDA: 1924

Title: Printed as if the first line of the poem in *An "Objectivists" Anthology* (1932).

5 and 47   Hibiscus is Wallace Stevens, who made frequent trips to Florida (T). See Jack Hardie, "Hibiscus and the Spaniard of the Rose: Williams' Dialogue with Wallace Stevens," WCWR, 4 (Fall 1978).

18   bungalows / bungalow   (*An "Objectivists" Anthology*)

22-24   (omitted in *An "Objectivists" Anthology*)

41   rime / time   (CEP) The source of the error was an unnoticed typist's mistake in Yale Za49.

42 and 31   WCW's friend Madeline Spence at the piano (T).

56   Hartley   The painter Marsden Hartley.

64   Marshal   "Martial" (T). Presumably the Roman epigrammatic poet.

71   Peggy   Peggy Ladd, a patient (T).

IN THE 'SCONSET BUS   Siasconset is a town on Nantucket Island.

*OUR (AMERICAN) RAGCADEMICIANS   *The New English Weekly* (July 1933).

3   Are we? more / Are we more   (*New English Weekly*) We follow the punctuation in the typescript (dated 3/8/33) at the Ransom Humanities Research Center, University of Texas.

*RHYMED ADDRESS: THE LOBSTER   Published in *The Westminster Magazine* (Autumn 1933) alongside Carl Rakosi's poem "The Lobster," which was dedicated to WCW.

THE FLOWERS ALONE

16   remains / remain   (*Active Anthology* [1933])

THE LOCUST TREE IN FLOWER   *Poetry* (Oct. 1933). A later version appeared in *An Early Martyr* (see p. 379). WCW printed the two versions together in CEP and in *More Power, Report of the Newark Public Library, 1946-1952* (Fall-Winter 1952), where there is an accompanying comment (see p. 538).

"I didn't think this gave a picture of the locust flower, so I had to cut it down . . . I literally cut out inessential lines" (T).

SONG (THE BLACK-WINGED GULL)   Titled "An Old Song" in *Poetry* (Oct. 1933) and *The Literary Digest* (Oct. 1933).

*A FOOT-NOTE   *Poetry* (Oct. 1933).

*THE ENTITY   An undated poem in the Buffalo collection (A97), first published by Martha Strom in *Journal of Modern Literature*, 11 (July 1984). WCW had been interested in the uses of "anti-poetic" materials since at least as early as *Spring and All*, but he was annoyed when Wallace Stevens—in his preface to WCW's *Collected Poems 1921-1931* (1934)—claimed that the "anti-poetic" was WCW's passion, an antidote to his sentimental leanings (see

IWWP 52). We have placed this poem in 1934 because of Stevens' preface, although it could have been written earlier.

THIS IS JUST TO SAY   "Tyler's interpretation is just nonsense!" (T). WCW is referring to Parker Tyler's article in *Briarcliff Quarterly*, 3 (Oct. 1946), where in a strained interpretation Tyler says that "the plums' 'death' (or formal disappearance and disintegration) was symbolically anticipated in the icy charm of their living flesh."

Florence Williams' "reply" to "This Is Just to Say" is included as a "Detail" in the partially published *Detail & Parody for the poem Paterson* (Buffalo D4); it first appeared in *The Atlantic Monthly* (Nov. 1982), p. 145. Since WCW chose to include the reply in his own sequence it seems likely that he took a note left by his wife and turned it into a "poem."

The following text is taken from a typescript (Buffalo A79):

Reply

(crumpled on her desk)

Dear Bill: I've made a
couple of sandwiches for you.
In the ice-box you'll find
blue-berries—a cup of grapefruit
a glass of cold coffee.

On the stove is the tea-pot
with enough tea leaves
for you to make tea if you
prefer—Just light the gas—
boil the water and put it in the tea

Plenty of bread in the bread-box
and butter and eggs—
I didn't know just what to
make for you. Several people
called up about office hours—

See you later. Love. Floss.

Please switch off the telephone.

*YOUNG WOMAN AT A WINDOW   WCW printed these two versions together in *The Westminster Magazine* (Autumn 1934) but subsequently reprinted only the "She sits with" version.

AN EARLY MARTYR AND OTHER POEMS (1935)

Dedication: "To John Coffee [Coffey]"
   "I should tell you about Coffey. He was a young radical who wanted to

help the poor, was convinced that they should be helped, and decided to do something about it. He was a poor Irish boy. He had nerve. He decided to steal goods from department stores and succeeded in doing it from Wanamaker's. His idea was to be arrested so that he could make his plea for the poor in court where he would get a lot of publicity. He wrote the police about his successful theft but they refused to let him go to court. Instead they put him in an insane asylum—in for life—but the place got too crowded eventually and they let him go. I identified myself in his defense. No one at that time would have thought of this as communistic—it was simply an unworldly dream and I was sympathetic to the dreamer and the dream. He finally came to realize that no matter how good his idea was, it wouldn't work. The poem 'An early martyr' tells about it, the factual details. The title poem is, in effect, a dedication" (IWWP 56).

In late 1919 Coffey had a brief love affair with the poet Louise Bogan. Conrad Aiken wrote from South Yarmouth, Mass., that "John Coffey and Max Bodenheim and Mrs. Bod., and one Louise Bogan . . . have all blown in in the last 24 hours, rolling in money, and have hired a house not far away" (*Selected Letters of Conrad Aiken*, ed. Joseph Killorin [New Haven, 1978], pp. 49-50). In early 1920 Coffey was arrested for theft (he specialized in valuable furs) and sent to the Matteawan State Hospital for the criminally insane. In April 1923 he and three other inmates escaped the institution after kidnapping two keepers and a chauffeur, but they were soon captured ("Mad Convicts Taken After Day At Large"). In all the newspaper reports of the escape Coffey is treated as a common criminal, "a fur thief from New York." By the mid-1930s Coffey had been released from Matteawan and was back in New York "being thrown out of basement bars when he began to prate his social sermons there" (A 299).

WCW and other writers took a romantic view of Coffey's exploits. In an article for *The Freeman*, "A Man Versus the Law" (23 June 1920), WCW defended Coffey's actions and his sanity: "What Coffey was after was definition, a light in the dark, a diagnosis, without which no advance of knowledge is possible and this the law could not allow concerning itself. . . . I have written this that attention may be called to John Coffey's logic and human devotion." Maxwell Bodenheim's 1924 novel *Crazy Man* presents Coffey as a Christ-figure; and in Aiken's novel *Conversation* (1940), based on Coffey's visit to South Yarmouth of twenty years before, "Jim Connor" (Coffey) is portrayed as an idealist. But Coffey himself took a different view of his past in a letter to Aiken praising *Conversation*: "I was glad to have your description of me . . . although I felt somewhat chagrined by your repetition of Bodenheim's rationalization that I stole from a desire to support 'genius' like his, as a kind of Robin Hood esthete. My main aim at the time was to make myself more articulate; that was why I consorted with you litterateurs. . . . I stole to finance my education . . . I wasn't naively unaware that Bodenheim was acting as parasitically toward me as I was acting toward the department stores. . . . Less larcenously yours, John Coffey" (*Selected Letters of Conrad Aiken*, p. 50).

AN EARLY MARTYR   Mrs. Williams recalled that *The Freeman* bought this poem "but lost their nerve and didn't publish it" (IWWP 56). If this is correct the poem dates from 1920, although in its final form the style is characteristic of Williams in the 1930s.

FLOWERS BY THE SEA   See first version, p. 352. Another version was published in *Modern Things,* ed. Parker Tyler (1934):

> When over the blossomy, sharp pasture's
> edge, unseen, the salt ocean
>
> lifts its form. Chickory and daisies,
> tied, released seem hardly flowers alone
>
> but color and a movement—or a shape
> perhaps. Whereas
>
> the sea is circled and sways harmlessly
> upon its plantlike stem—

ITEM   Presumably based on a contemporary newspaper photograph. "The importance of the individual—a pitiful, beaten creature as dear to me as anyone could be. Done with economy of line to give the telling impression—a defiance of conventional beauty. Proof you can make a poem out of anything. Goya's *Scenas de la Guerra* deeply moved me" (T).

THE LOCUST TREE IN FLOWER   See the first version, p. 366. In response to a reader's puzzlement over the poem WCW said: "It's the recurrence of the season—the whole history of May. . . . I cut out everything except the essential words to leave the thing as simple as possible and to make the reader concentrate as much as he can. Could anything be plainer?" (*More Power, Report of the Newark Public Library, 1946-1952* [Fall-Winter 1952]).

VIEW OF A LAKE   "I was inclined to trust the sequence of rhythm without punctuation. It was the Image, the significant image that made the poem. To put down something as a composition—not a story. Not in the stanzaic form. To be something of what I saw—the three little bitches gaping at the stalled traffic. I felt more kinship with them than with the stalled traffic" (T).
6   with / by   (*Artists' and Writers' Chapbook* [1935])
22   frock / smock   (*Chapbook*)
46-47   the three / with straight backs   "The Indians are notorious for their straight backs" (T).

TO A MEXICAN PIG-BANK   "On the mantel piece [a gift] from Marsden Hartley. . . . I was trying to make the Image rhythmically through the description which begins and ends the poem. I always liked it as very well described—an American image—some object, colorful and characteristic of Mexico. Back of everything I was doing was to get the design [in] it—unburdened" (T).

An earlier version was published in *Galaxy: An Anthology* (1934):

> To a Mexican
> pig-bank
>
> with a handle
> beside
>
> a small flock
> of clay
>
> sheep half
> its size
>
> a shepherd
> behind
>
> them—the
> pig
>
> is painted
> yellow
>
> with green
> ears
>
> and has a
> slot
>
> at the
> top—
>
> While from a
> base
>
> hair-pin
> wires
>
> hold up the
> sheep
>
> turning
> away—
>
> The shepherd
> wears
>
> a red
> blanket
>
> on his left
> shoulder

TO A POOR OLD WOMAN

12   Comforted / Comforted, relieved—   (*Smoke*, Autumn 1934)

*THE SADNESS OF THE SEA   A compressed version of the last part of poem "9/30" in *The Descent of Winter* (p. 292).

LATE FOR SUMMER WEATHER   "Expression of the truant thoughts about anything, but with the design always in view. I was composing—an attractive arrangement of the words" (T).
10   Fat   Lost   Ambling   [spacing of CCP has been restored]
12   upper town   "Passaic" (T)

PROLETARIAN PORTRAIT   "Ezra Pound wrote that he didn't like this because of the proletarian tone. He thought it was obvious and so what? 'She might have done as well in Russia as in Passaic' " (T).
In *Galaxy: An Anthology* (1934) the poem is titled "Study for a Figure representing Modern Culture" and the last five lines read:

> Her shoe in her hand she is looking
> intently into it—
>
> pulls out the paper insole to
> find the nail
>
> that was hurting her

TREE AND SKY   WCW on the changes from the *Poetry* version: "the fewer words the better" (T).
5   tree alone / tree stands alone   (*Poetry*, Oct. 1933)
6   on / upon   (*Poetry*, *Modern Things* [1934])
13   the unmoving / opens the unmoving   (*Poetry*, *Modern Things*)

THE RAPER FROM PASSENACK   Titled "The Raper from Hackensack" in *Alcestis* (Jan. 1935). "Literal description of the rape of a dear friend (a nurse) of mine, it [happened] after church. . . . What are you going to do with an incident like this? I write poetry. And it shows my human interest in the nurses. They'd flock to tell me everything. I used to love to hear their scuttlebutt" (T).

INVOCATION AND CONCLUSION   "I always thought that all things began with the relation of a man and a woman—a form of composition—something occurring around me—like the *Detail of Paterson*. Authentic details of my life. I had to get them down" (T).
Gloss to stanza 2: "an illiterate Italian girl" (T).
An earlier version in *Bozart-Westminster* (Spring-Summer 1935) ends with an additional stanza:

> Would you believe it?
> I never even knew what it was
> to be like other women
> till after the first
> six was born.

*GENESIS   Published in *An Early Martyr* and *Programme* No. 5 (May 1935).

*SOLSTICE   Appears only in *An Early Martyr*.

THE YACHTS   "I wrote the whole damn thing without a change. I was thinking of terza rima, but gave up rime—a *very* vague imitation of Dante. I was quickly carried away by my own feelings" (T). ". . . the yachts do not sink but go on with the race while only *in the imagination* are they seen to founder. It is a false situation which the yachts typify with the beauty of their movements while the real situation (of the poor) is desperate while 'the skillful yachts pass over' " (from notes by WCW filed in a folder with his letter to Henry W. Wells of 27 July 1955: General Manuscript Collection, Rare Book and Manuscript Library, Columbia University).
17   fleckless / feckless   In all printings before CEP and in the typescripts. But in a letter to Babette Deutsch of 9 March 1951 WCW wrote: "Fleckless, perhaps spotless, without fault—*not* feckless" (transcribed in T).

YOUNG LOVE   Titled "Young Romance" in *An Early Martyr*. See the first version on p. 200.

AN ELEGY FOR D. H. LAWRENCE
9-11   "D. H. Lawrence never answered me . . . [when] I wrote to him" (A 51).

SUNDAY   See first version, p. 353. "As Ezra Pound says: The poet must always be writing, even when he has nothing to write about—just for discipline. Much as Richard Strauss wrote his *Domestic Symphony*, which I heard in Germany in 1910—why not write a symphony using the noises in the house. And I put this feeling into this poem. Just finger exercises" (T).
24   Rutherford was on the Erie Railroad.

THE CATHOLIC BELLS
stanza 3 "Mrs. DeSmedt, [of] a Belgian family transplanted to Rutherford. This family is symbolized by The Bells. I had some understanding of what they were going through from the difficulties of my [own mother]" (T). The DeSmedts lived on Chestnut St. in Rutherford, across the street from the yellow-brick church of St. Mary (R. C.).
31   Concordia Halle   The old German Meeting Hall (now pulled down) in East Rutherford.

SIMPLEX SIGILUM VERI   See first version, p. 321.
3   the bank, a narrow building / a narrow building, the bank,   (*An Early Martyr* [1935], *Modern Things* [1934])
13-16   Version in *An Early Martyr* reads:

penholder on the brown marbled
field of the stained blotter

by an oystershell smudged with
cigarette ash. A primrose plant

17   gold-ringed / gold rimmed   (*An Early Martyr*)

TO BE HUNGRY IS TO BE GREAT   The poem is totally unpunctuated in *An Early Martyr* (1935).

A POEM FOR NORMAN MACLEOD   WCW admired the work of the younger poet and reviewed several volumes of his poetry, including *Horizons of Death* (1934). On 4 Sept. 1935 he wrote to Macleod: "You'll notice when you see it [*An Early Martyr*] that the last three poems, including the one about you, are in a different mood from the earlier ones. It's a mood I want to cultivate" (Mariani 371).
"I was very much in sympathy with Norman Macleod and his social attitudes to the poor. I felt that the revolution was coming. I was never in favor of the [Communist] Party, but I did think that some revolution [would come] which would bring down the socialites and give the poor people a chance. This treatment will take the bluff out of 'polite' talk. Norman was not 'polite': he was lowdown and acted that way—He was from Indian country" (T).

YOU HAVE PISSED YOUR LIFE   This poem was written in response to a letter from Ezra Pound berating WCW for having "pissed" his life away (Mariani 371 and T).

ADAM & EVE & THE CITY (1936)

Dedication: "To my wife"

TO A WOOD THRUSH

1-3   Singing across the orchard
in the stillness
before night, answered
by another from the depths
(*Smoke*, Autumn 1935)

8   it no / it was no   (*Smoke*)

11-12   What can I say that would
be wise enough or that
we share enough alike for
them to know you? Vistas
(*Smoke*)

FINE WORK WITH PITCH AND COPPER   The poem is "really telling about my struggle with verse" (IWWP 57).

A CHINESE TOY   Titled "Antique Engine" in *Smoke* (Autumn 1935).

ADAM and EVE   "are tributes to my father and mother" (IWWP 57).

ADAM   Line 68: *avia*, the reading in all printings, is changed to *tenia* in Thirlwall's copy of CEP.

ST. FRANCIS EINSTEIN OF THE DAFFODILS   See the first version, p. 130. "It is always spring time for the mind when great discoveries are made. Is not Einstein, at the same time, saintly in the purity of his scientific imagining? And if a saint it seems to me that the thorough logic which St. Francis saw as sparrows or donkeys, equally to be loved with whatever other living aspect of the world, would apply equally to Einstein's arrival in the United States a number of years ago to celebrate the event in the season's shapes and colors of that moment" (Author's Note in *Modern Poetry*, ed. Kimon Friar and John Malcolm Brinnin [New York, 1951], p. 546).
In the version published in *Modern Things* (1934) the first two stanzas are quite different:

> March
> has come at the time in fashion
> up out of the sea
> through the rippling daffodils
> in the foreyard of
> Liberty's Statue
> whose stonearms
> powerless against them
> the Venusremembering wavelets
> break into laughter
>
> "Sweet land"
> at last
> among the tormented fruit trees
> freedom
> for the daffodils—
> The unchained orchards
> shake their tufted flowers
> in a tearing wind
> rebellious, laughing—
> Einstein, tall as a violet
> in the latticearbor corner
> is tall as
> a blossomy peartree!

THE DEATH OF SEE   A poem about the suicide of the poet Harry Crosby (10 Dec. 1929). See Geoffrey Wolff, *Black Sun* (New York, 1976), and Joseph Evans Slate, "From the Front Page: A Note on Williams' 'The Death of See,'" WCWR, 3 (Spring 1977), 16-18. "M." is Stanley Mortimer, Crosby's artist

friend whose studio was used by Crosby for his final assignation with Jose-
phine Rotch (Mrs. Albert Bigelow). Crosby shot her and then himself. Morti-
mer discovered the bodies.

"Some of the newspaper errors may be traced to Stanley Mortimer's ac-
count. Abashed to find himself broadcast in the public prints as a 'complacent
friend,' and a kind of pander, he decided to invest himself with a casual man-
ner and memory. . . . He was particularly reticent with the New York
World, to whom he described Harry as a poet, 'but when or where his poems
were published Mortimer could not say' " (*Black Sun*, p. 291). "

10-15   artist's suite—
     Their bodies were
     found

     fully clothed
     and half covered
     by
     (*Modern Things* [1934])

22-33   poems were published
     M. could not
     say   .   .

     By which, not by
     the wind,
     snow

     trees, suddenly a
     clean world—
     Reprieve
     (*Modern Things*)

TO AN ELDER POET   "Emily Dickinson is the poet I had in mind" (WCW to
Harriet Monroe, 8 Dec. 1935; *Poetry* Archive, University of Chicago Library).

UNNAMED: FROM "PATERSON"   Titled in *Adam & Eve & The City* (1936)
"From the Poem 'Paterson.' " These vignettes anticipate the later *Detail &
Parody for the poem Paterson* (see the note on "Porous," p. 547).

THE CRIMSON CYCLAMEN   For information on Charles Demuth see the note
to the dedication of *Spring and All*, p. 500. Demuth was noted for his paint-
ings of flowers.

86-87   design—if not / the purpose, is explained [alteration in typescript
(Yale Za 49) from] design—though not / the purpose is explained (ADAM &
EVE and CCP)

TRANSLATIONS FROM THE SPANISH   For the source of these translations see the
note on "Translations from the Spanish" in *The Tempers*, p. 475.

1. CANCION (Lupercio de Argensola) From the first stanza of "Cancion del Mismo," which begins "Alivia sus fatigas."

*2. STIR YOUR FIELDS TO INCREASE ("Fertiliza tu vega").

*3. THE DAWN IS UPON US ("El alba nos mira"). See "IV. The day draweth nearer" in *The Tempers*, p. 14.

*4. TEARS THAT STILL LACKED POWER ("Lágrimas que no pudieron").

*5. POPLARS OF THE MEADOW ("Álamos del prado"). See "III. Poplars of the meadow" in *The Tempers*, p. 13.

PERPETUUM MOBILE: THE CITY
105   three hours   Present in all printed texts before CEP and in the corrected typescript (Yale Za49).

POEMS 1936-1939

THE YOUNG CAT AND THE CHRYSANTHEMUMS   Although this poem was only published in CLP, a note at Buffalo (A414) dates it from 1936. "12/20/36 8:40 P.M. This, in a slight poem, illustrates as well as can be shown in a simple manner, what I am after. W. C. Williams."

PATERSON: EPISODE 17   Parts of the poem were incorporated into *Paterson*, Book III (1949). See pp. 98, 104, 126-27 of the 1963 New Directions edition. In SP the poem is titled "Paterson: Episode from Book III."

ADVENT OF TODAY   In *William Zorach / Two Drawings William Carlos Williams / Two Poems* (1937) the first two stanzas read:

> South wind
> striking in
> a sea become winged
>
> torn spume
> scudding low
> trees inverted over trees

THE GIRL (WITH BIG BREASTS)   This poem is used as a "demonstration" in WCW's essay on modern poetry "The So-Called So-Called" (*Patroon*, May 1937). The following paragraphs frame the poem, which differs from the version in CLP.

> Those who invent the forms of their day are the major poets. Or even contribute toward that invention. Those who copy the forms of other days are the minor poets. But nobody reads history. They only interpret it—at so much a head.
> You'd think somebody with intelligence outside the art would perceive these things and make themselves useful by exhibiting

THE GIRL

with big breasts
in a blue sweater
was crossing the
street bareheaded
reading a paper
held up close
but stopped, turned
and looked down
as though
she had seen a coin
lying
on the pavement—

It isn't very good because it lacks metrical emphasis but it has a useful quality for study in that it presents a simple image in the same sort of light that the Athenian placed the Venus—only in not the same context.

The version in *William Zorach / Two Drawings William Carlos Williams / Two Poems* (1937) is identical to that in *Patroon* but divided into couplets.

CLASSIC SCENE   "Cf. [Charles] Sheeler's 'Classic Landscape' " (T). The painting is reproduced as Plate XVIII in Bram Dijkstra, *The Hieroglyphics of a New Speech* (1969).

THE SUN
2   and sea / and the sea   (*Life and Letters Today*, Summer 1937).

*WIND OF THE VILLAGE   Published in . . . *and Spain sings Fifty Loyalist Ballads Adapted by American Poets* (1937). This is an adaptation by WCW of Miguel Hernández's "Sentado Sobre Los Muertos" ("Seated above the dead"), which first appeared in 1937 in his volume *Viento Del Pueblo* (*Wind of the Village*). WCW was chairman of the Bergen County Medical Board to Aid Spanish Democracy (Mariani 401).

*SHE WHO TURNS HER HEAD   *Barometer* (Nov.-Dec. 1937).

*MAN AND NATURE   *Forum* (April 1938). An earlier version (Buffalo A193) was published by John C. Thirlwall in ND16 under the title "Roar and Clatter":

rushing on behind a
cataclysmic beacon
shake the glazed windows
and among hissings
and the loud clang
of a bell crash by
trailing the shaking

body. Gone. Leaving
only the cat that with
green eyes and dragging
tail slinks hesitant
across the endless
chasms of the streets

THE POOR
6 showing oak branches / showing branches (*The New Republic,* 15
June 1938).

LOVELY AD "An inconsequential poem—written in 2 minutes—as was (for
instance) The Red Wheel Barrow and most other very short poems" (T).

MIDDLE The last two stanzas of the version in CCP are on a second page
in the corrected typescript for CEP (Yale Za49), but are missing from Za50
and were therefore omitted by the printer. They have been restored here.

AT THE BAR This poem and the three following were subtitled "From
'Paterson'" in CCP. In CEP the four were grouped after "Unnamed: From
'Paterson.'" WCW clearly thought of them as part of his preliminary work
for the long poem.

MORNING The following passage (between line 28, "over shrubs," and line
29, "Level of") occurs in CCP but was cancelled by WCW on the typescript
for CEP (Yale Za49):

A big fish
outlined in red paint on a sheet of tin,
mouth and eyes: Sea Food.

57 *Pago, Pago!* "I pay, I pay!"
83 Jock Changed from "Balls," the CCP version, on the corrected type-
script (Yale Za49).

POROUS First published in *The New Yorker,* 17 Dec. 1938, p. 16. This
poem and the following four are in the 87-page typescript *Detail & Parody
for the poem Paterson* that WCW gave to James Laughlin on 9 March 1939.
A slightly different version of *Detail & Parody* is at Buffalo (D4). In the "de-
tails" and improvisations of this collection WCW was searching for a lan-
guage adequate to the long project he had been contemplating since at least
as early as 1927.
Fifteen poems from the typescript were published in the section "For the
Poem Patterson" of *The Broken Span* (1941).

*THE HALFWORLD First published in *Hika* (Gambier, Ohio), March 1939,
p. 15. Over twenty different versions of this poem can be found in Buffalo

(A131), *Detail & Parody*, and ND16. It obviously represents a period of great uncertainty and experimentation in WCW's career.

THE HARD LISTENER   First published in *Hika* (Gambier, Ohio), March 1939, p. 15.

THE RETURN TO WORK   First published in *The New Yorker*, 8 April 1939, p. 22.

THE LAST WORDS OF MY ENGLISH GRANDMOTHER   See the first version, p. 253. In *Furioso* (Summer 1939) the poem is preceded by this note: "(Born Emily Dickinson, at Chichester, England, 1837; died, Grace Hospital, New Haven, Dec. 1, 1920)." The maiden name of WCW's grandmother was probably Dickenson, but after his discovery of Emily Dickinson's poetry WCW often used that spelling. "Emily Dickinson, her name was. Isn't that amazing?" (*Writers at Work: The Paris Review Interviews*, 3rd series, ed. George Plimpton [New York, 1967], p. 12).

Appendix C: Tables of Contents

COLLECTED POEMS, 1921-1931 (1934)

POEMS

All the Fancy Things
Hemmed-in Males
Brilliant Sad Sun
Young Sycamore
It Is a Living Coral
To
This Florida: 1924
The Sun Bathers
The Cod Head
Struggle of Wings
Down-town
Winter
The Waitress
The Bull
In the 'Sconset Bus
Poem (As the cat)
The Jungle
The Lily
On Gay Wallpaper
The Source
Nantucket
The Winds
Lines on Receiving *The Dial*'s Award
The Red Lily
The Attic Which Is Desire:
Interests of 1926
This Is Just to Say
Birds and Flowers
Full Moon

DELLA PRIMAVERA TRASPORTATA AL MORALE

April (the beginning)
The Trees
The Birds' Companion
The Sea-Elephant
Rain

549

SOUR GRAPES, 1921

THE COLLECTED EARLIER POEMS (1951)

An asterisk (*) indicates poems published after 1938 that are not included in the present volume.

THE WANDERER

THE TEMPERS

STRUGGLE OF WINGS

Struggle of Wings

THE DESCENT OF WINTER

IMPROMPTU: THE SUCKERS

Impromptu: The Suckers

COLLECTED POEMS 1934

Acknowledgments

This edition could not have been completed in its present form without generous assistance from many individuals and institutions. Our largest debt is to James Laughlin, who first conceived the idea of a new edition of Williams' poetry and helped at every stage of its development. We are most grateful to the staff of New Directions, and especially to our editor Peggy Fox, whose intelligent handling of the complicated manuscript made this a better book.

Our deepest scholarly debt is to Emily Mitchell Wallace, who shared with us her unparalleled knowledge of Williams' publishing career. Her *Bibliography of William Carlos Williams* was our indispensable guide in gathering and arranging the poems. We are also greatly indebted to Paul Mariani, both for personal advice and for the rich information contained in his monumental biography, *William Carlos Williams: A New World Naked*. In the earlier stages of the edition we received invaluable assistance from James Longenbach, who located and photocopied most of the poems. We also wish to thank Daniel Goldberg, Jeff Huber, Catherine Levesque, and Lois Nesbitt for their help with our research. Tony Bavington, David Frail, and Dennis M. Read drew our attention to important materials used in the edition.

William Eric Williams and Paul Williams were unusually generous with their time and knowledge, helping us with many details of their father's early life in Rutherford. We also wish to give special thanks to the family of the late John C. Thirlwall, who allowed us to examine the copy of *Collected Earlier Poems* that contains Williams' annotations from the 1950s.

The staff of the Rare Book Room in Princeton University's Firestone Library were remarkably helpful throughout the making of this edition. We also wish to give particular thanks to the staff of the Beinecke Rare Book and Manuscript Library, Yale University, and especially to David Schoonover; to Cathy Henderson and the staff of the Harry Ransom Humanities Research Center at the University of Texas; and to Robert J. Bertholf and the staff of the Poetry/Rare Books Collection at the University of Buffalo. The descriptive catalogue of the Buffalo collection compiled by Neil Baldwin and Steven L. Meyers was extraordinarily helpful.

Other libraries that have assisted us are: The Free Public Library, Rutherford, N. J.; The New York Public Library; The Library of Congress; The Starr Library of Middlebury College; The Newberry Library; The Joseph Regenstein Library of the University of Chicago; The Huntington Library; The Lilly Library, Indiana University; the Rare Book and Manuscript Library, Columbia University; The Golda Meir Library, University of Wisconsin-Milwaukee; Kent State University Library, Dept. of Special Collections; The Alderman Library, University of Virginia; the University of Arkansas Library, Special Collections; the Morris Library, Southern Illinois University at Carbondale; the Amherst College Library; the Rare Books Room, University of Colorado at Boulder; Northwestern University Library; the Kenneth Spencer Research Library, University of Kansas; the Pennsylvania State University Library; the University of Minnesota Library; the University of Saskatchewan Library; Department of Special Collections, University of California Library, Los Angeles; the University of Delaware Library; The George Arents Research Library, Syracuse University; Special Collections, the Library of Washington University in St. Louis; the University of Washington Library; the Dartmouth College Library; Special Collections, Van Pelt Library, University of Pennsylvania.

Princeton University and the College of William and Mary provided assistance in the form of research grants. Finally, we wish to acknowledge the generous support of the Marguerite Eyer Wilbur Foundation and the special interest taken by its vice-president William Walter Longstreth.

INDEX OF TITLES

[The numbered poems of *Spring and All* are indexed under their titles in *Collected Earlier Poems* (see pp. xi-xii). The untitled poems in *The Descent of Winter* are not included in this index, but are listed in the Index of First Lines. Titles of poetic sequences are in capital letters.]

INDEX OF FIRST LINES

[Although in some of Williams' poems the title is syntactically the first line, we have confined this index to the lines that follow titles. When a first line is very short, usually one or two words, we have supplied the following line or lines.]

575